Cisco Unified Computing System (UCS)

A Complete Reference Guide to the Data Center Virtualization Server Architecture

Silvano Gai

Tommi Salli

Roger Andersson

Cisco Press

800 East 96th Street

Indianapolis, Indiana 46240 USA

Cisco Unified Computing System (UCS)
A Complete Reference Guide to the Data Center Virtualization Server Architecture

Silvano Gai
Tommi Salli
Roger Andersson

Copyright© 2010 Cisco Systems, Inc.

Published by:

Cisco Press

201 West 103rd Street

Indianapolis, IN 46290 USA

Printed in the United States of America   3 4 5 6 7 8 9 0

Third Printing September 2010

Library of Congress Cataloging-in-Publication Data

Gai, Silvano.

  Unified computing system (UCS) : a data center virtualization server /

Silvano Gai, Tommi Salli, Roger Andersson.

      p. cm.

  Includes bibliographical references.

  ISBN 978-1-58714-193-5 (pbk.)

  1. Virtual computer systems. 2. Parallel processing (Electronic

computers) I. Salli, Tommi, 1977- II. Andersson, Roger, 1970- III.

Title.

  QA76.9.V5G35 2010

  004'.35-dc22

2010016455

ISBN-10: 1-58714-193-0

ISBN-13: 978-1-58714-193-5

Warning and Disclaimer

This book is designed to provide information about the Cisco Unified Computing System (UCS). Every effort has been made to make this book as complete and as accurate as possible, but no warranty or fitness is implied.

The information is provided on an "as is" basis. The authors, Cisco Press, and Cisco Systems, Inc., shall have neither liability nor responsibility to any person or entity with respect to any loss or damages arising from the information contained in this book or from the use of the discs or programs that may accompany it.

The opinions expressed in this book belong to the author and are not necessarily those of Cisco Systems, Inc.

Feedback Information

At Cisco Press, our goal is to create in-depth technical books of the highest quality and value. Each book is crafted with care and precision, undergoing rigorous development that involves the unique expertise of members from the professional technical community.

Readers' feedback is a natural continuation of this process. If you have any comments regarding how we could improve the quality of this book, or otherwise alter it to better suit your needs, you can contact us through e-mail at feedback@ciscopress.com. Please make sure to include the book title and ISBN in your message.

We greatly appreciate your assistance.

Corporate and Government Sales

Cisco Press offers excellent discounts on this book when ordered in quantity for bulk purchases or special sales. For more information, please contact: U.S. Corporate and Government Sales 1-800-382-3419 corpsales@pearsontechgroup.com

For sales outside of the U.S., please contact: International Sales 1-317-581-3793 international@pearsontechgroup.com

Trademark Acknowledgments

All terms mentioned in this book that are known to be trademarks or service marks have been appropriately capitalized. Cisco Press or Cisco Systems, Inc. cannot attest to the accuracy of this information. Use of a term in this book should not be regarded as affecting the validity of any trademark or service mark.

Publisher: Paul Boger

Cisco Press Program Manager: Anand Sundaram

Associate Publisher: David Dusthimer

Cisco Representative: Eric Ullanderson

Executive Editor: Mary Beth Ray

Managing Editor: Sandra Schroeder

Project Editor: Mandie Frank

Editorial Assistant: Vanessa Evans

Compositor: Studio Galou, LLC

CISCO

Americas Headquarters	Asia Pacific Headquarters	Europe Headquarters
Cisco Systems, Inc.	Cisco Systems (USA) Pte. Ltd.	Cisco Systems International BV
San Jose, CA	Singapore	Amsterdam, The Netherlands

Cisco has more than 200 offices worldwide. Addresses, phone numbers, and fax numbers are listed on the Cisco Website at www.cisco.com/go/offices.

CCDE, CCENT, Cisco Eos, Cisco HealthPresence, the Cisco logo, Cisco Lumin, Cisco Nexus, Cisco StadiumVision, Cisco TelePresence, Cisco WebEx, DCE, and Welcome to the Human Network are trademarks; Changing the Way We Work, Live, Play, and Learn and Cisco Store are service marks; and Access Registrar, Aironet, AsyncOS, Bringing the Meeting To You, Catalyst, CCDA, CCDP, CCIE, CCIP, CCNA, CCNP, CCSP, CCVP, Cisco, the Cisco Certified Internetwork Expert logo, Cisco IOS, Cisco Press, Cisco Systems, Cisco Systems Capital, the Cisco Systems logo, Cisco Unity, Collaboration Without Limitation, EtherFast, EtherSwitch, Event Center, Fast Step, Follow Me Browsing, FormShare, GigaDrive, HomeLink, Internet Quotient, IOS, iPhone, iQuick Study, IronPort, the IronPort logo, LightStream, Linksys, MediaTone, MeetingPlace, MeetingPlace Chime Sound, MGX, Networkers, Networking Academy, Network Registrar, PCNow, PIX, PowerPanels, ProConnect, ScriptShare, SenderBase, SMARTnet, Spectrum Expert, StackWise, The Fastest Way to Increase Your Internet Quotient, TransPath, WebEx, and the WebEx logo are registered trademarks of Cisco Systems, Inc. and/or its affiliates in the United States and certain other countries.

All other trademarks mentioned in this document or website are the property of their respective owners. The use of the word partner does not imply a partnership relationship between Cisco and any other company. (0812R)

About the Authors

Silvano Gai, who grew up in a small village near Asti, Italy, has more than twenty-seven years of experience in computer engineering and computer networks. He is the author of several books and technical publications on computer networking as well as multiple Internet Drafts and RFCs. He is responsible for 30 issued patents and 50 patent applications. His background includes seven years as a full professor of Computer Engineering, tenure track, at Politecnico di Torino, Italy and seven years as a researcher at the CNR (Italian National Council for Scientific Research). For the past thirteen years, he has been in Silicon Valley where in the position of Cisco Fellow, he was an architect of the Cisco Catalyst family of network switches, of the Cisco MDS family of storage networking switches, and of the Nexus family of data center switches. Silvano teaches a course on the topics of this book at Stanford University.

Tommi Salli, who was born and raised in Finland, has close to 20 years of experience working with computers. He has extensive server and application background from companies like SUN Microsystems and VERITAS Software, which later got bought by Symantec from where he moved to Nuova Systems that got bought by Cisco. He has held different positions from Sales Engineer to Technology Scouting in the office of CTO from product management to architect and during his journey, he has been responsible for seven patent applications. He started his career in Finland, and for the past five years, he has been in Silicon Valley and is currently working for Cisco systems as a Technical Marketing Engineer.

Roger Andersson was born in Stockholm, Sweden. He has spent 20 years in the computer industry in both Sweden and the United States. Roger's experience includes more than 12 years in the CLARiiON Engineering Division at EMC and five years at VERITAS/ Symantec where Roger worked as a Technical Product Manager focusing on systems management, server, and application automated provisioning. Roger is currently working at Cisco as a Manager, Technical Marketing, where he is focused on the system management aspects of a Unified Computing System.

Dedications

To my wife Antonella, my daughters Eleonora and Evelina,
and my son Marco

To my wife Sari, my daughter Tara, and my son Sean

To my wife Kristine

And to our parents for their support in the early journey

Acknowledgments

This book is the result of a collaborative effort inside and outside Cisco®. Many people have contributed, and in particular, the authors want to express gratitude to the following:

Contributors and Reviewers:

- Arvie Martin
- Bill Minto
- Billy Moody
- Brian Shlisky
- Burhan Masood
- Carlos Pereira
- Christopher Paggen
- Christopher Travis
- Claudio DeSanti
- Corey Rhoades
- Damien Philip
- Dan Hanson
- Dan Lenoski
- Dante Malagrino
- Dave Berry
- David Cramer
- David Jansen
- David Lawler
- Diane McSweeney
- Dinesh Dutt
- Dino Farinacci
- Donna Helliwell
- Eamon O'Neill
- Ed Bugnion
- Eric Stephenson
- Ezequiel Aiello
- Fabio Ingrao
- Fausto Vaninetti
- Garth O'Mara
- Gilles Chekroun
- Gina Golden
- Glenn Charest
- Harpreet Bains
- Irene Golbery
- James Birkinshaw
- Jason Chang
- Jason Garbis
- Jason Waxman
- Jeff Ells
- Jeff Pishny
- Jeffrey Webb
- Jerome Simms
- Joe Vaccaro
- John Flood
- John McDonough
- Jose Martinez
- JR Rivers
- Justin Cooke
- Kathy Hickey
- Landon Curt Noll
- Leslie Menegaz
- Leslie Xu
- Liz Stine
- Louis Watta

- Luca Cafiero
- Madhu Somu
- Manoj Wadekar
- Mario Mazzola
- Matthew Kmiecik
- Matthew Taylor
- Mauricio Arregoces
- Maurizio Portolani
- Michelangelo Mazzola
- Mike Dvorkin
- Mike Galles
- Mike Liu
- Page Tagizad
- Pamela V. Snaith
- Philip Manela
- Prem Jain
- Ranga Bakthavathsalam
- Rich Lau
- Richard L. Morris
- Richard Tattoli
- Robert Bourassa
- Robert Burns
- Shannon Poulin
- Soni Jiandani
- Stephen Elliot
- Stephen Thorne
- Steve Abbott
- Steve Lemme

- Sunil Ahluwalia
- Susan Kawaguchi
- Suzanne Stout
- Tanvir Hussain
- Tjerk Bijlsma
- Tom Spencer
- Victor Moreno
- Walter Dey
- Wendy Payne

Silvano's wife Antonella has patiently reviewed the manuscript hunting for errors. Thank You.

Finally, we would like to acknowledge Julie Totora (www.paperumbrella.com) who helped us redraw most of the graphics.

Contents

Preface

This book is the result of the work done by the authors initially at Nuova Systems and subsequently at Cisco Systems on Project California, officially known as Cisco Unified Computing Systems (UCS).

UCS is a innovative technology platform that consolidates many traditional data center technical skill sets into one system. For this reason, the authors, from three very different backgrounds (and even different countries), have decided to combine their knowledge to publish this book together.

The book describes UCS from an educational view: We have tried to provide updated material about all server components and new data center technologies, as well as how these components and technologies are used to build a state of the art data center server.

We wish to express our thanks to the many engineering and marketing people from both Nuova Systems and Cisco Systems with whom we have collaborated with during the recent years.

UCS would not have been possible without the determination of the Cisco management team. They understood the opportunity for Cisco in entering the server market and decided to pursue it. Our gratitude goes out to them.

Nomenclature

Engineering projects are identified from inception to announcement by fantasy names that are often names of geographical places to avoid any trademark issue. Project California is not an exception. Project California or simply "California" is the name of the overall systems and city names, such as Palo and Menlo, are used to identify specific components.

Before the launch, Cisco decided to assign project California the official name of "Unified Computing System (UCS)", but the term California will continue to be used informally.

Cisco UCS Manager

The Cisco UCS Manager software integrates the components of the Cisco Unified Computing System into a single, seamless entity. The UCS Manager is described in Chapter 7.

Cisco UCS 6100 Series Fabric Interconnects

The Cisco UCS 6100 Series Fabric Interconnects are a family of line-rate, low-latency, lossless 10 Gigabit Ethernet, Cisco Data Center Bridging, and Fiber Channel over Ethernet (FCoE) switches, designed to consolidate the I/O at the system level. The Fabric Interconnects are described in Chapter 5.

Cisco UCS 2100 Series Fabric Extenders

The Cisco UCS 2100 Series Fabric Extender provides an extension of the I/O fabric into the blade server enclosure providing a direct 10 Gigabit Cisco Data Center Bridging connection between the blade servers and the Fabric Interconnects, simplifying diagnostics, cabling, and management. The Fabric Extenders are described in Chapter 5.

Cisco UCS 5100 Series Blade Server Enclosures

The Cisco UCS 5100 blade server Enclosures physically house blade servers and up to two fabric extenders. The Blade Server Enclosures are described in Chapter 5.

Cisco UCS B-Series Blade Servers

The Cisco UCS B-Series blade servers are designed for compatibility, performance, energy efficiency, large memory footprints, manageability, and unified I/O connectivity. They are based on Intel® Xeon® 5500 (Nehalem-EP), 5600 (West-mere-EP), and 7500 (Nehalem-EX) series processors (described in Chapter 2). The blade servers are described in Chapter 5.

Cisco UCS C-Series Rack Servers

The Cisco UCS C-Series rack servers are designed for compatibility, performance, energy efficiency, large memory footprints, manageability, expandability, and unified I/O connectivity. They are based on Intel® Xeon® 5500 (Nehalem-EP), 5600 (Westmere-EP), and 7500 (Nehalem-EX) series processors (described in Chapter 2). The rack servers are described in Chapter 6.

Cisco UCS Adapters

The Cisco UCS Adapters are installed on the UCS B-Series blade servers in order to provide I/O connectivity through the UCS 2100 Series Fabric Extenders. The different adapters are described in Chapter 4.

Chapter 1

Introduction

UCS is one of the largest endeavors ever attempted by Cisco®. It is a data center computing solution that is not a simple "me too" design, but rather a radical paradigm shift.

When we started this book, we were focused on describing UCS and pointing to other books for the reference material. Unfortunately, after repeated visits to the Stanford University bookstore and other prominent bookstores in Silicon Valley, we were unable to identify any updated reference books. Consequently, we have included this reference data ourselves.

The result is a book that consists of 50% reference material applicable to any server architecture and 50% specific to the UCS. The reference material includes updated processor, memory, I/O, and virtualization architectures.

UCS has a large ecosystem of partners, several of which have provided material for this book. We thank these partners for their contributions and help in making this book a reality.

With any book, there is always the question of how much time is spent in proof-reading it and making it error free. We wanted this book to be ready for Cisco Live, Las Vegas, July 2010. This has put a hard limit on the spell checking and improvement on graphics. If you find any error, or you have any advice for improvement, please email them to ca-book@ip6.com.

Finally, this book is neither a manual, nor a standard, nor a release note, nor a product announcement. This book was written to explain the concepts behind UCS to a large audience. It is not authoritative on anything; please reference the appropriate official documents when evaluating products, designing solutions, or conducting business. The authors do not provide any guarantee of the correctness of the content and are not liable for any mistake or imprecision.

Data Center Challenges

Data centers are the heartbeat of large corporations IT infrastructures. A typical Fortune 500 company runs thousands of applications worldwide, stores petabytes (10^{15}) of data, and has multiple data centers along with a disaster recovery plan in place. However, this huge-scale infrastructure often comes at a huge cost!

Data centers require expensive real estate, they use a lot of power, and in general they are expensive to operate.

To have a better understanding of how large data centers can become, reference [35] contains examples like:

- Google® The Dalles (OR) facility 68,680 Sq Ft (6,380 m²)
- Microsoft® Quincy, 470,000 Sq Ft (43,655 m²), 47 MWatts
- Yahoo® Wenatchee & Quincy, 2 Million Sq Ft (185,800 m²)
- Terremark®–NOTA, 750,000 Sq Ft (68,6767 m²), 100MWatts

These first few sections will analyze these issues in more detail.

Environmental Concerns—"Green"

You have probably noticed that green is everywhere these days: in the news, politics, fashion, and technology; data centers are no exception. The U.S. Environmental Protection Agency and the U.S. Department of Energy have a joint program to help businesses save money while protecting the environment through energy efficient products: It is called ENERGY STAR [40]. The money saving can be estimated by checking the average retail price of electricity [42].

ENERGY STAR is a proven energy management strategy that helps measure current energy performance, setting goals, tracking savings, and rewarding improvements. For example, the ENERGY STAR 4.0 standard that took effect in July 2007 requires power supplies in desktops, laptops, and workstations, to be 80% efficient for their load range. In addition, it places limits on the energy used by inactive devices, and requires systems to be shipped with power management features enabled.

Another effort, called Climate Savers® smart computing [41], started in the spirit of WWF (World Wildlife Fund) Climate Savers program. It has mobilized over a dozen companies since 1999 to cut CO_2 emissions, demonstrating that reducing emissions is part of a good business. Their mission is to reduce global CO_2 emissions from computer operation by 54 million tons per year, by 2010. This is equivalent to the annual output of 11 million cars or 10–20 coal-fired power plants.

Participating manufacturers commit to producing products that meet specified power-efficiency targets, and members commit to purchasing power-efficient computing products.

Climate Savers Computing Initiative starts with the ENERGY STAR 4.0 specification for desktops, laptops, and workstation computers and gradually increases the efficiency requirements in the period 2007–2011.

UCS is compliant with Energy Star and is designed to meet the power-efficiency targets of Climate Savers from day one.

Server Consolidation

In trying to save energy, it is always important to have a balanced approach between "every watt counts" and "let's target first the big consumers".

Speaking about the former, I remember a friend of mine telling me that he was drilling holes in the handle of his toothbrush before leaving for a long hiking trip, in order to reduce as much as possible the weight to carry.

The equivalent is to try to optimize as much as possible any component that uses power in a data center. For example, the networks elements consume approximately 14% of the overall power. By making them 50% more efficient (a goal very difficult to achieve), we will save 7% of the power.

Speaking about the latter, servers are the greatest power consumers in the data center and often most of the servers are very lightly loaded. Figure 1-1 shows an example of performance to power ratio for a generic server (courtesy of spec.org). From the figure, it is evident that if the load on the server is less than 60–70% the performance to power ratio is unacceptably low. Modern processors have techniques like "SpeedStep" to reduce power consumption on lightly loaded processors, but still the power consumed by the processor is only a fraction of the

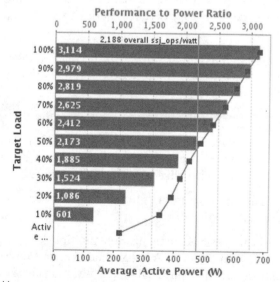

Figure 1-1   http://www.spec.org example

power consumed by the server. This implies that the major way to save power is to decommission lightly loaded servers and replace them with virtual machines.

Some statistics speak of an overall server utilization ranging from 5% to 10%. Let's assume that the servers use 70% of the power and that we reduce this number by a factor of five: Load will increase to 25–50% and power will be reduced to 14%, with a net saving of 56%.

The two techniques used in combination will produce even larger results. The key technology for reducing the number of servers is "server virtualization".

Virtualization

Virtualization is a broad and overused term that refers to the abstraction of computer and network resources. For example, VLAN (Virtual LAN) and VSAN (Virtual SAN) are forms of network virtualization.

What is becoming increasingly important for data centers is server virtualization, in particular hardware-assisted server virtualization. Wikipedia® defines it as: "*Hardware-assisted virtualization is a virtualization approach that enables efficient full virtualization using help from hardware capabilities, primarily from the host processors.*" Full virtualization is used to simulate a complete hardware environment, or virtual machine, in which an unmodified "guest" operating system (using the same instruction set as the host machine) executes in complete isolation. Hardware-assisted virtualization was first implemented on the IBM® System/370®, and was recently (2007) added to x86 processors (Intel VT® or AMD-V®).

According to Gartner, "*Virtualization is the highest impact trend changing infrastructure and operations through 2012. It will change how you manage, how and what you buy, how you deploy, how you plan, and how you charge [36].*" Several studies by the research firm IDC also support this claim. The firm reports 22 percent of servers today as being virtualized and expects that number to grow to 45 percent over the next 12 to 18 months [37]. Another IDC study predicts that the number of logical servers generated on virtualized servers will surpass the number of non-virtualized physical server units by 2010 [38].

Examples of virtualization solutions in X86-based processor systems include VMware® vSphere/ESX®, Microsoft Hyper-V®, Linux® KVM®, and Linux® Xen®.

With efficient hardware-assisted virtualization, multiple low-usage servers can be virtualized (i.e., transformed into a Virtual Machine) and multiple VMs can be run simultaneously on the same physical server. VMs can also be moved from one server to another for load balancing or disaster recovery.

Organizations worldwide are already beginning to take advantage of this model. The 2007 IDC study, for example, showed that 50% of all VMware ESX® users had adopted VMotion capability [39]. This technology enables live migration—moving guests from one physical server to another with no impact to end users' experience. By giving IT managers the ability to move guests on the fly, live migrations make it easier to balance workloads and manage planned and unplanned downtimes more efficiently.

UCS, with its large memory footprint and native virtualization support, may help cut the number of servers by one order of magnitude, thus achieving an even larger power saving.

Real Estate Power and Cooling

In building a new data center the number of servers that can be installed per square foot (square meter) is the result of many considerations, a primary one being how much cooling can be provided. In fact, all the power consumed by the data center equipment is transformed into heat that needs to be removed by the air conditioning systems.

Current data centers range from 50 to 200 Watts per square foot (500 to 2,000 W/m^2), which is optimal for current cooling technologies. New data centers are designed in the 300 to 500 Watts per square foot (3 to 5 KW/m^2). They require expensive cooling technologies that must be uninterruptible, since with such a high power load, the rise of temperature in the case of a fault in the cooling system can be as high as 25° F (14° C) per minute.

The Watts available per square foot have a direct correlation with the amount of Watts available on a per rack basis. With a rack every 40–60 square feet (4–6 m^2), current data centers have 2 to 10 KW/rack and future design may go as high as 12–25 KW/rack [35].

Cabling

Cabling is another big topic in data center designs. A mix of copper cables and fiber optics has been used until now, with two major physical topologies named Top of Rack (ToR) and End of Row (EoR).

The EoR approach places the network equipment (mainly LAN and SAN switches) at the end of the row and utilizes switches with a higher port count (128–512 ports) in the attempt to reduce the number of network devices that need to be managed. This implies longer cables with different lengths from the servers to the networking equipment. At 1 Gbps, these cable could be copper, but at 10 Gbps, fiber may be the only solution.

While a fiber cable may be cheaper than a copper cable, when installation and transceivers are considered (a fiber connection cost may exceed $3,000), if two or four links are used per server, this will exceed the cost of the server, without considering the cost of the switch ports.

In contrast, the ToR approach places the networking equipment as close as possible to the servers, typically at the top of each rack or every few racks. ToR switches are typically a lower port count (26–52 ports) fixed configuration switches. Distance from the servers to the ToR switches are limited typically to 33 feet (10 meters) and copper cables can easily be deployed, even with 10Gbps speed, resulting in all copper cabling within a rack. Fibers are used to connect the ToR switches to the central networking equipment (e.g., switches and Fibre Channel directors). All the servers connected to the same ToR switch share the cost of these fibers. This approach has one major trade-off, which is the increase in management points from the previous EoR architecture.

In both cases, cabling is a significant portion of the CAPEX (capital expenditure) of a data center and it restricts airflow in the rack and under the floor, negatively impacting cooling effectiveness (OPEX: operating expenditure). Figure 1-2 shows an extreme example of "spaghetti cabling."

In the past, three different parallel networks were deployed in the data center: Ethernet for LAN traffic, Fibre Channel for SAN traffic, and a separate Ethernet LAN for management. Sometimes additional dedicated networks have also been deployed—for example, a separate Ethernet or Fibre Channel network for backups and Infiniband for High Performance Computing. In recent next, generation

Figure 1-2   Cabling gone wrong

data center architectures, Ethernet has emerged as the enabling technology for the unified network design. Terms like Unified Fabric, I/O consolidation, and FCoE (Fibre Channel over Ethernet) are used to indicate the adoption of Ethernet as the sole network in the data center. This, of course, greatly simplifies cabling.

UCS is a system designed according to the ToR approach; all the servers that compose a UCS are connected to two Fabric Interconnects that are placed at the top of one or every few racks, and they communicate by using a Unified Fabric approach, thus greatly minimizing the cabling.

Disaster Recovery

Disaster strikes unexpectedly and large organizations must have a disaster recovery plan in place. This plan may be required by law to comply with government regulations. Data centers are no exception and they must be replicated at safe distances to minimize the possibility that both data centers could be affected by the same disaster. This implies replicating storage and servers and being able to restart the computing services on the backup data center in a minimal amount of time, known as Recovery Time Objective (RTO).

Virtualization is again our friend, since it allows moving Virtual Machines (VMs) from one site to another. Often VM movement is possible only inside the same layer 2 network (e.g., VLAN) since the MAC and IP addresses of the virtual server are part of the VM and in most cases they must be preserved during the movement.

As data centers have grown immensely in size over the past 10–15 years, there has been a reluctance to rely on Spanning Tree Protocol (STP) as the underlying technology for stability across an entire facility. To contain STP, layer 3 boundaries have been put in place to create PODS or borders between different zones within a data center facility in order to limit the effect of a dramatic layer 2 event, such as a STP loop or broadcast storm.

However, VMs have created a renewed interest in layer 2 networks that at one point seemed to be losing ground to layer 3 networks. Inside the data center, this will require replacing the spanning tree protocol with a more efficient layer 2 multipath solution. The IETF TRILL project [18] is a good example of this evolution: It proposes IS-IS in conjunction with MAC-in-MAC encapsulation to enable layer 2 multipathing. Efficient techniques to extend layer 2 networks across two or more data centers must also exist, and we discuss these in the following section on network virtualization.

Finally, a simple way to move server configurations from one data center to another must exist. In a UCS, the identity of the various components (MAC, addresses, UUIDs, WWNs, etc.) are not burned in the hardware, but contained in a configuration file. This allows the administrator to recreate an identical UCS in a disaster recovery site by simply moving the configuration file.

Network Virtualization

The role of the network in the virtualization space should address two complementary aspects: first, the use of network functionality in support of virtualized compute environments, and second the virtualization of the network elements.

When planning for disaster recovery or managing workloads across multiple data center facilities, larger and pervasive Layer 2 networks provide a multitude of operational advantages.

Larger and multi-site layer 2 networks should not create an unnecessary operational burden and should maintain the scalability and stability provided today by IP networks.

A promising solution is the evolution of technologies based upon the concept of "MAC routing", which enables VPN solutions in which Layer 2 connectivity can be provided between separate Layer 2 domains, while preserving all the benefits of an IP-based interconnection. This is a significant step forward in data center interconnection solutions.

In MAC routing, Layer 2 reachability information is distributed in a control protocol much like that used in a Layer 3 network. This protocol learning is the cornerstone to maintaining the failure containment and loop-free path diversity characteristics of an IP network while still providing Layer 2 connectivity. There are techniques in MAC routing to ensure that reconvergence events, broadcasts and unknown unicast flooding can be localized and kept from propagating to multiple data centers.

In the MAC routing model, traffic forwarding is done natively in IP, which makes the solution transport agnostic. The network architect now has the freedom of leveraging any Layer 1, Layer 2, or Layer 3 service between their data centers. The key here is that the operational model does not change from one transport to another. Thus, there are not any complex interactions between the transport core and the overlaid Layer 2 extensions. This is a big departure from the transport restrictions imposed by current label-switched VPN technologies. In short, MAC routing is totally transparent to the core and therefore minimizes the impact on design and operations that the extension of Layer 2 may impose on the network.

The Nexus 7000 is the first Cisco platform that provides MAC routing functionality at the L2/L3 boundary, maintaining the benefits of L3 routing between Layer 2 domains that may require Layer 2 connectivity. The Layer 3 intelligence may be realized in the underlying IP core or on the overlay control plane itself, allowing inter-domain Layer 2 traffic to inherit the wide variety of enhancements traditionally seen in a Layer 3 network. Some examples include: loop-free multipathing that enables load distribution for high-bandwidth interconnect, optimal Multicast replication, single control plane for multicast and unicast, Fast Re-route with Equal Cost Multi-Path routing.

MAC routing enables Layer 2 VPN solutions, which by extension enable Layer 3 VPN solutions. These are used more and more in order to virtualize the network itself and realize the consolidation benefits of a virtual network environment.

Desktop Virtualization

An important form of virtualization is desktop virtualization. Many large corporations have thousands of desktops distributed in multiple sites that are complex to install and maintain. The alternative has been to provide a terminal server service, but this deprives the users from a full PC desktop experience.

Desktop virtualization or Virtual Desktop Infrastructure (VDI) proposes to give the system administrator and the end users the best of both worlds, i.e.—a full PC experience for the users that is centrally provisioned and managed by the systems administrators.

With desktop virtualization, the system managers can provide new applications, upgrade existing ones, and upgrade or patch the operating systems of all the desktops in a centralized manner. Data is also stored in a consistent way and can be backed-up and restored centrally.

Companies like VMware®, Microsoft®, and Citrix® have proposed a few different approaches. They all have services running in a data center, often on virtual machines, and different kinds of desktops that range from classical PCs, to laptops, to thin clients. They vary in where the applications are run, the degree of flexibility they provide to the user, how anonymous the desktops are, and the technologies used to install applications and to communicate between the desktops and the servers.

The Remote Desktop Protocol (RDP) has been used in many installations and other solutions are appearing on the market, but a clearly winning architecture has not yet emerged.

UCS is a platform that can run tens of thousands of virtual machines on a single system comprised of hundreds individual nodes and it is therefore perfectly suited to host large desktop virtualization environments.

Cloud Computing

Cloud computing is a popular term used to indicate an economic way to run applications. The idea is to use a "cloud" composed of commodity servers, storage, and networking equipment. The cloud runs applications on demand, through a flexible management system that can seamlessly scale resources up or down as an application demands [43], [44].

With cloud computing, applications can be accessed from anywhere, at anytime. Clouds may be private to an enterprise or public. The most well-known example of public cloud computing is probably Amazon® EC2®.

Of course, not all applications are suited for public clouds. Significant concerns exist in relation to data security. Regulatory requirements can mandate keeping multiple copies of data in different geographical locations. Other concerns include latency and application availability.

For these reasons, many customers are evaluating the possibility to create private clouds inside their enterprises as a way to build a cost-effective data center infrastructure, suitable for on-demand application deployment. This should significantly increase server utilization.

Moreover, customers are starting to require servers that are "anonymous"—i.e., that can be easily repurposed. In addition, these new servers must be capable of supporting a high number of virtual machines, of easily moving them from one server to another, and have a management system that is policy-driven and provides a rich API interface (to interface with the cloud software).

Cisco UCS is a server designed with cloud computing in mind.

Evolution of Data Centers

This section describes the evolution of data center server architectures.

Stand-Alone Servers

Also known as discrete servers, they are independent servers that have a proprietary form factor. They may range from a desk-side PC to a large mainframe. They all have the basic components shown in Figure 1-3, but they may have a different number of processors, amount of memory, I/O capacity, expansion slots, and integrated storage.

The largest ones run multiple different applications and support a large number of users. Often they use some form of virtualization software that allows running multiple operating systems at the same time. However, no matter how powerful a discrete server is, it has scalability issues in both its physical limits and the operating system that it can provide for a specific application use case.

To overcome the scalability limitations, two different approaches have been used: scale-up and scale-out.

Figure 1-3　Server components

Scale-Up

Scale-up, aka scale vertically, is a term used to indicate a scaling strategy based on increasing the computing power of a single server by adding resources in term of more processors, memory, I/O devices, etc.

Such vertical scaling of existing systems also enables them to leverage virtualization technology more effectively, as it provides more resources for the hosted operating systems and applications.

Scale-up limits the number of management points, potentially easing security policy enforcement.

While attractive for some applications, most data centers prefer to use standard components and adopt a scale-out approach.

Scale-Out

Scale-out, aka scale horizontally, is a term used to indicate a scaling strategy based on increasing the number of servers. It has the big advantage that the administrator can more easily re-purpose compute as required.

Scale-out strategies are commonly adopted in association with Intel X86 servers. These types of servers, based on the PC architecture, have seen in the recent years a continued price drop and performance increase. These "commodity" systems have now reached a computing capacity sufficient to run the majority of applications present in data centers. They may also be interconnected in clusters to perform HPC (High Performance Computing) applications in scientific fields like modeling and simulation, oil and gas, seismic analysis, and biotechnology, previously possible only on mainframes or supercomputers.

The scale-out model has created an increased demand for shared data storage with very high I/O performance, especially where processing of large amounts of data is required, such as for databases.

Scale-Up vs. Scale-Out

There are trade-offs between the two models.

Scale-up requires dedicated and more expensive hardware and provides a limited number of operating system environments, and there are limitations on the amount of total load that a server can support. It has the advantage of having few management points and a good utilization of resources and therefore it tends to be more power and cooling efficient than the scale-out model.

Scale-out dedicates each server to a specific application. Each application is limited by the capacity of a single node, but each server can run the most appropriate OS for the application with the appropriate patches applied. There is no application interference and application performance is very deterministic. This approach clearly explodes the number of servers and it increases the management complexity.

Rack-Optimized Servers

With scale-out constantly increasing the number of servers, the need to optimize their size, airflow, connections, and to rationalize installation becomes obvious.

Rack-optimized servers were the first attempt to solve this problem (see Figure 1-4). Also known as rack-mounted servers, they fit in 19-inch wide racks and their height is specified in term of Rack Unit (RU), one rack unit being 1.75 in (44.45 mm) high. A typical Intel-based server fits in one RU and it dissipates approximately 500 Watts. The racks are typically 42 RUs, but it is normally impossible to provide enough power and cooling to fill an entire rack with servers.

Typical data centers have 5 to 10 KW of power and cooling available per rack and therefore 10 to 20 servers are installed in a rack. The remaining space is filled with patch panels. Sometimes ToR (Top of the Rack) switches are installed to aggregate the traffic generated by the servers present in few adjacent racks. In other designs larger EoR (End of Row) switches are used to connect all the servers in a row and in hybrid schemes ToR/EoR.

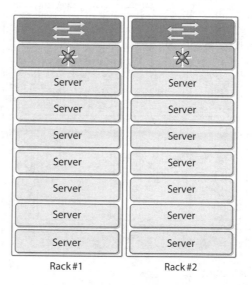

Figure 1-4   Rack-mounted servers

The benefits of this approach are rational space utilization and high flexibility: the relative large server size allows adopting the latest processor with a larger memory, and several I/O slots. The weaknesses are in the lack of cabling rationalization, in the serviceability that is not easy, and in the lack of power and cooling efficiency, since each server has its own power supplies and fans.

Rack-mounted servers are just a simple repackaging of conventional servers in a form factor that allows installing more servers per square foot of data center floor, but without significant differences in functionality.

At the time of this writing (March 2010), rack-optimized servers account for approximately 50% of the overall server market.

Blade Servers

Blade servers were introduced as a way to optimize cabling and power efficiency of servers compared to rack mounted. Blade server chassis are 6 to 12 RUs and can host 6 to 16 computing blades, plus a variety of I/O modules, power supplies, fans, and chassis management CPUs (see Figure 1-5).

Blade server advantages are shared chassis infrastructure (mainly power and cooling), rationalization in cabling, and the capability to monitor the shared infrastructure. The number of management points is reduced from one per server to one per chassis, but the chassis is often an added artificial point of aggregation.

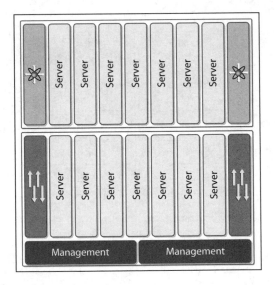

Figure 1-5   Blade servers

The concept of chassis is not of primary importance, for example, when defining a pool of servers to be used for a particular application or for virtualization.

Blade servers cannot host generic PCI cards, but require "mezzanine cards" that have proprietary form factors. This limits the I/O options when compared to rack-mounted servers.

At the time of this writing (March 2010), blade servers account for approximately 10% of the overall server markets, but their adoption is accelerating and this percentage is growing rapidly.

Server Sprawl

Today, most servers run a single OS (commonly some form of Windows® or Linux®) and a single application per server (see Figure 1-6). This deployment model leads to "server sprawl", i.e., a constantly increasing number of servers with an extremely low CPU utilization, as low as 5% to 10% average utilization. This implies a lot of waste in space, power, and cooling.

The benefits of this deployment model are isolation (each application has guaranteed resources), flexibility (almost any OS/application can be started on any server), and simplicity (each application has a dedicated server with the most appropriate OS version). Each server is a managed object, and since each server runs a single application, each application is a managed object.

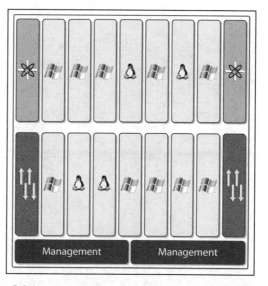

Figure 1-6   Single OS/application per server

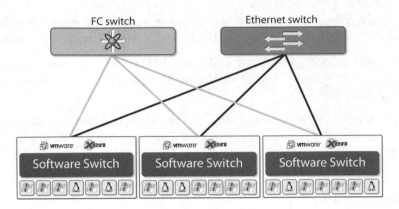

Figure 1-7   Server virtualization

This architecture allows the consistent setting of differentiated policies for the different applications. The network has one (or more) physical port for each application, and on that port, it can ensure QoS, ACLs, security, etc. This works independently from the fact that the switches are inside the blade server or outside.

Nonetheless, server sprawl is becoming rapidly unacceptable due to the waste of space, power, and cooling. In addition, the management of all these servers is an administrator nightmare as well as very expensive.

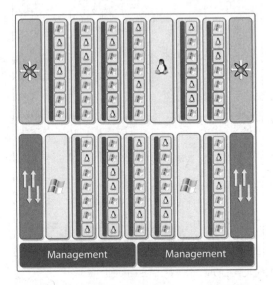

Figure 1-8   Virtualization deployed on a blade server

Virtualization

Virtualization is one of key technologies used to reduce server sprawl and it has been heavily adopted by organizations throughout the world. As opposed to the chassis being a container, with virtualization a server is a container of multiple logical servers (see Figure 1-7 and Figure 1-8). The virtualization software contains a software switch that is equivalent to the physical switch present in a chassis. The advantages of server virtualization are utilization, mobility, and availability. The disadvantages are lack of distributed policies, security, diagnostics, and performance predictability.

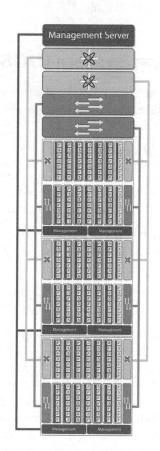

Figure 1-9   Blade servers interconnected by external switches

Server Deployment Today

All of the server evolutions described up to now have mainly been "an evolution of size" and not a significant change in the model. Scale-up means larger servers; scale-out means more servers and therefore more network infrastructure. For example, Figure 1-9 shows three blade servers, running virtualization, mounted in a rack, and interconnected by external switches.

Management tools are very often an afterthought: They are applied to servers, not deeply integrated with them. This causes a growth in the number of tools required to manage the same server set, and in general, it is difficult to maintain policy coherence, to secure, and to scale.

Unified Computing System (UCS)

The Cisco Unified Computing System (UCS), aka Project California, is an attempt to eliminate, or at least reduce, the limitations present in current server deployments.

Cisco's definition for Unified Computing is:

> *"Unified Computing unifies network virtualization, storage virtualization, and server virtualization into one, within open industry standard technologies and with the network as the platform."*

UCS is a component of the Cisco Data Center 3.0 architecture. It is a scalable compute platform, based on the natural aggregation point that exists in any data center: the network.

UCS is composed of fabric interconnects that aggregate a set of blade chassis and rack servers.

Compared to blade servers, it is an innovative architecture. It removes unnecessary switches, adapters, and management modules—i.e., it has 1/3 less infrastructure compared to classical blade servers. This results in less power and cooling and fewer management points, which leads to an increased reliability. For example, Figure 1-10 shows a UCS with 40 blades. When compared with the three blade servers of Figure 1-9 (42 blades total), six Ethernet switches, six Fibre Channel Switches, and six management modules are no longer needed. This equates in power and cooling saving, but also in a reduced number of management points.

The saving increases with a larger number of blades. A single UCS may grow as large as 320 blades. Figure 1-11 shows a single UCS with 280 blades, hosted in 7 racks. In this configuration, there is no single point of failure.

The most important technology innovations introduced in UCS are:

- **Embedded management:** UCS does not require a separate management server, since it has an embedded management processor that has global visibility on all the elements that constitute a UCS. This guarantees coordinated control and provides integrated management and diagnostics.

- **Unified Fabric:** UCS is the first server completely designed around the concept of Unified Fabric. This is important since different applications have different I/O requirements. Without Unified Fabric, it is difficult to move applications from one server to another while also preserving the appropriate I/O requirement. Unified Fabric not only covers LAN, SAN, and HPC, but also the management network.

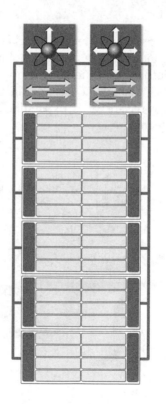

Figure 1-10   A UCS

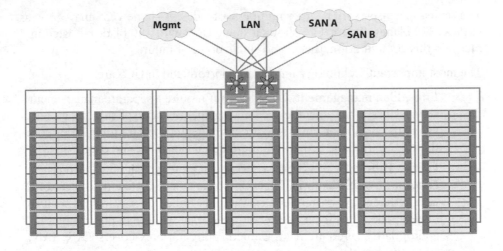

Figure 1-11   A multi-rack UCS

■ **Optimized virtualized environment:** Designed to support a large number of virtual machines not only from the point of view of scale, but
also from policy enforcement, mobility, control, and diagnostics. This
is achieved by working simultaneously on the three axis of Figure 1-12;
i.e., by using state of the art CPUs, expanding the memory, and adopting
sophisticated I/O techniques.

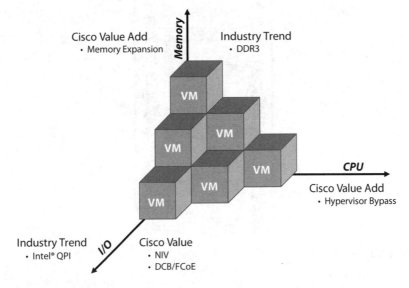

Figure 1-12   Virtualization improvements

- **Fewer servers with more memory:** The UCS computing blades using Cisco Memory Expansion Technology can support up to four times more memory when compared to competing servers with the same processor. More memory enables faster database servers and more virtual machines per server, thus increasing CPU utilization. Fewer CPUs with more utilization lower the cost of software licenses.

- **Stateless computing:** Server attributes are no longer tied to physical hardware that enables seamless server mobility. The blades and the blade enclosures are completely stateless. UCS also puts a lot of attention on network boot (LAN or SAN) with the boot order configurable as a part of the service profile.

- **Hybrid system:** A UCS can be composed of a mixture of blades and rack servers and they can all be managed by the UCS Manager.

Since the management is embedded, there is no need to have a separate server for the management software with the required hardware configuration and OS patches, or to have complex installation procedures that are prone to error and that can cause system downtime.

UCS is not only a single management point, it is a single system. All UCS features are made available to any computing blade or rack server that is added. UCS has a comprehensive model-driven architecture, in which all components are designed to integrate together.

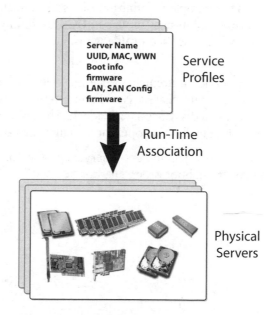

Figure 1-13 Service profile

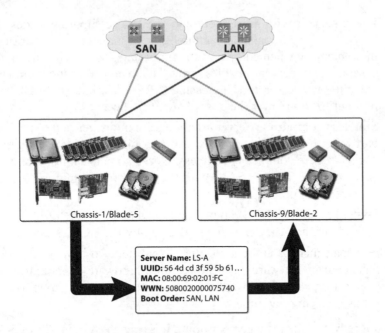

Figure 1-14 Service profile movements

At the core of the UCS architecture is the concept of a "Service Profile"—i.e., a template that contains the complete definition of a service including server, network, and storage attributes. Physical servers in UCS are totally anonymous and they get a personality when a service profile is instantiated on them (see Figure 1-13).

This greatly simplifies service movement, since a service profile can be simply moved from one blade in one chassis (see Figure 1-14, Chassis-1/Blade-5) to another blade in another chassis (Chassis-9/Blade 2). The uniform I/O connectivity based on Unified Fabric makes this operation straightforward.

The figures illustrate only few parameters; a service profile contains many more, like BIOS version and setting, boot order, etc.

Chapter 2

Server Architectures

Processor, memory, and I/O are the three most important subsystems in a server from a performance perspective. At any given point in time, one of them tends to become a bottleneck from the performance perspective. We often hear of applications that are CPU-bound, memory-bound, or I/O-bound.

In this chapter, we will examine these three subsystems with particular reference to servers built according to the IA-32 (Intel® Architecture, 32-bit), often generically called x86 architecture. In particular, we will describe the most recent generation of Intel® processors compatible with the IA-32 architecture; i.e., the Intel® microarchitecture (formerly known by the codename Nehalem).[1]

The Nehalem microarchitecture (see "Intel Microarchitectures" in Chapter 2, page 45) and its variation, the Westmere microarchitecture, include three families of processors that are used on the Cisco UCS: the Nehalem-EP, the Nehalem-EX, and the Westmere-EP. Table 2-1 summarizes the main characteristics of these processors.

Table 2-1 UCS Processors

	Nehalem-EP	Westmere-EP	Nehalem-EX	Nehalem-EX
Commercial Name	Xeon® 5500	Xeon® 5600	Xeon® 6500	Xeon® 7500
Max Sockets Supported	2	2	2	8
Max Cores per Socket	4	6	8	8
Max Threads per Socket	8	12	16	16
MB Cache (Level 3)	8	12	18	24
Max # of Memory DIMMs	18	18	32	128

---

1 The authors are thankful to Intel Corporation for the information and the material provided to edit this chapter. Most of the pictures are courtesy of Intel Corporation.

Figure 2-1   An Intel® Xeon® 5500 Processor

The Processor Evolution

Modern processors or CPUs (Central Processing Units) are built using the latest silicon technology and pack millions of transistors and megabytes of memory on a single die (blocks of semiconducting material that contains a processor).

Multiple dies are fabricated together in a silicon wafer; each die is cut out individually, tested, and assembled in a ceramic package. This involves mounting the die, connecting the die pads to the pins on the package, and sealing the die.

At this point, the processor in its package is ready to be sold and mounted on servers. Figure 2-1 shows a packaged Intel® Xeon® 5500.

Sockets

Processors are installed on the motherboard using a mounting/interconnection structure known as a "socket." Figure 2-2 shows a socket used for an Intel® Processor. This allows the customers to personalize a server motherboard by installing processors with different clock speeds and power consumption,

The number of sockets present on a server motherboard determines how many processors can be installed. Originally, servers had a single socket, but more recently, to increase server performance, 2-, 4-, and 8-socket servers have appeared on the market.

In the evolution of processor architecture, for a long period, performance improvements were strictly related to clock frequency increases. The higher the clock frequency, the shorter the time it takes to make a computation, and therefore the higher the performance.

Figure 2-2   An Intel® processor socket

As clock frequencies approached a few GigaHertz, it became apparent the physics involved would limit further improvement in this area. Therefore, alternative ways to increase performance had to be identified.

Cores

The constant shrinking of the transistor size (Nehalem uses a 45-nanometer technology; Westmere uses a 32-nanometer technology) has allowed the integration of millions of transistors on a single die. One way to utilize this abundance of transistors is to replicate the basic CPU (the "core") multiple times on the same die.

Multi-core processors (see Figure 2-3) are now common in the market. Each processor (aka socket) contains multiple CPU cores (2, 4, 6, and 8 are typical numbers). Each core is associated with a level 1 (L1) cache. Caches are small fast memories used to reduce the average time to access the main memory. The cores generally share a larger level 2 (L2) or level 3 (L3) cache, the bus interface, and the external die connections.

In modern servers, the number of cores is the product of the number of sockets times the number of cores per socket. For example, servers based on Intel® Xeon® Processor 5500 Series (Nehalem-EP) typically use two sockets and four cores per sockets for a total of eight cores. With the Intel® Xeon® 7500 (Nehalem-EX), 8 sockets each with 8 cores are supported for a total of 64 cores.

Dual CPU Core Chip

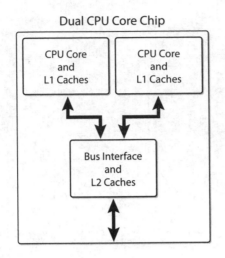

Figure 2-3   Two CPU cores in a socket

Figure 2-4 shows a more detailed view of a dual-core processor. The CPU's main components (instruction fetching, decoding, and execution) are duplicated, but the access to the system buses is common.

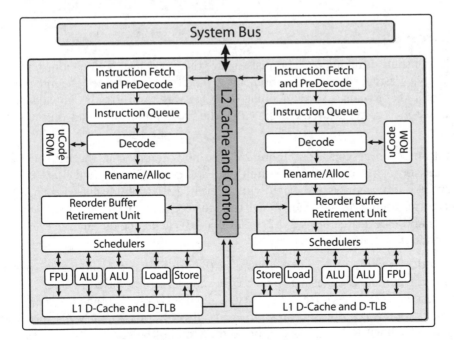

Figure 2-4   Architecture of a dual-core processor

Threads

To better understand the implication of multi-core architecture, let us consider how programs are executed. A server will run a kernel (e.g., Linux®, Windows®) and multiple processes. Each process can be further subdivided into "threads". Threads are the minimum unit of work allocation to cores. A thread needs to execute on a single core, and it cannot be further partitioned among multiple cores (see Figure 2-5).

Processes can be single-threaded or multi-threaded. A process that is single thread process can execute in only one core and is limited by the performance of that core. A multi-threaded process can execute on multiple cores at the same time, and therefore its performance can exceed the performance of a single core.

Since many applications are single-threaded, a multi-socket, multi-core architecture is typically convenient in an environment where multiple processes are present. This is always true in a virtualized environment, where a hypervisor allows consolidating multiple logical servers into a single physical server creating an environment with multiple processes and multiple threads.

Intel® Hyper-Threading Technology

While a single thread cannot be split between two cores, some modern processors allow running two threads on the same core at the same time. Each core has multiple execution units capable of working in parallel, and it is rare that a single thread will keep all the resources busy.

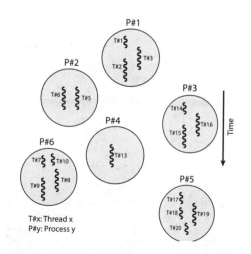

Figure 2-5   Processes and threads

Figure 2-6 shows how the Intel® Hyper-Threading Technology works. Two threads execute at the same time on the same core, and they use different resources, thus increasing the throughput.

Front-Side Bus

In the presence of multi-sockets and multi-cores, it is important to understand how the memory is accessed and how communication between two different cores work.

Figure 2-7 shows the architecture used in the past by many Intel® processors, known as the Front-Side Bus (FSB). In the FSB architecture, all traffic is sent across a single, shared bidirectional bus. In modern processors, this is a 64-bit wide bus that is operated at 4X the bus clock speed. In certain products, the FSB is operated at an information transfer rate of up to 1.6 GT/s (Giga Transactions per second, i.e., 12.8 GB/s).

The FSB is connected to all the processors and to the chipset called the Northbridge (aka MCH: Memory Controller Hub). The Northbridge connects the memory that is shared across all the processors.

One of the advantages of this architecture is that each processor has knowledge of all the memory accesses of all the other processors in the system. Each processor can implement a cache coherency algorithm to keep its internal caches in synch with the external memory and with the caches of all other processors.

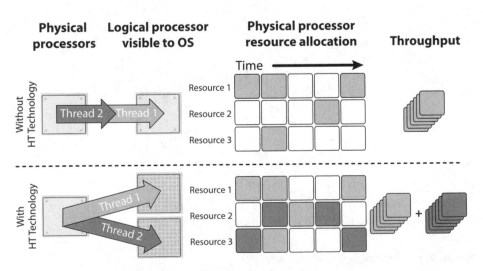

Figure 2-6   Intel® Hyper-Threading Technology

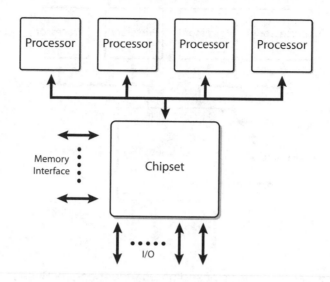

Figure 2-7   A server platform based on a front-side bus

Platforms designed in this manner have to contend with the shared nature of the bus. As signaling speeds on the bus increase, it becomes more difficult to implement and connect the desired number of devices. In addition, as processor and chipset performance increases, the traffic flowing on the FSB also increases. This results in increased congestion on the FSB, since the bus is a shared resource.

Dual Independent Buses

To further increase the bandwidth, the single shared bus evolved into the Dual Independent Buses (DIB) architecture depicted in Figure 2-8, which essentially doubles the available bandwidth.

However, with two buses, all the cache consistency traffic has to be broadcasted on both buses, thus reducing the overall effective bandwidth. To minimize this problem, "snoop filters" are employed in the chipset to reduce the bandwidth loading.

When a cache miss occurs, a snoop is put on the FSB of the originating processor. The snoop filter intercepts the snoop, and determines if it needs to pass along the snoop to the other FSB. If the read request is satisfied with the other processor on the same FSB, the snoop filter access is cancelled. If the other processor on the same FSB does not satisfy the read request, the snoop filter determines the next course of action. If the read request misses the snoop filter, data is returned directly from memory. If the snoop filter indicates that the target cache line of the

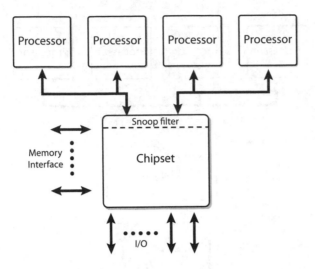

Figure 2-8   A server platform based on Dual Independent Buses

request could exist on the other FSB, the snoop filter will reflect the snoop across to the other segment. If the other segment still has the cache line, it is routed to the requesting FSB. If the other segment no longer owns the target cache line, data is returned from memory. Because the protocol is write-invalidate, write requests must always be propagated to any FSB that has a copy of the cache line in question.

Dedicated High-Speed Interconnect

The next step of the evolution is the Dedicated High-Speed Interconnect (DHSI), as shown in Figure 2-9.

DHSI-based platforms use four independent FSBs, one for each processor in the platform. Snoop filters are employed to achieve good bandwidth scaling.

The FSBs remains electrically the same, but are now used in a point-to-point configuration.

Platforms designed using this approach still must deal with the electrical signaling challenges of the fast FSB. DHSI drives up also the pin count on the chipset and require extensive PCB routing to establish all these connections using the wide FSBs.

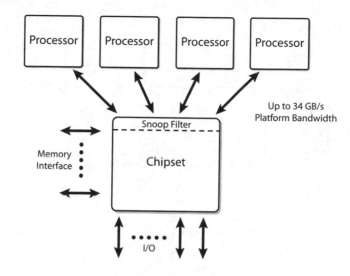

Figure 2-9   A server platform based on DHSI

Intel® QuickPath Interconnect

With the introduction of the Intel Core i7 processor, a new system architecture has been adopted for many Intel products. This is known as the Intel® QuickPath Interconnect (Intel® QPI). This architecture utilizes multiple high-speed uni-directional links interconnecting the processors and the chipset. With this architecture, there is also the realization that:

- A common memory controller for multiple sockets and multiple cores is a bottleneck.
- Introducing multiple distributed memory controllers would best match the memory needs of multi-core processors.
- In most cases, having a memory controller integrated into the processor package would boost performance.
- Providing effective methods to deal with the coherency issues of multi-socket systems is vital to enabling larger-scale systems.

Figure 2-10 gives an example functional diagram of a processor with multiple cores, an integrated memory controller, and multiple Intel® QPI links to other system resources.

In this architecture, all cores inside a socket share IMCs (Integrated Memory Controllers) that may have multiple memory interfaces (i.e., memory buses).

IMCs may have different external connections:

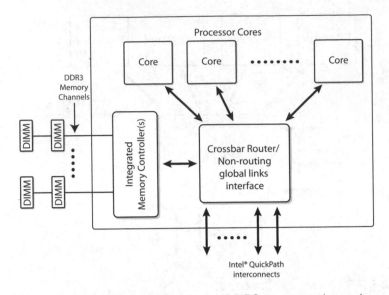

Figure 2-10   Processor with Intel® QPI and DDR3 memory channels

- DDR3 memory channels: In this case, the DDR3 DIMMs (see the next section) are directly connected to the sockets, as shown in Figure 2-12. This architecture is used in Nehalem-EP (Xeon 5500) and Westmere-EP (Xeon 5600).

- High-speed serial memory channels, as shown in Figure 2-11. In this case, an external chip (SMB: Scalable Memory Buffer) creates DDR3 memory channels where the DDR3 DIMMs are connected. This architecture is used in Nehalem-EX (Xeon 7500).

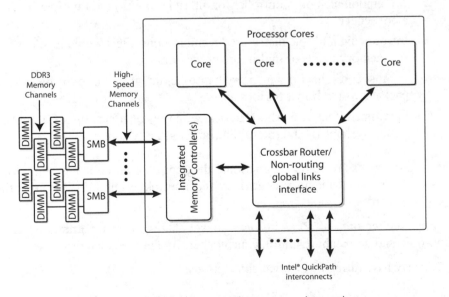

Figure 2-11   Processors with high-speed memory channels

IMCs and cores in different sockets talk to each other using Intel® QPI.

Processors implementing Intel® QPI also have full access to the memory of every other processor, while maintaining cache coherency. This architecture is also called "cache-coherent NUMA (Non-Uniform Memory Architecture)"—i.e., the memory interconnection system guarantees that the memory and all the potentially cached copies are always coherent.

Intel® QPI is a point-to-point interconnection and messaging scheme that uses a point-to-point differential current-mode signaling. On current implementation, each link is composed of 20 lanes per direction capable of up to 25.6 GB/s or 6.4 GT/s (Giga Transactions/second); (see "Platform Architecture" in Chapter 2, page 46).

Intel® QPI uses point-to-point links and therefore requires an internal crossbar router in the socket (see Figure 2-10) to provide global memory reachability. This route-through capability allows one to build systems without requiring a fully connected topology.

Figure 2-12 shows a configuration of four Intel® Nehalem EX, each processor has four QPI and interconnects with the three other processors and with the Boxboro-EX chipsets (SMB components are present, but not shown).

The Memory Subsystem

The electronic industry has put a significant effort into manufacturing memory subsystems capable of keeping up with the low access time required by modern processors and the high capacity required by today's applications.

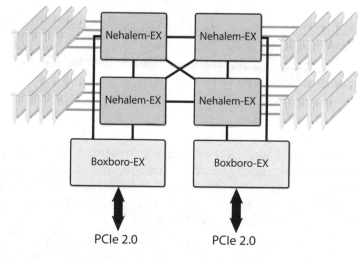

Figure 2-12   Four-socket Nehalem EX

Before proceeding with the explanation of current memory subsystems, it is important to introduce a glossary of the most commonly used terms:

- RAM (Random Access Memory)
- SRAM (Static RAM)
- DRAM (Dynamic RAM)
- SDRAM (Synchronous DRAM)
- SIMM (Single Inline Memory Module)
- DIMM (Dual Inline Memory Module)
- UDIMM (Unbuffered DIMM)
- RDIMM (Registered DIMM)
- DDR (Double Data Rate SDRAM)
- DDR2 (Second Generation DDR)
- DDR3 (Third Generation DDR)

In particular, the Joint Electron Device Engineering Council (JEDEC) is the semiconductor engineering standardization body that has been active in this field. JEDEC Standard 21 [21], [22] specifies semiconductor memories from the 256 bits SRAM to the latest DDR3 modules.

The memory subsystem of modern servers is composed of RAMs (Random Access Memories), i.e., integrated circuits (aka ICs or chips) that allow the data to be accessed in any order, in a constant time, regardless of its physical location. RAMs can be static or dynamic [27], [28], [29], [30].

SRAMs

SRAMs (Static RAMs) are generally very fast, but smaller capacity (few megabytes) than DRAM (see next section), and they have a chip structure that maintains the information as long as power is maintained. They are not large enough to be used for the main memory of a server.

DRAMs

DRAMs (Dynamic RAMs) are the only choice for servers. The term "dynamic" indicates that the information is stored on capacitors within an integrated circuit. Since capacitors discharge over time, due to leakage currents, the capacitors need to be recharged ("refreshed") periodically to avoid data loss. The memory controller is normally in charge of the refresh operations.

SDRAMs

SDRAMs (Synchronous DRAMs) are the most commonly used DRAM. SDRAMs have a synchronous interface, meaning that their operation is synchronized with a clock signal. The clock is used to drive an internal finite state machine that pipelines memory accesses. Pipelining means that the chip can accept a new memory access before it has finished processing the previous one. This greatly improves the performance of SDRAMs compared to classical DRAMs.

DDR2 and DDR3 are the two most commonly used SDRAMs (see "DDR2 and DDR3" in Chapter 2, page 41 [23]).

Figure 2-13 shows the internal architecture of a DRAM chip.

The memory array is composed of memory cells organized in a matrix. Each cell has a row and a column address. Each bit is stored in a capacitor (i.e., storage element).

To improve performance and to reduce power consumption, the memory array is split into multiple "banks." Figure 2-14 shows a 4-bank and an 8-bank organization.

DDR2 chips have four internal memory banks and DDR3 chips have eight internal memory banks.

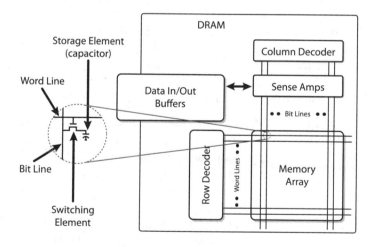

Figure 2-13 Internal architecture of a DRAM chip

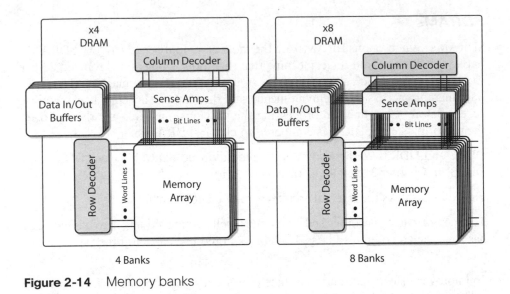

Figure 2-14 Memory banks

DIMMs

Multiple memory chips need to be assembled together to build a memory subsystem. They are organized in small boards known as DIMMs (Dual Inline Memory Modules).

Figure 2-15 shows the classical organization of a memory subsystem [24]. For example, a memory controller connects four DIMMs each composed of multiple DRAM chips. The memory controller (that may also integrate the clock driver) has an address bus, a data bus, and a command (aka control) bus. It is in charge of reading, writing, and refreshing the information stored in the DIMMs.

Figure 2-16 is an example of the connection between a memory controller and a DDR3 DIMM. The DIMM is composed of eight DRAM chips, each capable of storing eight bits of data for a total of 64 bits per memory word (width of the memory data bus). The address bus has 15 bits and it carries, at different times, the "row address" or the "column address" for a total of 30 address bits. In addition, three bits of bank address allow accessing the eight banks inside each DDR3 chip. They can be considered equivalent to address bits raising the total addressing capability of the controller to eight Giga words (i.e., 512 Gbits, or 64 GB). Even if the memory controller has this addressing capability, the DDR3 chips available on the market are significantly smaller. Finally, RAS (Row Address Selection), CAS (Column Address Selection), WE (Write Enabled), etc. are the command bus wires.

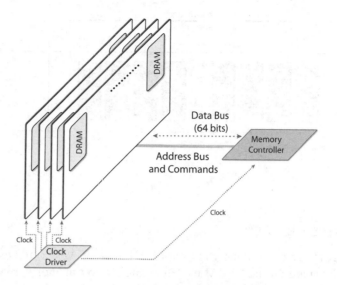

Figure 2-15   Example of a memory subsystem

Figure 2-17 shows a schematic depiction of a DIMM.

The front view shows the eight DDR3 chips each providing eight bits of information (normally indicated by "x8"). The side view shows that the chips are on one side of the board for a total of eight chips (i.e., 64 bits).

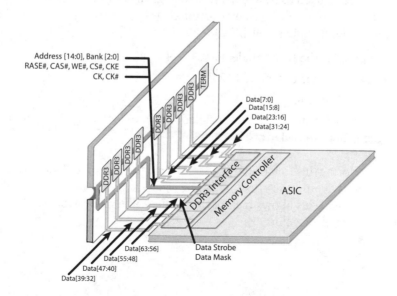

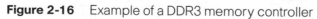

Figure 2-16   Example of a DDR3 memory controller

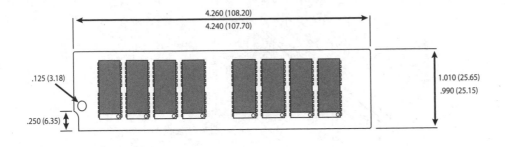

Figure 2-17   A DIMM

ECC and Chipkill®

Data integrity is a major concern in server architecture. Very often extra memory chips are installed on the DIMM to detect and recover memory errors. The most common arrangement is to add 8 bits of ECC (Error Correcting Code) to expand the memory word from 64 to 72 bits. This allows the implementation of codes like the Hamming code that allows a single-bit error to be corrected and double-bit errors to be detected. These codes are also known as SEC/DED (Single Error Correction / Double Error Detection).

With a careful organization of how the memory words are written in the memory chips, ECC can be used to protect from any single memory chip that fails and any number of multi-bit errors from any portion of a single memory chip. This feature has several different names [24], [25], [26]:

- Chipkill® is the IBM® trademark.
- Oracle® calls it Extended ECC.
- HP® calls it Chipspare®.
- A similar feature from Intel is called Intel® x4 Single Device Data Correction (Intel® x4 SDDC).

Chipkill® performs this function by bit-scattering the bits of an ECC word across multiple memory chips, such that the failure of any single memory chip will affect only one ECC bit. This allows memory contents to be reconstructed despite the complete failure of one chip.

While a complete discussion of this technology is beyond the scope of this book, an example can give an idea of how it works. Figure 2-18 shows a memory controller that reads and writes 128 bits of useful data at each memory access, and 144 bits when ECC is added. The 144 bits can be divided in 4 memory words of 36 bits. Each memory word will be SEC/DED. By using two DIMMs, each with 18 4-bit chips, it is possible to reshuffle the bits as shown in Figure 2-18. If a chip fails, there will be one error in each of the four words, but since the words are SEC-DEC, each of the four words can correct an error and therefore all the four errors will be corrected.

Memory Ranks

Going back to how the DIMMs are organized, an arrangement of chips that produce 64 bits of useful data (not counting the ECC) is called a "rank". To store more data on a DIMM, multiple ranks can be installed. There are single, dual, and quad-ranks DIMMs. Figure 2-19 shows three possible organizations.

In the first drawing, a rank of ECC RAM is built using nine eight-bit chips, a configuration that is also indicated 1Rx8. The second drawing shows a 1Rx4 arrangement in which 18 four-bit chips are used to build one rank. Finally, the third drawing shows a 2Rx8 in which 18 eight-bit chips are used to build two ranks.

Memory ranks are not selected using address bits, but "chip selects". Modern memory controllers have up to eight separate chip selects and therefore are capable of supporting up to eight ranks.

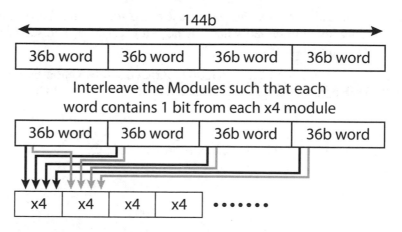

Figure 2-18   A Chipkill® example

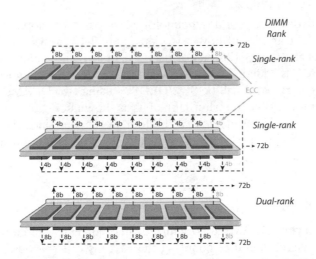

Figure 2-19   DIMMs and memory ranks

UDIMMs and RDIMMs

SDRAM DIMMs are further subdivided into UDIMMs (Unbuffered DIMMs) and RDIMM (Registered DIMMs). In UDIMMs, the memory chips are directly connected to the address and control buses, without any intermediate component.

RDIMM have additional components (registers) placed between the incoming address and control buses and the SDRAM components. These registers add one clock cycle of delay but they reduce the electrical load on the memory controller and allow more DIMM to be installed per memory controller.

RDIMM are typically more expensive because of the additional components, and they are usually found in servers where the need for scalability and stability outweighs the need for a low price.

Although any combination of Registered/Unbuffered and ECC/non-ECC is theoretically possible, most server-grade memory modules are both ECC and registered.

Figure 2-20 shows an ECC RDIMM. The registers are the chips indicated by the arrows; the nine memory chips indicate the presence of ECC.

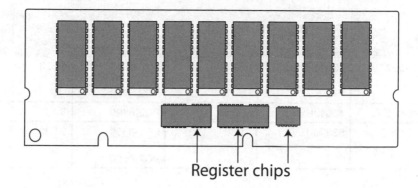

Register chips

Figure 2-20   ECC RDIMM

DDR2 and DDR3

The first SDRAM technology was called SDR (Single Data Rate) to indicate that a single unit of data is transferred per each clock cycle. It was followed by the DDR (Double Data Rate) standard that achieves nearly twice the bandwidth of SDR by transferring data on the rising and falling edges of the clock signal, without increasing the clock frequency. DDR evolved into the two currently used standards: DDR2 and DDR3.

DDR2 SDRAMs (double-data-rate two synchronous dynamic random access memories) operate at 1.8 Volts and are packaged in 240 pins DIMM modules. They are capable of operating the external data bus at twice the data rate of DDR by improved bus signaling.

The rules are:

- Two data transfers per DRAM clock
- Eight bytes (64 bits) per data transfer

Table 2-2 shows the DDR2 standards.[2]

Table 2-2   DDR2 DIMMs

Standard name	DRAM clock	Million data transfers per second	Module name	Peak transfer rate GB/s
DDR2-400	200 MHz	400	PC2-3200	3.200
DDR2-533	266 MHz	533	PC2-4200	4.266

continues

2   Some of the DDR2 modules have two names, depending on the manufacturer.

Standard name	DRAM clock	Million data transfers per second	Module name	Peak transfer rate GB/s
DDR2-667	333 MHz	667	PC2-5300 PC2-5400	5.333
DDR2-800	400 MHz	800	PC2-6400	6.400
DDR2-1066	533 MHz	1,066	PC2-8500 PC2-8600	8.533

DDR3 SDRAMs (double-data-rate three synchronous dynamic random access memories) improve over DDR2 in the following areas:

- Reduced power consumption obtained by reducing the operating voltage to 1.5 volts.
- Increased memory density by introducing support for chips from 0.5 to 8 Gigabits; i.e., rank capacity up to 16 GB.
- Increased memory bandwidth by supporting a burst length = 8 words, compared to the burst length = 4 words of DDR2. The reason for the increase in burst length is to better match the increased external data transfer rate with the relatively constant internal access time. As the transfer rate increases, the burst length (the size of the transfer) must increase to not exceed the access rate of the DRAM core.

DDR3 DIMMs have 240 pins, the same number as DDR2, and are the same size, but they are electrically incompatible and have a different key notch location. In the future, DDR3 will also operate at faster clock rate. At the time of publishing, only DDR3-800, 1066, and 1333 are in production.

Table 2-3 summarizes the different DDR3 DIMM modules.

Table 2-3   DDR3 DIMMs

Standard name	RAM clock	Million data transfers per second	Module name	Peak transfer rate GB/s
DDR3-800	400 MHz	800	PC3-6400	6.400
DDR3-1066	533 MHz	1,066	PC3-8500	8.533
DDR3-1333	667 MHz	1,333	PC3-10600	10.667
DDR3-1600	800 MHz	1,600	PC3-12800	12.800
DDR3-1866	933 MHz	1,866	PC3-14900	14.900

The I/O Subsystem

The I/O subsystem is in charge of moving data from the server memory to the external world and vice versa. Historically this has been accomplished by providing in the server motherboards I/O buses compatible with the PCI (Peripheral Component Interconnect) standard. PCI was developed to interconnect peripheral devices to a computer system, it has been around for many years [1] and its current incarnation is called PCI-Express.

The Peripheral Component Interconnect Special Interest Group (PCI-SIG) is in charge of the development and enhancement of the PCI standard.

PCI Express®

PCI Express (PCIe®) [2] is a computer expansion card interface format designed to replace PCI, PCI-X, and AGP.

It removes one of the limitations that have plagued all the I/O consolidation attempts—i.e., the lack of I/O bandwidth in the server buses. It is supported by all current operating systems.

The previous bus-based topology of PCI and PCI-X is replaced by point-to-point connectivity. The resultant topology is a tree structure with a single root complex. The root complex is responsible for system configuration, enumeration of PCIe resources, and manages interrupts and errors for the PCIe tree. A root complex and its endpoints share a single address space and communicate through memory reads and writes, and interrupts.

PCIe connects two components with a point-to-point link. Links are composed of N lanes (a by-N link is composed of N lanes). Each lane contains two pairs of wires: one pair for transmission and one pair for reception.

Multiple PCIe lanes are normally provided by the SouthBridge (aka ICH: I/O Controller Hub) that implements the functionality of "root complex".

Each lane connects to a PCI Express endpoint, to a PCI Express Switch or to a PCIe to PCI Bridge, as in Figure 2-21.

Different connectors are used according to the number of lanes. Figure 2-22 shows four different connectors and indicates the speeds achievable with PCIe 1.1.

In PCIe 1.1, the lanes run at 2.5 Gbps (2 Gbps at the datalink) and 16 lanes can be deployed in parallel (see Figure 2-23). This supports speeds from 2 Gbps (1x) to 32 Gbps (16x). Due to protocol overhead, 8x is required to support a 10 GE interface.

PCIe 2.0 (aka PCIe Gen 2) doubles the bandwidth per lane from 2 Gbit/s to 4 Gbit/s and extends the maximum number of lanes to 32x. It is shipping at the time of writing. A PCIe 4x is sufficient to support 10 GE.

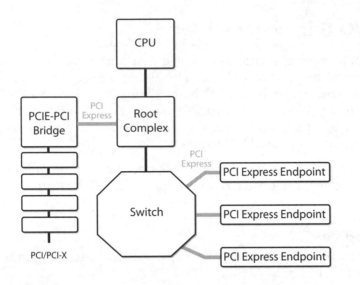

Figure 2-21   PCI-Express root complex

PCIe 3.0 will approximately double the bandwidth again. The final PCIe 3.0 specifications, including form factor specification updates, may be available by mid 2010, and could be seen in products starting in 2011 and beyond [3]. PCIe 3.0 will be required to effectively support 40 GE (Gigabit Ethernet), the next step in the evolution of Ethernet.

All the current deployments of PCI Express are Single Root (SR), i.e., a single I/O Controller Hub (ICH) controlling multiple endpoints.

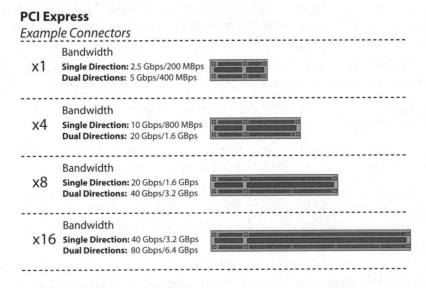

Figure 2-22   PCI Express connectors

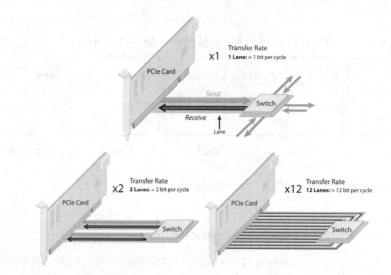

Figure 2-23   PCI Express lanes

Multi Root (MR) has been under development for a while, but it has not seen the light yet, and many question if it ever will, due to the lack of components and interest.

SR-IOV (Single Root I/O Virtualization) is another extremely relevant standard developed by PCI-SIG to be used in conjunction with Virtual Machines and Hypervisors. It is discussed in "DCBX: Data Center Bridging eXchange" in Chapter 3, page 73.

Intel Microarchitectures

The Cisco UCS uses the Intel® Processor belonging to the Nehalem and Westmere microarchitectures (more generally, the 32nm and 45nm Hi-k Intel® Core™ microarchitectures).

The Nehalem microarchitectures was introduced in servers in early 2009 and was one of the first architectures to use the new 45 nm (nanometer) silicon technology developed by Intel [32], [33], [34]. Nehalem processors span the range from high-end desktop applications, up through very large-scale server platforms. The codename is derived from the Nehalem River on the Pacific coast of northwest Oregon in the United States.

In Intel® parlance, processor developments are divided into "tick" and "tock" intervals, as in Figure 2-24. Tick is a technology that shrinks an existing processor, while tock is a new architecture done in the previous technology. Nehalem is the 45 nm tock. Westmere is the 32 nm tick following Nehalem.

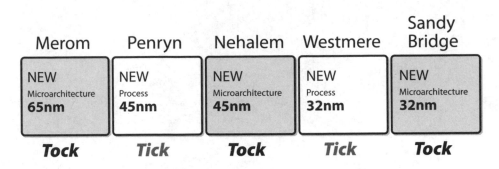

Figure 2-24   Intel® "Tick/Tock" processor development model

Nehalem and Westmere are a balance between different requirements:

- Performance of existing applications compared to emerging application (e.g., multimedia)
- Equally good support for applications that are lightly or heavily threaded
- Implementations that range from laptops to servers

They try to optimize for performance and at the same time reduce power consumption. This discussion is based on a nice Intel® Development Forum Tutorial [32]. In the rest of this chapter, the innovations are described in relation to the Nehalem microarchitecture, but they are also inherited in the Westmere architecture. There are few places where the architectures of Nehalem and Westmere differ and these will be highlighted.

Platform Architecture

It is the biggest platform architecture shift in about 10 years for Intel. The inclusion of multiple high-speed point-to-point connections, i.e., Intel® QuickPath Interconnect (see "Dedicated High-Speed Interconnect" in Chapter 2, page 30), along with the use of Integrated Memory Controllers (IMCs), is a fundamental departure from the FSB-based approach.

An example of a dual-socket Intel® Xeon® 5500 (Nehalem-EP) systems is shown in Figure 2-25. Please note the QPI links between the CPU sockets and from the CPU sockets to the I/O controller, and the memory DIMMs directly attached to the CPU sockets.

Integrated Memory Controller (IMC)

In Nehalem-EP and Westmere-EP, each socket has Integrated Memory Controller (IMC) that supports three DDR3 memory channels (see "DDR2 and DDR3" in Chapter 2, page 41). DDR3 memories run at higher frequency when compared with DDR2, thus higher memory bandwidth. In addition, for dual-socket architecture, there are two sets of memory controllers instead of one. All these improvements lead to a 3.4x bandwidth increase compared to the previous Intel® platform (see Figure 2-26).

This will continue to increase over time, as faster DDR3 becomes available. An integrated memory controller also makes a positive impact by reducing latency.

Power consumption is also reduced, since DDR3 is 1.5 Volt technology compared to 1.8 Volts of DDR2. Power consumption tends to go with the square of the voltage and therefore a 20% reduction in voltage causes approximately a 40% reduction in power.

Finally, the IMC supports both RDIMM and UDIMM with single, dual, or quad ranks (quad ranks is only supported on RDIMM; see "Memory Ranks" on page 39 and "UDIMMs and RDIMMs" on page 40, both from Chapter 2).

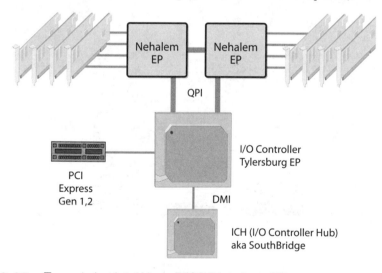

Figure 2-25   Two-socket Intel Xeon 5500 (Nehalem-EP)

Nehalem-EX has a similar, but not identical, architecture. In Nehalem-EX, there are two IMCs per socket. Each IMC supports two Intel® Scalable Memory Interconnects (SMIs) connected to two Scalable Memory Buffers (SMBs) for a total of four SMBs per socket (see Figure 2-27). Each SMB has two DDR3 buses, each connecting two RDIMMs. The total number of RDIMMs per socket is therefore sixteen.

The overall memory capacity of a Nehalem-EX system as a function of the number of sockets and of the RDIMM capacity is summarized in Table 2-4.

Table 2-4   Nehalem-EX Memory Capacity

	4GB RDIMM	8GB RDIMM	16GB RDIMM
2 sockets	128 GB	256 GB	512 GB
4 sockets	256 GB	512 GB	1 TB
8 sockets	512 GB	1 TB	2 TB

Intel® QuickPath Interconnect (QPI)

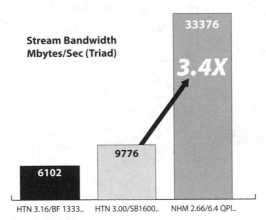

Figure 2-26   RAM bandwidth

Source: Intel Internal measurements—August 2008

HTN: Intel® Xeon® processor 5400 Series (Harpertown)

NHM: Intel® Core™ microarchitecture (Nehalem)

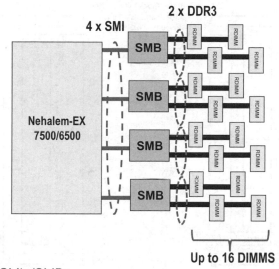

Figure 2-27   SMIs/SMBs

All the communication architectures have evolved over time from buses to point-to-point links that are much faster and more scalable. In Nehalem, Intel® Quick-Path Interconnect has replaced the front-side bus (see Figure 2-28).

Intel® QuickPath Interconnect is a coherent point-to-point protocol introduced by Intel®, not limited to any specific processor, to provide communication between processors, I/O devices, and potentially other devices such as accelerators.

The number of QPIs available depends on the type of processor. In Nehalem-EP and in Westmere-EP, each socket has two QPIs allowing the topology shown in Figure 2-25. Nehalem-EX supports four QPIs allowing many other glueless topologies, as shown in Figure 2-29.

The Intel® Xeon® processor 7500 is also compatible with third-party node controllers that are capable of interconnecting more than eight sockets for even greater system scalability.

CPU Architecture

Nehalem increases the instructions per second of each CPU by a number of innovations depicted in Figure 2-30.

Some of these innovations are self-explanatory; we will focus here on the most important one that deals with performance vs. power.

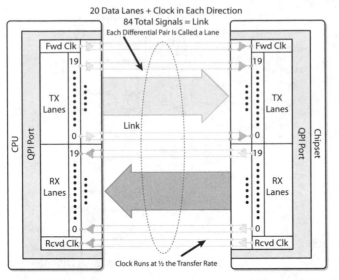

Figure 2-28 Intel® QPI

In comparing performance and power, it is normally assumed that a 1% performance increase with a 3% power increase is break-even. The reason is that it is always possible to reduce the voltage by 1% and reduce the power by 3% (see "Chip Design" in Chapter 2, page 61).

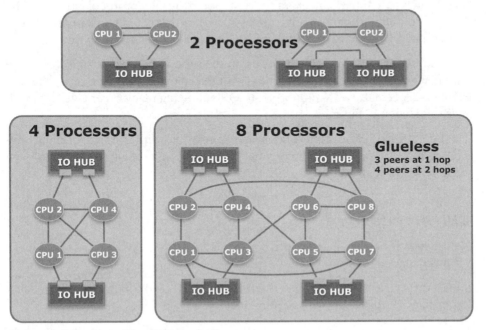

Figure 2-29 Nehalem-EX topologies

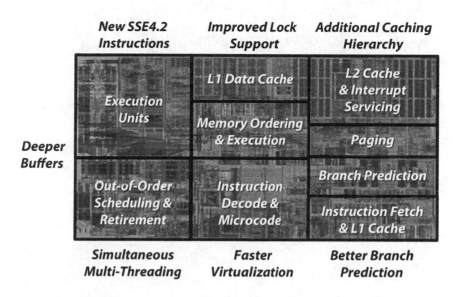

Figure 2-30   Nehalem microarchitecture innovations

The innovations that are important are those that improve the performance by 1% with only a 1% increase in power (better than break-even).

Intel® Hyper-Threading Technology (Intel® HT Technology)

Intel® Hyper-Threading Technology (Intel® HT Technology) is the capability of running simultaneously multiple threads on the same core, in the Nehalem/Westmere implementation two threads. This enhances both performance and energy efficiency (see "Intel® Hyper-Threading Technology" in Chapter 2, page 27).

The basic idea is that with the growing complexity of each execution unit, it is difficult for a single thread to keep the execution unit busy. Instead by overlaying two threads on the same core, it is more likely that all the resources can be kept busy and therefore the overall efficiency increases (see Figure 2-31). Hyper-Threading consumes a very limited amount of area (less than 5%), and it is extremely effective in increasing efficiency, in a heavily threaded environment. Hyper-Threading is not a replacement for cores; it complements cores by allowing each of them to execute two threads simultaneously.

Cache-Hierarchy

The requirement of an ideal memory system is that it should have infinite capacity, infinite bandwidth, and zero latency. Of course, nobody knows how to build such a system. The best approximation is a hierarchy of memory subsystems that go from larger and slower to smaller and faster. In Nehalem, Intel® added one level of hierarchy by increasing the cache layers from two to three (see Figure 2-32).

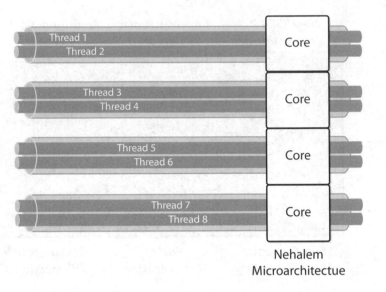

Nehalem
Microarchitectue

Figure 2-31   Intel® HT technology

Level one caches (L1) (Instruction and Data) are unchanged compared to previous Intel® designs. In the previous Intel® design, the level two caches (L2) were shared across the cores. This was possible since the number of cores was limited to two. Nehalem increments the number of cores to four or eight, and the L2 caches cannot be shared any longer, due to the increase in bandwidth and arbitration requests (potentially 8X). For this reason, in Nehalem Intel® added L2 caches (Instruction and Data) dedicated to each core to reduce the bandwidth toward the shared caches that is now a level three (L3) cache.

Core	Core	Core	Core
32k L1 I-cache	32k L1 I-cache	32k L1 I-cache	32k L1 I-cache
32k L1 D-cache	32k L1 D-cache	32k L1 D-cache	32k L1 D-cache
256k L2 cache data + Inst.	256k L2 cache data + Inst.	256k L2 cache data + Inst.	256k L2 cache data + Inst.

8 MB L3 cache

For all applications
to share

Inclusive cache policy to
minimize traffic from snoops

Figure 2-32   Cache hierarchy

Segmentation

Nehalem is designed for modularity. Cores, caches, IMC, and Intel® QPI are examples of modules that compose a Nehalem processor (see Figure 2-30).

These modules are designed independently and they can run at different frequencies and different voltages. The technology that glues all of them together is a novel synchronous communication protocol that provides very low latency. Previous attempts used asynchronous protocols that are less efficient.

Integrated Power Gate

This is a power management technique that is an evolution of the "Clock Gate" that exists in all modern Intel® processors. The clock gate shuts off the clock signals to idle logic, thus eliminating switching power, but leakage current remains. Leakage currents create leakage power consumption that has no useful purpose. With the reduction in channel length, starting approximately at 130 nm, leakage has become a significant part of the power, and at 45 nm, it is very important.

The power gate instead shuts off both switching and leakage power and enables an idle core to go to almost zero power (see Figure 2-33). This is completely transparent to software and applications.

The power gate is difficult to implement from a technology point of view. The classical elements of 45 nm technologies have significant leakage. It required a new transistor technology with a massive copper layer (7 mm) that was not done before (see Figure 2-34).

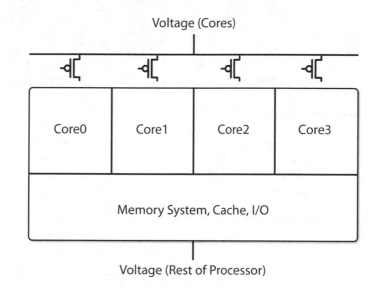

Figure 2-33   Nehalem power gate

The power gate becomes more important as the channel length continues to shrink, since the leakage currents continue to increase. At 22 nm, the power gate is essential.

Nehalem-EP and Westmere-EP have "dynamic" power-gating ability to turn core power off completely when the core is not needed for the given workload. Later, when the workload needs the core's compute capability, the core's power is reactivated.

Nehalem-EX has "static" power gating. The core power is turned off completely when the individual core is disabled in the factory, such as when an 8-core part is fused to make a 6-core part. These deactivated cores cannot be turned back on. On prior generations, such factory deactivated cores continued to consume some power. On Nehalem-EX, the power is completely shut off.

Power Management

Power sensors are key in building a power management system. Previous Intel® CPUs had thermal sensors, but they did not have power sensors. Nehalem has both thermal and power sensors that are monitored by an integrated microcontroller (PCU) in charge of power management (see Figure 2-35).

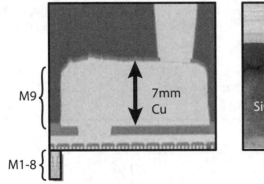

Very low resistance, package-like metal (M9) deposited on Silicon to create low on-resistance for power gate

Specialized, ultra-low leakage transistor developed for high off-resistance for power gate

Figure 2-34   Power gate transistor

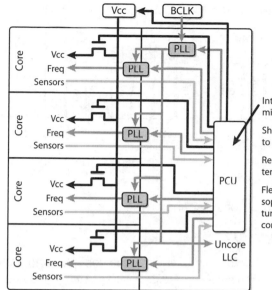

Figure 2-35   Power Control Unit

Intel® Turbo Boost Technology

Power gates and power management are the basic components of Intel® Turbo Boost Technology. Intel® Turbo Boost mode is used when the operating system requires more performance, if environmental conditions permit (sufficient cooling and power)—for example, because one or more cores are turned off. Intel® Turbo Boost increases the frequency of the active cores (and also the power consumption), thus increasing the performance of a given core (see Figure 2-36). This is not a huge improvement (from 3% to 11%), but it may be particularly valuable in lightly or non-threaded environments in which not all the cores may be used in parallel. The frequency is increased in 133MHz steps.

Figure 2-36 shows three different possibilities: In the normal case, all the cores operate at the nominal frequency (2.66 GHz); in the "4C Turbo" mode, all the cores are frequency upgraded by one step (for example, to 2.79 GHz); and in the "<4C Turbo" mode, two cores are frequency upgraded by two steps (for example, to 2.93 GHz).

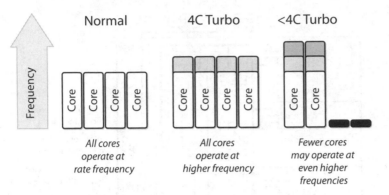

Figure 2-36   Intel® Turbo Boost Technology

Virtualization support

Intel® Virtualization Technology (VT) extends the core platform architecture to better support virtualization software—e.g., VMs (Virtual Machines) and hypervisors aka VMMs (Virtual Machine Monitors); see Figure 2-37.

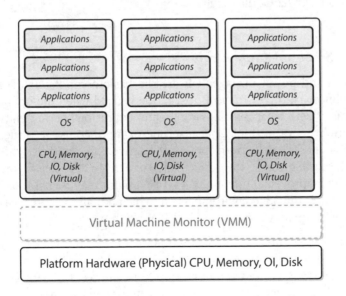

Figure 2-37   Virtualization support

VT has four major components:

- Intel® VT-x refers to all the hardware assists for virtualization in Intel® 64 and IA32 processors.
- Intel® VT-d for Directed I/O (Intel® VT-d) refers to all the hardware assists for virtualization in Intel chipset.
- Intel® VT-c for Connectivity (Intel® VT-c) refers to all the hardware assists for virtualization in Intel networking and I/O devices.
- VT Flex Migration to simplify Virtual Machine movement.

Intel® VT-x enhancements include:

- **A new, higher privilege ring for the hypervisor**—This allows guest operating systems and applications to run in the rings they were designed for, while ensuring the hypervisor has privileged control over platform resources.
- **Hardware-based transitions**—Handoff between the hypervisor and guest operating systems are supported in hardware. This reduces the need for complex, compute-intensive software transitions.
- **Hardware-based memory protection**—Processor state information is retained for the hypervisor and for each guest OS in dedicated address spaces. This helps to accelerate transitions and ensure the integrity of the process.

In addition, Nehalem adds:

- EPT (Extended Page Table)
- VPID (Virtual Processor ID)
- Guest Preemption Timer
- Descriptor Table Exiting
- Intel® Virtualization Technology FlexPriority
- Pause Loop Exiting

VT Flex Migration

FlexMigration allows migration of the VM between processors that have a different instruction set. It does that by synchronizing the minimum level of the instruction set supported by all the processors in a pool.

When a VM is first instantiated, it queries its processor to obtain the instruction set level (SSE2, SSE3, SSE4). The processor returns the agreed minimum instruction set level in the pool, not the one of the processor itself. This allows VMotion between processors with different instruction set.

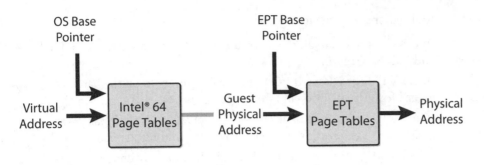

Figure 2-38   Extended page tables

Extended Page Tables (EPT)

EPT is a new page-table structure, under the control of the hypervisor (see Figure 2-38). It defines mapping between guest- and host-physical addresses.

Before virtualization, each OS was in charge of programming page tables to translate between virtual application addresses and the "physical addresses". With the advent of virtualization, these addresses are no longer physical, but instead local to the VM. The hypervisor needs to translate between the guest OS addresses and the real physical addresses. Before EPT, the hypervisors maintained the page table in software by updating them at significant boundaries (e.g., on VM entry and exit).

With EPT, there is an EPT base pointer and an EPT Page Table that allow it to go directly from the virtual address to the physical address without the hypervisor intervention, in a way similar to how an OS does it in a native environment.

Virtual Processor ID (VPID)

This is the ability to assign a VM ID to tag CPU hardware structures (e.g., TLBs: Translation Lookaside Buffers) to avoid flushes on VM transitions.

Before VPID, in a virtualized environment, the CPU flushes the TLB unconditionally for each VM transition (e.g., VM Entry/Exit). This is not efficient and adversely affects the CPU performance. With VPID, TLBs are tagged with an ID decided by the hypervisor that allows a more efficient flushing of cached information (only flush what is needed).

Guest Preemption Timer

With this feature, a hypervisor can preempt guest execution after a specified amount of time. The hypervisor sets a timer value before entering a guest and when the timer reaches zero, a VM exit occurs. The timer causes a VM exit directly with no interrupt, so this feature can be used with no impact on how the VMM virtualizes interrupts.

Descriptor Table Exiting

Allows a VMM to protect a guest OS from internal attack by preventing relocation of key system data structures.

OS operation is controlled by a set of key data structures used by the CPU: IDT, GDT, LDT, and TSS. Without this feature, there is no way for the hypervisor to prevent malicious software running inside a guest OS from modifying the guest's copies of these data structures. A hypervisor using this feature can intercept attempts to relocate these data structures and forbid malicious ones.

FlexPriority

This is a technique to improve performance on older 32-bit guest OS's. It was designed to accelerate virtualization interrupt handling thereby improving virtualization performance. FlexPriority accelerates interrupt handling by preventing unnecessary VMExits on accesses to the Advanced Programmable Interrupt Controller.

Pause Loop Exiting

This technique detects spin locks in multi-process guests to reduce "lock-holder preemption". Without this technique, a given virtual processor (vCPU) may be preempted while holding a lock. Other vCPUs that try to acquire lock will spin for entire execution quantum.

This technique is present in Nehalem-EX, but not in Nehalem-EP.

Advanced Reliability

A lot of the innovation in Nehalem-EX compared to Nehalem-EP is in the advanced reliability area or more properly RAS (Reliability, Availability, and Serviceability); see Figure 2-39.

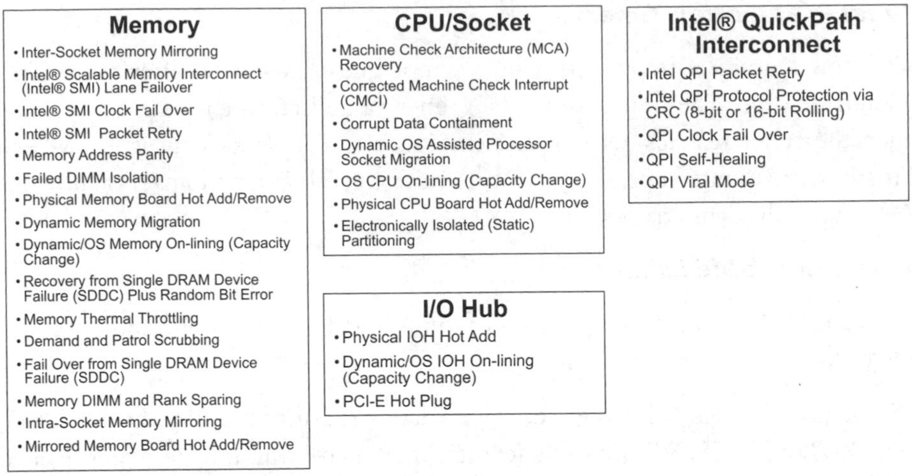

Memory

- Inter-Socket Memory Mirroring
- Intel® Scalable Memory Interconnect (Intel® SMI) Lane Failover
- Intel® SMI Clock Fail Over
- Intel® SMI Packet Retry
- Memory Address Parity
- Failed DIMM Isolation
- Physical Memory Board Hot Add/Remove
- Dynamic Memory Migration
- Dynamic/OS Memory On-lining (Capacity Change)
- Recovery from Single DRAM Device Failure (SDDC) Plus Random Bit Error
- Memory Thermal Throttling
- Demand and Patrol Scrubbing
- Fail Over from Single DRAM Device Failure (SDDC)
- Memory DIMM and Rank Sparing
- Intra-Socket Memory Mirroring
- Mirrored Memory Board Hot Add/Remove

CPU/Socket

- Machine Check Architecture (MCA) Recovery
- Corrected Machine Check Interrupt (CMCI)
- Corrupt Data Containment
- Dynamic OS Assisted Processor Socket Migration
- OS CPU On-lining (Capacity Change)
- Physical CPU Board Hot Add/Remove
- Electronically Isolated (Static) Partitioning

Intel® QuickPath Interconnect

- Intel QPI Packet Retry
- Intel QPI Protocol Protection via CRC (8-bit or 16-bit Rolling)
- QPI Clock Fail Over
- QPI Self-Healing
- QPI Viral Mode

I/O Hub

- Physical IOH Hot Add
- Dynamic/OS IOH On-lining (Capacity Change)
- PCI-E Hot Plug

Figure 2-39   Nehalem-EX RAS

In particular, all the major processor functions are covered by RAS, including: QPI RAS, I/O Hub (IOH) RAS, Memory RAS, and Socket RAS.

Corrected Errors are now signaled using the Corrected Machine Check Interrupts (CMCI).

An additional RAS technique is Machine Check Architecture-recovery (MCAr); i.e., a mechanism in which the CPU reports hardware errors to the operating system. With MCAr, it is possible to recover from otherwise fatal system errors.

Some features require additional operating system support and/or requires hardware vendor implementation and validation.

This technology is implemented only in Nehalem-EX.

Advanced Encryption Standard

Westmere-EP adds six new instructions for accelerating encryption and decryption of popular AES (Advanced Encryption Standard) algorithms. With these instructions, all AES computations are done by hardware and they are of course not only faster, but also more secure than a software implementation.

This enables applications to use stronger keys with less overhead. Applications can encrypt more data to meet regulatory requirements, in addition to general security, with less impact to performance.

This technology is implemented only in Westmere-EP.

Trusted Execution Technology

Intel® Trusted Execution Technology (TXT) helps detect and/or prevent software-based attacks, in particular:

- Attempts to insert non-trusted VMM (rootkit hypervisor)
- Attacks designed to compromise platform secrets in memory
- BIOS and firmware update attacks

Intel® TXT uses a mix of processor, chipset, and TPM (Trusted Platform Module) technologies to measure the boot environment to detect software attacks (see Figure 2-40).

This technology is implemented only in Westmere-EP.

Chip Design

When trying to achieve high performance and limit the power consumption, several different factors need to be balanced.

With the progressive reduction of the length of the transistor channel, the range of voltages usable becomes limited (see Figure 2-41).

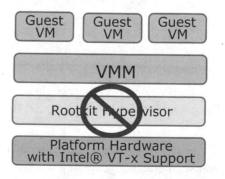

Helps prevent hijacking during boot

Figure 2-40   Intel® trusted execution technology

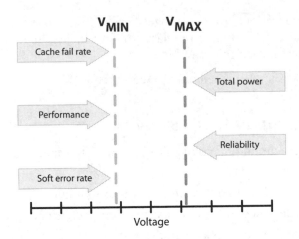

Figure 2-41   Voltage range

The maximum voltage is limited by the total power consumption and the reliability decrease associated with high power, the minimum voltage is limited mostly by soft errors especially in memory circuits.

In general, in CMOS design the performance is proportional to the voltage, since higher voltages allow higher frequency.

$$Performance \sim Frequency \sim Voltage$$

Power consumption is proportional to the frequency and the square of voltage:

$$Power \sim Frequency \; x \; Voltage^2$$

and, since frequency and voltage are proportional:

$$Power \sim Voltage^3$$

Energy efficiency is defined as the ratio between performance and power, and therefore:

$$Energy \; Efficiency \sim 1/Voltage^2$$

Therefore, from an energy-efficiency perspective, there is an advantage in reducing the Voltage (i.e., the power; see Figure 2-42) so big that Intel® has decided to address it.

Since the circuits that are more subject to soft error are memories, Intel® in Nehalem deploys a sophisticated error-correcting code (triple detect, double correct) to compensate for these soft errors. In addition, the voltage of the caches and the voltage of the cores are decoupled so the cache can stay at high voltage while the cores works at low voltage.

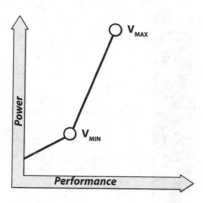

Figure 2-42   Power vs. performance

For the L1 and L2 caches, Intel® has replaced the traditional six transistors SRAM design (6-T SRAM) with a new eight transistors design (8-T SRAM) that decouples the read and write operations and allows lower voltages (see Figure 2-43).

Also, to reduce power, Intel® went back to static CMOS, which is the CMOS technology that consumes less power (see Figure 2-44).

Performance was regained by redesigning some of the key algorithm like instruction decoding.

Chipset Virtualization Support

In addition to the virtualization support provided inside Nehalem, other improvements have been implemented at the chipset/motherboard level to better support

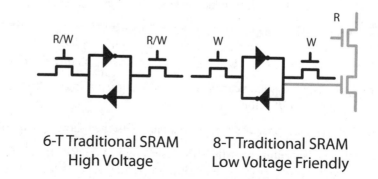

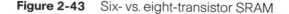

Figure 2-43   Six- vs. eight-transistor SRAM

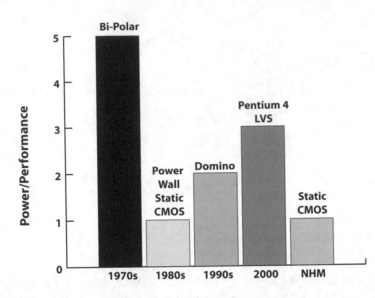

Figure 2-44   Power consumption of different technologies

virtualization. These improvements are important to increase the I/O performance in the presence of a hypervisor (in Intel parlance, the hypervisor is referred to as VMM: Virtual Machine Monitor).

Intel® VT-d for Direct I/O

Servers use an Input/Output Memory Management Unit (IOMMU) to connect a DMA-capable I/O bus (e.g., PCIe) to the main memory. Like a traditional MMU (Memory Management Unit), which translates CPU-visible virtual addresses to physical addresses, the IOMMU takes care of mapping device-visible virtual addresses to physical addresses. These units also provide memory protection from misbehaving devices.

A general requirement for I/O virtualization is the ability to isolate and restrict device accesses to the resources owned by the partition managing the device.

In 2008, Intel published a specification for IOMMU technology: Virtualization Technology for Directed I/O, abbreviated VT-d.

Intel® VT for Directed I/O provides VMM software with the following capabilities:

- **I/O device assignment:** For flexibly assigning I/O devices to VMs and extending the protection and isolation properties of VMs for I/O operations.

- **DMA remapping:** For supporting independent address translations for Direct Memory Accesses (DMA) from devices.

- **Interrupt remapping:** For supporting isolation and routing of interrupts from devices and external interrupt controllers to appropriate VMs.

- **Reliability:** For recording and reporting to system software DMA and interrupt errors that may otherwise corrupt memory or impact VM isolation.

Intel® VT-c for Connectivity

Intel® Virtualization Technology for Connectivity (Intel® VT-c) is a collection of I/O virtualization technologies that enables lower CPU utilization, reduced system latency, and improved networking and I/O throughput.

Intel® VT-c consists of platform-level technologies and initiatives that work together to deliver next-generation virtualized I/O:

- Virtual Machine Device Queues (VMDq) dramatically improves traffic management within the server, helping to enable better I/O performance from large data flows while decreasing the processing burden on the software-based Virtual Machine Monitor (VMM).

- Virtual Machine Direct Connect (VMDc) provides near native-performance by providing dedicated I/O to virtual machines, bypassing the software virtual switch in the hypervisor completely. It also improves data isolation among virtual machines, and provides flexibility and mobility by facilitating live virtual machine migration.

VMDq

In virtual environments, the hypervisor manages network I/O activities for all the VMs (Virtual Machines). With the constant increase in the number of VMs, the I/O load increases and the hypervisor requires more CPU cycles to sort data packets in network interface queues and route them to the correct VM, reducing CPU capacity available for applications.

Intel® Virtual Machine Device Queues (VMDq) reduces the burden on the hypervisor while improving network I/O by adding hardware support in the chipset. In particular, multiple network interface queues and sorting intelligence are added to the silicon, as shown in Figure 2-45.

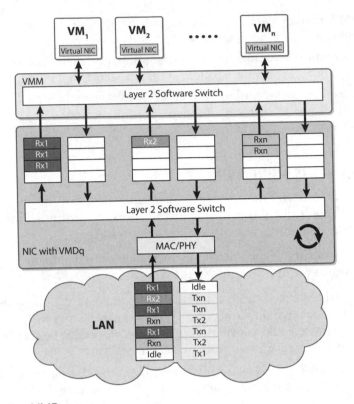

Figure 2-45   VMDq

As data packets arrive at the network adapter, a Layer 2 classifier/sorter in the network controller sorts and determines which VM each packet is destined for based on MAC addresses and VLAN tags. It then places the packet in a receive queue assigned to that VM. The hypervisor's layer 2 software switches merely routes the packets to the respective VM instead of performing the heavy lifting work of sorting data.

As packets are transmitted from the virtual machines toward the adapters, the hypervisor layer places the transmit data packets in their respective queues. To prevent head-of-line blocking and ensure each queue is fairly serviced, the network controller transmits queued packets to the wire in a round-robin fashion, thereby guaranteeing some measure of Quality of Service (QoS) to the VMs.

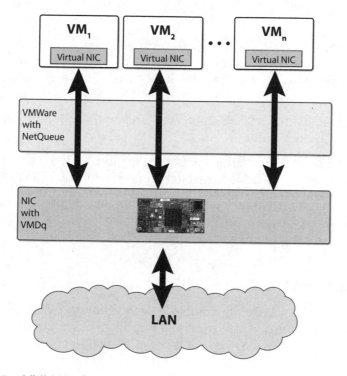

Figure 2-46   VMM NetQueue

NetQueue®

To take full advantage of VMDq, the VMMs needs to be modified to support one queue per Virtual Machine. For example, VMware® has introduced in its hypervisor a feature called NetQueue that takes advantage of the frame, sorting capability of VMDq. The combination of NetQueue and VMDq offloads the work that ESX has to do to route packets to virtual machines; therefore, it frees up CPU and reduces latency (see Figure 2-46).

VMQ®

VMQ is Microsoft's Hyper-V® queuing technology that makes use of the VMDq capabilities of the Intel Ethernet controller to enable data packets to be delivered to the VM with minimal handling in software.

VMDc®

Virtual Machine Direct Connect (VMDc) enables direct networking I/O assignment to individual virtual machines (VMs). This capability improves overall networking performance and data isolation among VMs and enables live VM migration.

VMDc complies with the Single Root I/O Virtualization (SR-IOV) standard; see "SR-IOV" in Chapter 3, page 83.

The latest Intel® Ethernet server controllers support SR-IOV to virtualize the physical I/O port into multiple virtual I/O ports called Virtual Functions (VFs).

Dividing physical devices into multiple VFs allows physical I/O devices to deliver near-native I/O performance for VMs. This capability can increase the number of VMs supported per physical host, driving up server consolidation.

VMDirectPath®

When VMDq and VMDc are combined with VMware® VMDirectPath, the ESX/vSphere hypervisor is bypassed in a way similar to a "kernel bypass", the software switch inside the hypervisor is not used, and data is directly communicated from the adapter to the vNICs (virtual NICs) and vice versa. See "VN-Link" in Chapter 3, page 90, and in particular Figure 3-20.

Chapter 3

UCS Enabling Technologies

Unified Fabric

The terms Unified Fabric or I/O consolidation are synonymous and refer to the ability of a network (both switches and host adapters) to use the same physical infrastructure to carry different types of traffic that typically have different traffic characteristics and handling requirements.

From the network side, this equates in having to install and operate a single network instead of three. From the hosts side, fewer CNAs (Converged Network Adapters) replace and consolidate NICs (Network Interface Cards), HBAs (Host Bus Adapters), and HCAs (Host Channel Adapters). This results in a lower number of PCIe slots required on rack-mounted servers, and it is particularly beneficial in the case of blade servers, where often only a single mezzanine card is supported per blade.

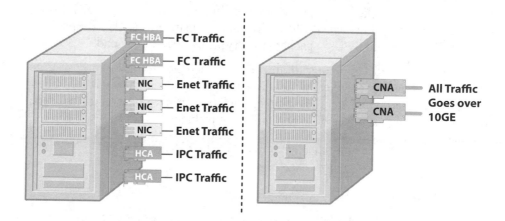

Figure 3-1   Server with Unified Fabric connections

Customers benefits are:

- Great reduction, simplification, and standardization of cabling.
- Absence of gateways that cause bottleneck and are a source of incompatibilities.
- Less power and cooling.
- Reduced cost.

Figure 3-1 shows an example where two FC HBAs, three Ethernet NICs, and two IB HCAs are replaced by two CNAs (Converged Network Adapters).

The biggest challenge of I/O consolidation is to satisfy the requirements of different traffic classes within a single network without creating "traffic interference"; i.e., the possibility of one class of traffic to starve another.

Deployments worldwide of IPv4 and IPv6 on Ethernet-based networks have resulted in it becoming the de facto standard for all LAN traffic [4]. Too much investment has been done in this area and too many applications assume that Ethernet is the underlying network for this to change. This traffic is characterized by a large number of flows. Typically, these flows are not very sensitive to latency, but this is changing rapidly and latency must be taken into serious consideration. An increasing number of applications are also sensitive to latency jitter.

Block storage traffic must follow the Fibre Channel (FC) model. Again, large customers have massive investment in FC infrastructure and management. Storage provisioning often relies on FC services like naming, zoning, etc. In FC, losing frames is not an option, since SCSI is extremely sensitive to packet drops. This traffic is characterized by large packet sizes, typically 2KB in payload.

IPC (Inter Processor Communication) traffic is characterized by a mix of large and small messages. It is typically latency sensitive, especially the short messages. IPC traffic is used in "clusters"; i.e., interconnections of two or more computers. In the data center, examples of server clustering include:

- Availability clusters (e.g., Symantec®/Veritas® VCS®, MSCS®)
- Clustered file systems
- Clustered databases (e.g., Oracle® RAC®)
- VMware® virtual infrastructure services (e.g., VMware® VMotion, VMware® HA)

Cluster technologies usually require a separate network to guarantee that normal network traffic does not interfere with latency requirements. Clusters are not as dependent on the underlying network technology, provided that it is low cost, it offers high bandwidth, it is low latency, and the adapters provide zero-copy mechanisms (i.e., they avoid making intermediates copies of packets).

10 Gigabit Ethernet

10GE (10 Gigabit Ethernet) is the network of choice for I/O consolidation. During 2008, the standard reached the maturity status and low-cost cabling solutions are available. Fiber continues to be used for longer distances, but copper is deployed in the data center to reduce the costs.

Switches and CNAs have standardized their connectivity using the small form factor plus pluggable (SFP+) transceiver. SFP+ are used to interface a network device mother board (switches, routers, or CNAs) to a fiber optic or copper cable.

Unfortunately, due to the complexity of encoding and decoding 10GE traffic onto and from a copper twisted pair (IEEE 10GBASE-T), an enormous number of transistors are required, especially when the distance approaches 100 meters (328 feet). This translates to a significant power requirement and into additional delay (see Figure 3-2). The heat given off and power consumed by a 10GBaseT port makes it difficult to produce high-density line cards; e.g., 48 ports.

A more practical solution in the data center, at the rack level, is to use SFP+ with Copper Twinax cable (defined in Annex of SFF-8431, see [6]). This cable is very flexible; approximately 6 mm (1/4 of an inch) in diameter, and it uses the SFP+ as the connectors. Twinax cables are low cost, use little power, and introduce negligible delay. Copper Twinax cables are limited to 10 meters (33 feet) that is sufficient to connect a few racks of servers to a common top of the rack switch.

Technology	Cable	Distance	Power (Each Side)	Transceiver Latency (Link)
SFP+ C Copper	Twinax	10m	0.1W	0.1µs
SFP+ USR ultra short reach	MM OM2 MM OM3	10m 100m	1W	0
SFP+ SR short reach	MM 62.5µm MM 50µm	82m 300m	1W	0
10GBASE	Cat6 Cat6a/7 Cat6a/7	55m 100m 30m	8W 8W 4W	2.5µs 2.5µs 1.5µs

Figure 3-2   10GE cabling options

Starting in 2011, the 10GBASE-T technology will mature, and competitive products will start to appear on the market. At that point, 10GBASE-T will become a viable alternative to Copper Twinax.

Lossless Ethernet

To satisfy the requirements of Unified Fabric, Ethernet has been enhanced to operate both as a "lossless" and "lossy" network. This classification does not consider the fact that Ethernet can still lose frames due to transmission errors, but in a controlled environment, such as a data center, where links are limited in length, these loses are extremely rare.

Fibre Channel and IB (InfiniBand) are examples of lossless networks; they have a link level signaling mechanism to keep track of buffer availability at the other end of the link. This mechanism allows the sender to send a frame only if a buffer is available at the receiving end and therefore the receiver never needs to drop frames. Avoiding frame drops is mandatory for carrying block storage traffic over Ethernet, since storage traffic does not tolerate frame loss. SCSI was designed with the assumption that SCSI transactions are expected to succeed and that failures are so rare that is acceptable to recover slowly in such an event.

Terminology

DCB (Data Center Bridging) is a term used by IEEE to collectively indicate the techniques described in "PFC (Priority-Based Flow Control)" on page 72, "DCBX: Data Center Bridging eXchange" on page 73, and "Bandwidth Management" on page 74, all in Chapter 3.

The terms CEE (Converged Enhanced Ethernet) and DCE (Data Center Ethernet) have also been used to group these techniques under common umbrellas, but are now obsolete.

PFC (Priority-Based Flow Control)

Following these requirements, Ethernet has been enhanced by IEEE 802.1Qbb (priority-based flow control) and IEEE 802.3bd (frame format for priority-based flow control). According to these new standards, a physical link can be partitioned into multiple logical links (by extending the IEEE 802.1Q priority concept) and each priority can be configured to have either a lossless or a lossy behavior. This new mechanism was also previously known as PPP (Per Priority Pause) [8].

With PFC, an administrator can define which priorities are lossless and which are lossy. The network devices will treat the lossy priorities as in classical Ethernet and will use a per priority pause mechanism to guarantee that no frames are lost on the lossless priorities.

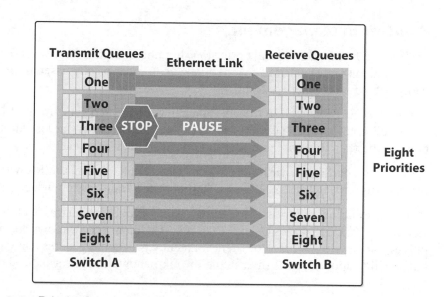

Figure 3-3 Priority flow control

If separate traffic classes are mapped to different priorities, there is no traffic interference. For example, in Figure 3-3, storage traffic is mapped to priority three and it is paused, while IPC traffic is mapped to priority six and it is being forwarded and so is IP traffic that is mapped to priority one.

PFC requires a more complex organization in the data plane that allows for resources, such as buffers or queues, to be allocated on a per-priority basis.

PFC is the basic technique required to implement I/O consolidation. Additional techniques make I/O consolidation deployable on a larger scale. The next paragraphs describe two additional components:

- Discovery Protocol (DCBX);
- Bandwidth Manager (ETS: Enhanced Transmission Selection).

DCBX: Data Center Bridging eXchange

DCBX is a discovery and configuration protocol that guarantees that both ends of an Ethernet link are configured consistently. DCBX works to configure correctly switch to switch links and switch to host links. This is to avoid "soft errors" that can be very difficult to troubleshoot.

DCBX discovers the capabilities of the two peers at each end of a link: It can check for consistency, it can notify the device manager in the case of configuration mismatches, and it can provide basic configuration in the case where one of the two peers is not configured. DCBX can be configured to send conflict alarms to the appropriate management stations.

Bandwidth Management

IEEE 802.1Q-2005 defines eight priorities, but not a simple, effective, and consistent scheduling mechanism. The scheduling goals are typically based upon bandwidth, latency, and jitter control.

Before this IEEE standard, products typically implemented some form of Deficit Weighted Round Robin (DWRR), but there was no consistency across implementations, and therefore configuration and interworking was problematic.

IEEE has standardized a hardware efficient scheduler (two-level DWRR with strict priority support) in IEEE 802.1Qaz ETS (Enhanced Transmission Selection) [12].

With this structure, it is possible to assign bandwidth based on traffic classes, for example: 40% LAN, 40% SAN, and 20% IPC. This architecture allows control not only of bandwidth, but also of latency. Latency is becoming increasingly important for IPC applications. An example of link bandwidth allocation is shown in Figure 3-4.

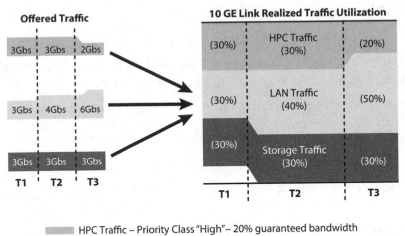

HPC Traffic – Priority Class "High" – 20% guaranteed bandwidth
LAN Traffic – Priority Class "Medium" – 50% guaranteed bandwidth
Storage Traffic – Priority Class "Medium High" – 30% default bandwidth

Figure 3-4 Bandwidth manager

FCoE (Fibre Channel over Ethernet)

FCoE is described in detail in a book from Silvano Gai and Claudio DeSanti [17].

FCoE (Fibre Channel over Ethernet) is a standard developed by the FC-BB-5 working group of INCITS T11 [13], [14], [15]. FCoE, being based on the FC protocol dominant in storage networks, is able to provide a true I/O consolidation solution based on Ethernet.

The idea behind FCoE is simple—to implement I/O consolidation by carrying each FC frame inside an Ethernet frame. The encapsulation is done on a frame-by-frame basis and therefore keeps the FCoE layer stateless and it does not require fragmentation and reassembly.

FCoE traffic shares the physical Ethernet links with other traffic, but it is run on a lossless priority to match the lossless behavior guaranteed in Fibre Channel by buffer-to-buffer credits.

Figure 3-5 shows an example of I/O consolidation using FCoE in which the only connectivity needed on the server is Ethernet, while separate backbones can still be maintained for LAN and SAN.

FCoE has the advantage of being completely part of the Fibre Channel architecture and it is therefore able to provide seamless integration with existing FC SANs, allowing reuse of existing FC SAN tools and management constructs.

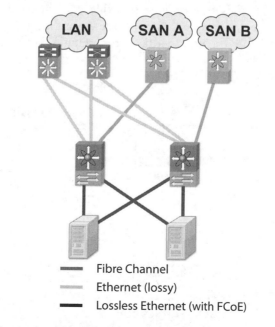

Figure 3-5   Example of Unified Fabric with FCoE

Figure 3-6 shows that an FCoE-connected server is just a SCSI initiator over FCP/ FC, exactly as if the server were connected over native FC. The same applies to FCoE connected storage arrays: They act just as SCSI targets.

Another notable advantage of FCoE is that it requires no gateway. In fact, the encapsulation/de-encapsulation functions simply add or remove an Ethernet envelope around a FC frame. The FC frame remains untouched and the operation is stateless. Figure 3-6 shows a comparison of FCoE with iSCSI from the absence/ presence of a gateway.

The management tools that customers use to manage and maintain their SANs today can be used in an FCoE environment. From a storage administrator per-spective, zoning is a basic provisioning function that is used to give hosts access to storage. FCoE switches provide the same unmodified zoning functionality ensuring that storage allocation and security mechanisms are unaffected. The same consideration applies to all other Fibre Channel services, such as dNS, RSCN, and FSPF.

The FCoE encapsulation is shown in Figure 3-7. Starting from the inside out, there is the FC Frame that can be up to 2 KB, hence the requirement to support jumbo frame sizes up to 2.5 KB. The FC frame contains the original FC-CRC. This is extremely important, since the FC frame and its CRC remain unmodified end-to-end, whether they are being carried over FC or over FCoE. Next is the FCoE header and trailer that mainly contain the encoded FC start of frame and end of frame (in native, FC these are ordered sets that contain code violation and therefore they need to be re-encoded, since a code violation cannot appear in the middle of a frame). Finally the Ethernet header contains Ethertype = FCoE and

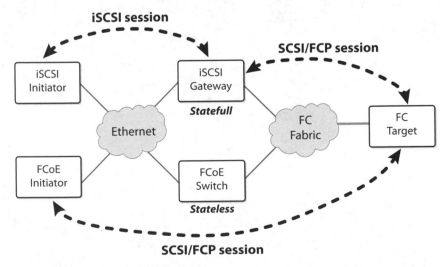

Figure 3-6   No gateway in FCoE

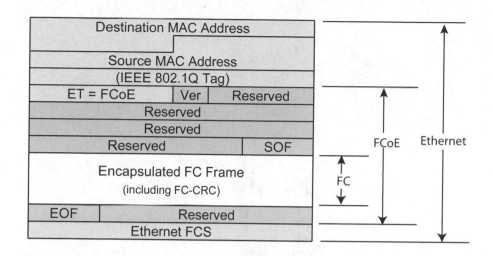

Figure 3-7   FCoE frame format

the Ethernet trailer contains the FCS (Frame Control Sequence). The reserved bits have been inserted so that the Ethernet payload is greater or equal to the minimum Ethernet Payload (46 bytes) in the presence of minimum-size FC frames (28 bytes).

In FC, all the links are point-to-point, while Ethernet switches creates "clouds". With the term cloud, we refer to an Ethernet multi-access network, a broadcast domain (not to be confused with cloud computing).

Figure 3-8 shows a classical blade server deployment where two Ethernet switches inside the blade server create two "Ethernet clouds" to which multiple FCoE capable end stations are connected. It is therefore necessary to discover among the end stations connected to a cloud that are FCoE capable. For this reason, FCoE is really two different protocols:

- FCoE itself is the data plane protocol. It is used to carry most of the FC frames and all the SCSI traffic. This is data intensive and typically it is switched in hardware.

- FIP (FCoE Initialization Protocol) is the control plane protocol. It is used to discover the FC entities connected to an Ethernet cloud and by the hosts to login to and logout from the FC fabric. This is not a data intensive protocol and it is typically implemented in software on the switch supervisor processor.

The two protocols have two different Ethertypes. Figure 3-9 shows the steps of FIP that lead to a successful FLOGI and to the possibility of exchanging SCSI traffic using FCoE.

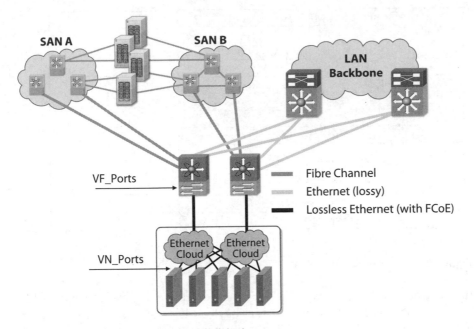

Figure 3-8   Ethernet clouds inside blade servers

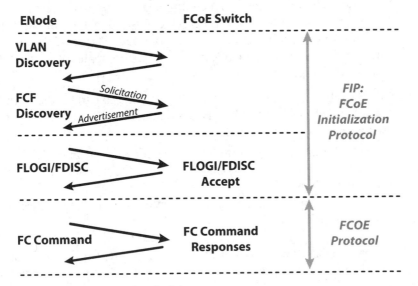

Figure 3-9   FCoE initialization ladder

Once the initialization phase is completed, virtual ports are created. The term "virtual" refers to an FC port that is implemented on a network that is not native FC. Therefore, FC-BB-5 defines:

- VN_Port (Virtual N_Port): An N_Port over an Ethernet link
- VF_Port (Virtual F_Port): An F_Port over an Ethernet link
- VE_Port (Virtual E_Port): An E_Port over an Ethernet link

Figure 3-8 shows the position of the VF_Ports and VN_Port in a classical blade server deployment.

The ENode typically implements the VN_Port. ENodes are commercially called CNAs (Converged Network Adapters). They are PCI Express adapters that contain both HBA and NIC functionality, as shown in Figure 3-10.

The unification occurs only on the network-facing side, since two separate PCI-Express devices are still presented to the server. Figure 3-11 shows how Windows views a dual port CNA within domain manager:

- In the "Network Adapters" section of the Device Manager, it sees two Ethernet NICs.
- In the "SCSI and RAID controllers" section of the Device Manager, it sees two Fibre Channel adapters.

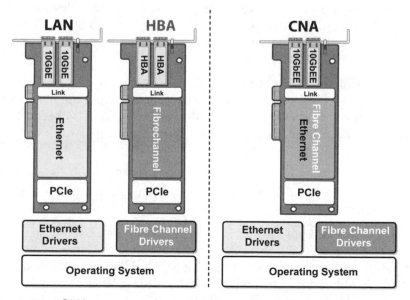

Figure 3-10   CNAs

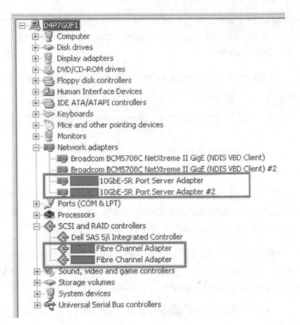

Figure 3-11   Windows view of a CNA

From the SCSI perspective, the host is incapable of distinguishing whether SCSI is running over FCoE or native FC.

The high availability of Ethernet will be dealt with at a lower level using NIC teaming (Windows) or bonding (Linux), while the high availability of Fibre Channel will be dealt with at a much higher level using storage multipath software (e.g., EMC® PowerPath® or Veritas® DMP®).

CNAs are available as regular PCI Express boards or in mezzanine form factor for blade servers. CNAs will soon start to appear on the motherboard in an arrangement often referred to as LOM (LAN On Motherboard). As LOM becomes available, there will be an even greater adoption of FC/FCoE, as businesses leverage the cost benefits that LOM provides.

FCoE can also be implemented entirely in software. This may be particularly interesting for servers that perform non-I/O intensive operations, but that have a need to access storage arrays.

A complete software implementation of FCoE exists in an open-source project (www.Open-FCoE.org) [13]. This has been accepted into the Linux kernel as part of the 2.6.29 release. It will soon start to appear in Linux distributions such as RedHat® or SuSE® and later possibly also in Microsoft® Windows®.

Virtualization

One of the most overused terms in the computer and network industry is "virtualization". It is used in conjunction with servers, platforms, resources, applications, desktops, networks, etc.

The following sections describe the relation between server virtualization and network virtualization and how this is relevant to the UCS.

Server Virtualization

The times when a server had a single CPU, a single Ethernet card (with a unique MAC address), and a single operating system are long gone. Today servers are much more complex. They contain multiple sockets (see "Sockets" in Chapter 2 on page 24) with each socket containing multiple cores (see "Cores" in Chapter 2 on page 25) and each core being capable of running one or more threads simultaneously. These servers have significant I/O demands and they use multiple NICs (Network Interface Cards) to connect to various networks, and to guarantee performance and high availability. These NICs are evolving to support SR-IOV (see"SR-IOV" in Chapter 3 on page 83) and server virtualization.

Server virtualization is a technique that allows use of all the available cores without modifying/rewriting the applications. VMware® ESX®/vSphere®, Linux® XEN®, and Microsoft® Hyper-V® are well-known virtualization solutions that enable multiple Virtual Machines (VMs) on a single server through the coordination of a hypervisor.

A VM is an instantiation of a logical server that behaves as a standalone server, but it shares the hardware and network resources with the other VMs.

The hypervisor implements VM to VM communication using a "software switch" module, this creates a different model compared to standalone servers.

Standalone servers connect to one or more Ethernet switches through dedicated switch ports (see Figure 3-12). Network policies applied to these Ethernet switch ports (dashed line in Figure 3-12) are effectively applied to the single standalone servers.

A logical server running in a VM connects to the software switch module in the hypervisor and this in turn connects to one or more Ethernet switches (see Figure 3-13). Network policies applied to the Ethernet switch ports (dashed line in Figure 3-13) are not very effective, since they are applied to all the VMs (i.e., logical servers) and cannot be differentiated per VM.

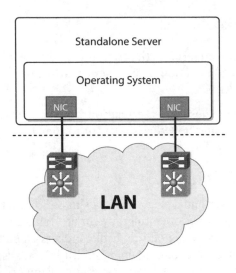

Figure 3-12 Standalone server

Attempts to specify such policies in term of source MAC addresses are also not effective, since the MAC addresses used by VMs are assigned by the virtualization software and can change over time. Moreover, this opens the system to MAC address spoofing attacks; for example, a VM may try to use the MAC address assigned to another VM.

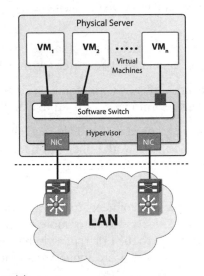

Figure 3-13 Virtual machines

Virtualization software can also move the VMs between different physical servers making the management of network policies even more challenging. The number of VMs tends to be much larger than the number of physical servers and this creates scalability and manageability concerns. For these reasons, alternative solutions have been identified to avoid using a software switch inside the hypervisor, but still allowing VM to VM communication.

SR-IOV

The PCI-SIG (Peripheral Component Interconnect - Special Interest Group) has a subgroup that produces specifications for NIC cards supporting I/O Virtualization (IOV). SR-IOV (Single Root IOV) deals with native I/O Virtualization in PCI Express topologies where there is a single root complex. These devices are designed to work in conjunction with server virtualization by allowing multiple VMs to share PCI Express devices, potentially bypassing the hypervisor ("PCI Express®" in Chapter 2 on page 43).

The IEEE Standard Effort

IEEE project 802.1 has been in charge of standardizing Ethernet switching behavior. IEEE 802.1Qbh is an addition approved in November 2009 to cover "Port Extenders".

A Port Extender (see Figure 3-14) attaches to a MAC port of an 802.1Q bridge (Controlling Bridge) and provides additional MAC ports (Downlink Interfaces) that are logically ports of the 802.1Q bridge to which it is attached.

This solution applies to both physical and virtual network scenarios. Port Extenders can be cascaded through multiple layers (see Figure 3-14, top-right).

All packets flow from Port Extender (PE) through the Controlling Bridge (CB) allowing consistent forwarding and policy enforcement for all traffic

The Controlling Bridge acts as centralized management point for its collection of Port Extenders.

Port Extenders act as an access device and can be implemented in NICs, blade switches, Top of Rack switches, hypervisor modules, etc.

Cisco fully supports the IEEE 802.1Qbh standard effort that can be seen as an evolution of Cisco VNTag architecture (see "VN Tag" in Chapter 3 on page 86) and more in general an integral part of the VN-Link architecture (see"VN-Link" in Chapter 3 on page 90).

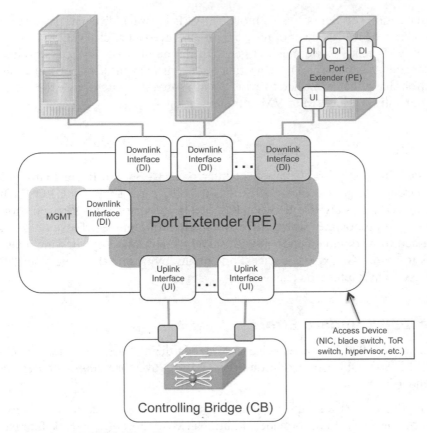

Figure 3-14   IEEE 802.1Qbh Port Extender

Port Extenders and Virtualization

When Port Extenders are combined with virtualization software, they allow the delegation of complex and performance critical data path functions to external Ethernet switches, as shown in Figure 3-15. The Ethernet switches are responsible of ensuring feature consistency to all VMs, independent of where they are located—i.e., of which Hypervisor/Physical-Server the VM resides in.

The number of switches to be managed does not increase, since there are no switches inside the NICs. In addition, the need for the network managers to manage a server component (i.e., the hypervisor switch) is no longer present.

NIC designers can now use the available logical gates to provide better performance to ULP, by improving data movement and ULP features like TCP offload, RDMA, and FC/SCSI.

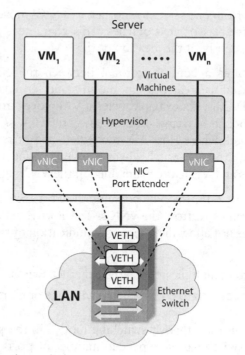

Figure 3-15   VEB in the switch

The Port Extender approach requires developing a new Ethernet tagging scheme between the NIC and the Ethernet switch to indicate the vNIC (virtual NIC) associated within the frame. Cisco Systems has pioneered the VNTag (Virtual NIC Tag) scheme, and IEEE 802.1Qbh will use it as a base for the standard.

This scheme moves the interfaces from the VMs to an external Ethernet switch and makes them virtual. These new virtual interfaces are also called vEth (virtual Ethernet) ports and the Ethernet switch operates on them if they were physical ports. Whatever an Ethernet switch can do on a physical port, it can do it on a VEth port.

This new tag binds a vNIC to a VEth port and vice versa. Policies are applied to VEth ports and therefore to vNICs. Policies may include ACLs (Access Control Lists), traffic management (for example, parameters for PFC and ETS), authentication, encryption, etc.

The VNTag is much more difficult to spoof than a MAC address, since it is inserted by the NIC or the hypervisor and not by the VM.

When a VM moves from one server to another, its vNICs moves with it, the VEth ports moves with their associated policies. This guarantees feature and policy consistency independently of the location of the VM.

This approach requires a control protocol between the NIC and the Ethernet switch that is used to create, assign, modify, and terminate the relationship between vNICs and vEths. For example, when a VM moves from Host-A to Host-B, this control protocol is in charge of terminating the vNICs/VEths relationships on the Ethernet switch where Host-A is connected, and of recreating equivalent relationships on the Ethernet switch where Host-B is connected. Policies associated with the vNICs and VEths are maintained in the VM migration.

Going back to Figure 3-15, the NIC contains the Port Extender that is responsible to dispatch frames to/from the vNICs. The Port Extender is not a switch and therefore it does not allow the direct communication of two vNICs. The Port Extender allows:

- One vNIC to communicate with the Ethernet switch.
- The Ethernet switch to communicate with one or more vNICs.

There is no change in the Ethernet switching model; in the presence of a VEth port, the Ethernet switch has an expanded number of ports, one for each connected vNIC. The Ethernet switch functionality for the virtual ports remains unchanged.

VNTag

The VNTag (Virtual NIC tag) is an Ethernet tag inserted into the Ethernet frame immediately after the MAC-DA (Destination Address) and MAC-SA (Source Address) pair (see Figure 3-16). The IEEE MACsec (authentication and encryption) tag may precede it.

VNTag is needed to augment the forwarding capability of an Ethernet switch and make it capable to operate in a virtualized environment. Classical Ethernet switches do not support the forwarding of frames where the source and destination MAC address are on the same port and therefore do not support forwarding frames between two VMs connected on the same switch port. VNTag solves this and other issues by creating a virtual Ethernet interface per each VM on the switch. Since the switch is capable of forwarding between these virtual Ethernet interfaces, it is capable of forwarding between VMs connected on the same physical port.

VNTag is a six-byte tag whose format is shown in Figure 3-17. The VNTag is used between the Ethernet switch and the Port Extender. Its main concept is the "vif" (virtual interface identifier). The vif appears in the VNTag as src_vif (source vif) and dst_vif (destination vif).

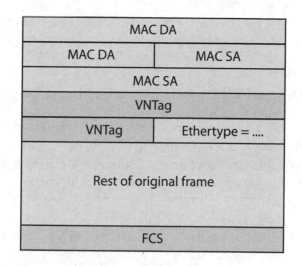

Figure 3-16 VNTag applied to an Ethernet frame

It starts with two bytes of Ethertype = VNTag in order to identify this particular type of tag. The next four bytes have the following meaning:

- v: version[2]—Indicates the version of the VNTag protocol carried by this header, currently version zero.
- r: reserved[1]—This field is reserved for future use.
- d: direction[1]—d = 0 indicates that the frame is sourced from a Port Extender to the Ethernet switch. d = 1 indicates that the frame is sourced from the Ethernet switch to a Port Extender (one or more vNICs).

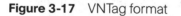

Figure 3-17 VNTag format

- dst_vif[14] and p: pointer[1]—These fields select the downlink interface(s) that receives a frame when sent from the Ethernet switch to the Port Extender. As such, they are meaningful when d = 1. When d = 0, these fields must be zero.
- p = 0 indicates that dst_vif selects a single vNIC, typically used for unicast frames. p = 1 indicates that dst_vif is an index into a virtual interface list table; this case is used for multicast frame delivery.
- src_vif[12]—Indicates the vNIC that sourced the frame. src_vif must be set appropriately for all frames from a Port Extender to the Ethernet switch (d = 0). In addition, src_vif may be set for frames headed toward the Port Extender (d = 1) as indicated by looped.
- l: looped[1]—Indicates that the Ethernet switch looped back the frame towards the Port Extender that originated it. In this situation, the Port Extender must ensure that the vNIC indicated by src_vif does not receive the frame, since it has originated the frame.

The vif is just an identifier of the association between a vNIC and a VEth on a given link. It has a meaning that is local to the link (physical port of the Ethernet switch), but it is not unique in the network. If the VM moves, the vNIC and the VEth move with it. The existing association between the vNIC and the VEth on the current link is terminated and a new association is created on the new link. Because vifs are local to a particular link, the vif used to identify the association on the new link may differ from the vif previously used before the move.

The implementation of VNTag can be done either in hardware by a VNTag capable NIC (for example, Cisco Palo supports VNTag, see "Cisco® Palo" in Chapter 4 on page 124) or in software by the hypervisor.

The Port Extender is found in server NICs, but it can also be implemented as a separate box that acts as a remote multiplexer toward an Ethernet switch. This box is commonly called a "Fabric Extender".

Fabric Extenders

The Fabric Extender is a standalone implementation of a Port Extender and it uses VNTag toward the upstream Ethernet switches. The Fabric Extender can also be viewed as a remote line-card of an Ethernet switch or as an Ethernet multiplexer/ de-multiplexer. These remote line cards are used to increase the number of ports available without increasing the number of management points. Being a simple box that is managed by the upstream switch, it also reduces the overall cost of the solution.

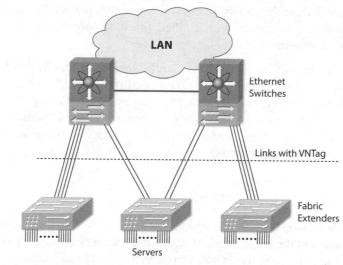

Figure 3-18   Fabric Extenders

Figure 3-18 shows three Fabric Extenders connected to two Ethernet switches. Note that the links that cross the dashed line use the VNTag encapsulation.

A Fabric Extender can be a one RU (Rack Unit) box with 48 x 1GE downfacing ports toward the servers and 4 x 10GE uplinks toward the Ethernet switches. In this particular example, the Fabric Extender uses 48 vifs to identify each 1GE ports and it does not use VNTag on the 1GE interfaces.

The uplinks of the Fabric Extender can be bundled together using EtherChannels. In Figure 3-18, the left-most and right-most Fabric Extenders have the four uplinks bundled together toward a single Ethernet switch; the center Fabric Extender has the four uplinks bundled together into a single EtherChannel, but connected in pairs to two separate Ethernet switches.

For example, a data center switch like the Cisco Nexus 5000 has the hardware capability to support 20 Fabric Extenders providing a total number of 960 x 1GE ports, with a single point of management, in 24 RUs. The Nexus 5000 and attached Fabric Extenders create a single switch domain on the network. The Nexus 5000 performs all the management plane functions and no local configuration or software image is stored on the Fabric Extenders themselves.

Another example is a Fabric Extender with 32 x 10GE downfacing ports toward the servers and 8 x 10GE uplinks toward the Ethernet switches. In this particular example, the Fabric Extender uses 256 vifs, and dynamically assign them to the 32 x 10GE ports that also use VNTag on the links toward the servers. This illustrates the possibility to aggregate links that already use VNTag.

Twenty of these Fabric Extenders, in association with a pair of Nexus switches, can provide 640 x 10GE ports, with Unified Fabric support, in 24 RUs, with a single point of management.

The Fabric Extender can be placed close to the servers so that low cost copper connections can be used between the servers and the Fabric Extender. Alternatively, the Ethernet switches can be placed at the end-of-row using more expensive fiber connections between the Fabric Extender and the Ethernet switches. The resulting solution, though oversubscribed, provides a cost-effective 10GE solution that can be centrally managed.

VN-Link

Cisco® Systems and VMware® collaborated to develop the Virtual Network Link (VN-Link) to address the issues of virtualization-aware networking. VN-Link simplifies the management and administration of a virtualized environment by bringing the server and the network closer together. VN-Link delivers network-wide VM visibility and mobility along with consistent policy management.

VN-Link and the Nexus 1000v

The Nexus1000V is the first implementation of the VN-Link architecture. It is a Cisco software switch embedded into the VMware® vSphere/ESX hypervisor. It is compliant with VMware® vNDS (virtual Network Distributed Switch) API that was jointly developed by Cisco Systems and VMware.

vNetwork DS includes not only the support for VN-Link and VNTag, but also VMDirectPath and NetQueue (see "Intel® VT-c for Connectivity" on page 65 in Chapter 2).

VM policy enforcement is applied to and migrated with the VM when a VMotion or DRS (Distributed Resource Scheduler) move a VM. Not only the policies are moved with the VM, but also all the statistical counters, the Netflow status and ERSPAN sessions.

Network Policies are called "Port Profiles" and are created on the Nexus 1000v by the network administrator using, for example, CLI commands. Port Profiles are automatically populated inside VMware® VC (Virtual Center). Port Profiles are visible inside VMware® Virtual Infrastructure Client as "Port Groups" and the server administrator can assign them to vNICs and therefore ultimately to VMs.

Port Profiles are the constructs in VN-Link that enable a collaborative operational model between the server administrator and the network administrator without requiring the use of a new management tool.

VEths and Port Profiles are the basic building blocks to enable automated VM connectivity and mobility of policies; i.e., to allow the interface configuration, interface state, and interface statistics to move with a virtual machine from server to server, as VMotion or DRS occurs. This also guarantees that security and connectivity policies are persistent.

Nexus 1000V is a member of the Nexus family of switches and it runs NX-OS. Figure 3-19 shows the basic components: the "Nexus 1000V VEM" (Virtual Ethernet Module) is installed in VMware® ESX® and remotely configured and managed by the Nexus 1000V VSM (Virtual Supervisor Module) that runs in an NX-OS appliance (virtual or physical) or in a Nexus family switch, like the Nexus 5000 or the Nexus 7000. The dashed lines in Figure 3-19 indicate the management and configuration relationship between the VEMs and VSM. A single VSM can manage multiple VEMs. In addition, it maintains the VMware® Virtual Center provisioning model for server administration.

Being part of the Nexus family, the Nexus 1000V provides many value added features like ACLs, QoS marking and queueing, Cisco TrustSec, CDP v2, Netflow V9, Port Profiles, Cisco CLI, XMP API, SNMP Read/Write, detailed interface counters and statistics, Port Security, etc. It also supports ERSPAN (Encapsulated Remote SPAN) to allow traffic to mirror the traffic of a VM to an external sniffer located centrally in the data center even during the VM migration.

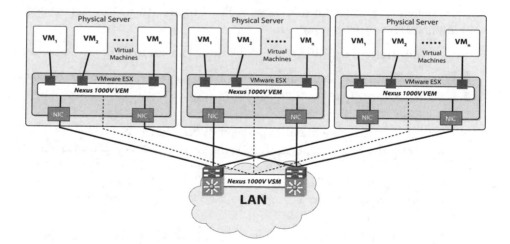

Figure 3-19   Nexus 1000V

VN-Link and the UCS

An alternative approach is to replace the switch inside the hypervisor with a Port Extender capable of supporting the VNTag/VN-Link architecture. In this case, either the Nexus 5000 switch or the UCS 6100 Fabric Interconnect operates as a controlling bridge (see "The IEEE Standard Effort" in Chapter 3, page 83) using VNTag (see "VNTag" in Chapter 3, page 86) between the Port Extender in the server and the Nexus 5000/UCS 6100.

The Port Extender is in charge of tagging the frames leaving the VM and this can happen in one of two ways:

- Inserting the VNTag in the hypervisor software switch (either the Nexus 1000V or the VMware® switch) and then forward the packet to the Nexus 5000/UCS 6100, or
- Having an SR-IOV NIC capable of adding VNTag in hardware.

This second approach is clearly superior from the performance perspective, since it does not consume CPU resources in the hypervisor and can potentially enable hypervisor bypass.

The external behavior and benefits are the same as using VN-Link on the Nexus 1000V; however, with the Nexus 5000, all the Ethernet features (switching, ACLs, ERSPAN, QoS, etc.) are performed completely in hardware at wire rate.

Network Policies are still defined in terms of Port Profiles. All VMotion/DRS and VN-Link features are also supported.

Figure 3-20 illustrates three different possibilities, from left to right:

- The Nexus 1000V solution described in the previous section: The Nexus 1000V does software switching and applies all the Ethernet features, by using the server processor.
- VNTag in hardware without hypervisor bypass: Each vNIC is mapped to a vEth, the vNIC supports SR-IOV, the switch (Nexus 5000/UCS 6100) applies all the Ethernet features in hardware. This can be achieved without touching the VM and it supports all the VMware features. This feature is supported, for example, in Cisco Palo (see "Cisco® Palo" in Chapter 4, page 124).
- VNTag in hardware with hypervisor bypass: This is similar to the previous solution, but the hypervisor is completely bypassed for higher performance. VMDirectPath allows VMware® vSphere/ESX® to bypass the hypervisor and map the physical NICs directly to the virtual machines. It currently requires an additional driver in the VM and it does not support VMotion (this limitation will be removed in a future release of vSphere).

Software Switching   **VNTag in Hardware**   **VNTag in Hardware**
Nexus 1000V   **with VM DirectPath**

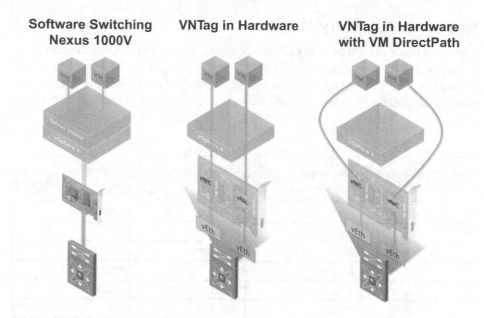

Figure 3-20   VN-Link and UCS

Memory Expansion

With the growing computing capacity of modern CPUs, memory often becomes the bottleneck limiting server performance. This is true both for memory speed and memory size.

Each server socket has a limited number of memory sockets and speeds with which it can connect to. For example, the Intel® Xeon 5500 (Nehalem-EP) processor used on the first generation of the UCS has a supported configuration in which each of the three memory channel per socket is capable of connecting to eight ranks of memory on two DDR3 RDIMMs (see "UDIMMs and RDIMMs" in Chapter 2, page 40). At the time of writing (February 2010), the largest RDIMM on the market is 16 GB, but the price is still incredibly high. 8 GB DIMMs are commonly used; i.e., 16 GB per bus, and 48 GB per socket.

Speed vs. Capacity

There is a trade-off between speed and capacity. The maximum speed supported in Nehalem-EP varies from 800 MTps, to 1066 MTps (MTps = Million Transfers per second), to 1333 MTps (see Table 3-1), depending on how many sockets are installed per memory channel, how many are populated, and how many ranks are present per DIMM.

Table 3-1   Trade-Off of DIMM Speed vs. Capacity

DIMM Slots per Channel	DIMM Populated per Channel	Million Data Transfer per Second	Ranks per DIMM
2	1	800, 1066, 1333	SR, DR
2	1	800, 1066	QR
2	2	800, 1066,	SR, DR
2	2	800	SR, DR, QR
3	1	800, 1066, 1333	SR, DR
3	1	800, 1066	QR
3	2	800, 1066	SR, DR
3	2	800	SR, DR, QR
3	3	800	SR, DR

SR: Single Rank, DR: Double Rank, QR: Quad Rank

Similar tables apply to Westmere-EP and Nehalem-EX.

Capacity vs. Cost

Another important consideration is the cost of the DIMM per GB. This cost does not grow linearly between generations. For example, the prices shown in Table 3-2 are the list prices at the time this book was written.

Table 3-2 DDR3 DIMM List Price

Capacity	List Price	List Price / GB
2 GB	125 USD	65.5 USD/GB
4 GB	300 USD	75 USD/GB
8 GB	1,200 USD	150 USD/GB

While there is not much difference in the price/GB using 2 or 4 GB RDIMMs, 8 GB RDIMMs come at a substantial premium.

How Much Memory Is Required?

Memory requirements are hard to quantify in absolute terms, but guidelines can be given for applications.

Memory Requirements

Let us consider the typical memory requirements shown in Table 3-3 for operating systems.

Table 3-3 OS Memory Requirements

Operating System	Typical	High Performance
Windows 7	2 GB – 4 GB	2 GB – 8 GB
Windows Vista	1 GB – 4 GB	2 GB – 8 GB
Windows XP	512 MB – 2 GB	1 GB – 4 GB
Windows 2000	256 MB – 1 GB	512 MB – 2 GB
Windows 2003 32 bits	1 GB – 2 GB	2 GB – 4 GB
Windows 2003 64 bits	2 GB – 4 GB	4 GB – 8 GB
Windows 2008 64 bits	2 GB – 8 GB	8 GB – 16 GB
Linux	512 MB – 2 GB	2 GB – 8 GB
Macintosh OS X	512 MB – 2 GB	1 GB – 4 GB

These numbers may not look too bad at first compared to the capacity of current DIMM. When considered in a Virtual Machine environment, they are multiplied by the number of VMs and they often exceed the capacity of current DIMMs, before the CPU becomes a bottleneck (more on this later).

Memory on Servers

When considering server memory requirements, the goal is to have enough physical memory compared to active virtual memory, so that memory pagination can be avoided. Virtual memory is paged to disk, and this is a slow process. If intense pagination occurs, significant performance degradation is unavoidable.

Memory also depends on the number and speed of processors. A server with more cores processes information faster and requires more memory than a server with fewer cores.

64-bit operating systems also use more memory than their 32-bit predecessors.

Memory requirements, while clearly dependent on the number of users, depend more heavily on the type of applications being run. For example, text-based applications tend to require less memory than GUI/graphic-based applications.

The applications that tend to use less memory are applications like directory services (DNS, DHCP, or LDAP servers) that perform a very specific task. 1 GB to 2 GB can be reasonable.

Communication servers (like IP phones, voice servers, and email/fax servers) are intermediate memory users in the 2 GB to 4 GB range.

Web server memory mainly depends on the number of concurrent users and the required response time; they are in the 2 GB to 4 GB range.

Application server memory is in a similar range as web servers, and it greatly depends on the application and on the number of users.

Database servers are in general the most memory intensive and can use the maximum amount of memory a server can provide to cache the database content, thus dramatically improving performance. They start at 4 GB for small databases.

Some engineering tools are memory-bound on the complexity of the model they can simulate; the larger the memory on the server, the larger the circuit they can simulate or the more accurate the analysis they perform. In the same class are tools for oil and energy and biotech research.

Memory on Virtualized Servers

The amount of memory installed in a server may be insufficient in a virtualized environment where multiple virtual machines run on the same processor. Each virtual machine consumes memory based on its configured size, plus a small amount of additional overhead memory for virtualization [20].

Hypervisors typically allow specifying a minimum and a maximum amount of memory per VM: The minimum is guaranteed to be always available; the maximum can be reached as a function of the state of the other VMs. This technique is called memory over-commitment, and it is useful when some virtual machines are lightly loaded while others are more heavily loaded, and relative activity levels vary over time.

Certain minimums must be guaranteed to avoid errors. For example, Windows® XP and RedHat® Enterprise Linux 5 both requires at least 512 MB.

In practice, most production environments allocate from 2 GB/VM to 4 GB/per VM. Using this assumption, Table 3-4 analyzes how many VMs can be run on a Nehalem-EP/Westmere-EP CPU socket assuming 2 DIMMs per memory channel are populated.[1]

Table 3-4   VMs per Socket

	Total Memory	2 GB/VM	4 GB/VM	Estimated List Price	List Price per 2 GB/VM
Inexpensive 2 GB DIMM	12 GB	6	3	750 USD	125 USD
Medium Price 4 GB DIMM	24 GB	12	6	1,800 USD	150 USD
Expensive 8 GB DIMM	48 GB	24	12	7,200 USD	300 USD

This table illustrates how either expensive DIMMs are needed to run a significant number of VMs or few VMs can be run per socket with the possibility of not fully utilizing all the cores. For example, 3 VMs will not fully utilize the 4 cores of a Nehalem socket and even 6 or 12 VMs may not be enough, unless they run CPU-intensive workloads.

In the Intel® Microarchitecture (Nehalem), memory controllers are integrated on the processor socket and therefore memory can only be added with additional sockets, but this does not solve the original issue of increasing the memory per socket.

---

1   This is only an example, since the amount of memory per VM is extremely dependant on the applications.

NUMA

Non-Uniform Memory Access or Non-Uniform Memory Architecture (NUMA) is a computer memory design used in multiprocessors, where the memory access time depends on the memory location relative to a processor. Under NUMA, a processor can access its own local memory faster than non-local memory; that is, memory local to another processor or memory shared between processors [31].

The Intel® Xeon 5500, 5600, and 7500 (Nehalem-EP, Westmere-EP, and Nehalem-EX) processor family supports NUMA and allows a core to access the memory locally connected to the memory channels of its socket or to access the memory connected to another socket via the QPI interconnect. Access times are of course different; for example, the memory local to the processor socket can be accessed in ~63 nanoseconds, while the memory connected to another processor socket can be accessed in ~102 ns.

The particular type of NUMA supported by Nehalem is "cache-coherent NUMA"; i.e., the memory interconnection system guarantees that the memory and all the potentially cached copies are always coherent.

The Nehalem support of NUMA is a key enabling technology for the UCS solution described in the next section.

The UCS Approach

UCS addresses the need for larger memories with dedicated computing blades that have an increased number of memory sockets. This may seem in contradiction with what shown in Table 3-1, where the limitation in number of memory modules is reported.

The limit on the number of memory sockets is not directly related to the addressing capability of the processor (Nehalem is capable of addressing larger memories). Electrical issues, DRAM device density, and details of the processor's pinout are the real limiting factors. Each memory socket on a memory channel adds parasitic capacitance, and the DIMMs inserted on the memory sockets further load the memory bus. The load increase results in lower speed operation. Three DIMMs directly attached on the bus is the practical upper limit given the speeds required for DDR3 operation. Additionally, memory capacity is limited by the maximum number of ranks (eight) that the Nehalem processor can directly address on each memory channel, and by the density of the DRAM devices that comprise each rank. Finally, there are details in the number and type of control signals generated by the Nehalem CPU that limit the number of directly attached DIMMs to two or three.

When a larger memory system is desired, UCS uses Cisco ASICs called the "Catalina chipset" to expand the number of memory sockets that can be connected to each single memory bus. These ASICs are inserted between the processor and the DIMMs on the memory bus, minimizing the electrical load, and bypassing the control signal limitations of the Nehalem CPU design.

The achieved expansion factor is 4X: Using 8GB DIMMs, a Nehalem socket can connect up to 192 GB of RAM and a dual-processor socket blade can host up to 384 GB of RAM (see a Windows screenshot in Figure 3-21). The DIMMs are unmodified JEDEC standard DDR3 RDIMMs. This expansion is done at the electrical level and it is completely transparent to the operating systems and its applications. The BIOS is extended to initialize and monitor the ASICs and to perform error reporting.

In order to increase the number of memory sockets without sacrificing memory bus clock speed, the Catalina chipset adds a small amount of latency to the first word of data fetched from memory. Subsequent data words arrive at the full memory bus speed with no additional delay. For example, in a typical Nehalem configuration, the memory latency grows from ~63 nanoseconds to ~69 nanoseconds (+10%), but it is still well below the 102 nanoseconds (+62%) required to access the memory on a different socket, and is orders of magnitude below the time required to fetch data from disk.

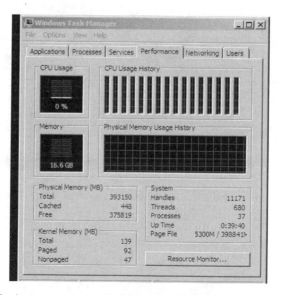

Figure 3-21   Windows running with 384 GB of RAM

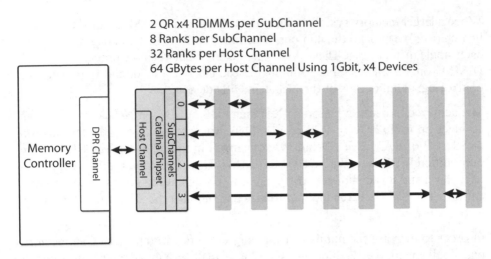

2 QR x4 RDIMMs per SubChannel
8 Ranks per SubChannel
32 Ranks per Host Channel
64 GBytes per Host Channel Using 1Gbit, x4 Devices

Figure 3-22   The Catalina ASIC chipset

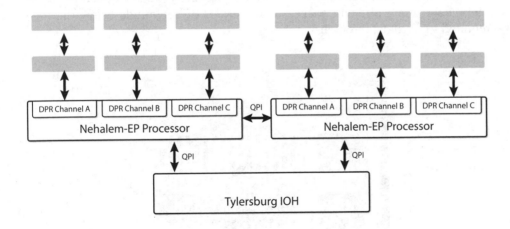

Figure 3-23   Nehalem system without memory expansion

Figure 3-22 illustrates how each memory channel is buffered and expanded to four sub-channels.

Each sub-channel can support two SR (Single Rank), DR (Dual Rank), or QR (Quad-Rank) x4 DIMMs. "x4" refers to the data width of the DRAM chips in bits.

Figure 3-23 and Figure 3-24 show a comparison between a classical two-socket Nehalem system and a two-socket expanded system.

The Catalina chipset was originally designed for the memory channels of the Nehalem-EP processor, but since these channels are standard DDR3 buses, it can work on any DDR3 busses. Therefore, it can be used as well in conjunction with Westmere-EP and Nehalem-EX.

The UCS Advantage

UCS with the adoption of the Catalina chipset, multiplies the number of memory sockets available by four while introducing minimal latency. This solution uses standard DDR3 DIMMs.

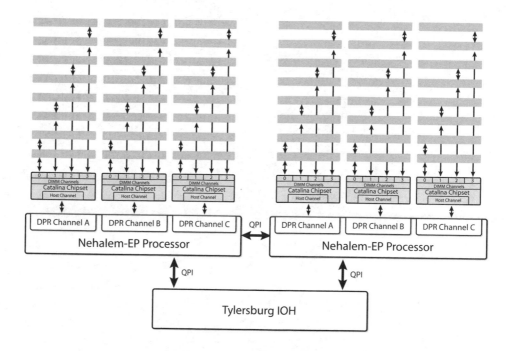

Figure 3-24 Nehalem system with memory expansion

This can be exploited in two different ways:

- Building the largest memories possible using the highest density DIMMs. This may be particularly appropriate for applications that are more memory intensive, such as large databases and engineering tools like large circuit synthesis and simulation.
- Building a medium to large memory configuration using inexpensive DIMMs.

In both cases, the final customer obtains the best price/performance ratio.

Chapter 4

I/O Adapters

Historically, server I/O connectivity to storage, local area networks, and other servers have been accommodated by hardware and software specifically designed and dedicated to the application, each with different traffic characteristics and handling requirements. Server access to storage in enterprises has been largely satisfied by Storage Area Networks (SAN) based on Fibre Channel. Server access to networking devices is almost exclusively satisfied by local networks (LAN) based on Ethernet. Lastly, server-to-server connectivity, or inter-process communication (IPC) for high performance computing (HPC), is being satisfied with InfiniBand. While each of these technologies serves their application needs very well, the specialization results in the need for enterprise servers to support multiple dedicated specialized networks with unique dedicated hardware. All these networks in the data center often require physically redundant backup connections, which compounds the problem and introduces double the amount of NICs, HBAs, and HCAs into the network.

In recent years, server density has increased and server manufacturers are providing more compute power in smaller and smaller packaging. "Green" concerns (see "Environmental Concerns—'Green'" in Chapter 1, page 2) have sparked a strong emphasis on reduced power consumption and cooling. Servers one "RU" in height and bladed chassis-based servers are pushing the density envelope. The trend toward higher and higher densities is resulting in tremendous incentive to provide consolidated I/O. Consolidated I/O can result in fewer unique I/O adapters, translating to less power consumption and heat dissipation, as well as reduced, simplified, common cabling.[1]

Players in this new consolidated I/O market are the classical Ethernet NIC vendors that are adding storage capabilities to their devices and HBA vendors that are adding Ethernet support.

UCS uses several different I/O adapters, all in mezzanine form factor. This chapter presents some of them that are available at the time of writing or in future releases. Please consult the UCS documentation to verify availability.

---

1   The authors thank QLogic® for providing most of the text of this section.

Disclaimer

The material contained in this chapter has been provided by the I/O adapter man-ufacturers. For this reason, the presentation of the different I/O adapters are not homogeneous and even the terminology used differs from adapter to adapter. The authors understand that this can cause some confusion in the reader.

The Intel® Approach

Virtualization focuses on increasing service efficiency through flexible resource management. In the near future, this usage model will become critical to data centers, allowing IT managers to use virtualization to deliver high-availability solutions with the agility to address disaster recovery and real-time workload bal-ancing so they can respond to the expected and the unexpected.[2]

Dynamic load balancing requires the ability to easily move workloads across mul-tiple generations of platforms without disrupting services. Centralized storage becomes a key requirement for virtualization usage models. 10GE (10 Gigabit Ethernet) supports storage implementations of iSCSI SAN as well as NAS today. Fibre Channel over Ethernet (FCoE) solutions extend the 10GE to seamlessly interoperate with existing Fibre Channel SAN installations. Consolidating storage traffic over 10GE using FCoE simplifies the network and provides a cost effective mean to enable virtualization usage.

In addition to virtualization, many bandwidth hungry applications require 10GE NICs. 10GE provides the bandwidth needed by High Performance Computing (HPC) applications, clustered databases, image rendering, and video applications.

10 Gigabit Ethernet NIC Solutions

Intel® launched one of the first PCI-X based 10GE adapter to the market back in 2003. Since then, new PCIe (PCI Express, see "PCI Express®" in Chapter 2, page 43) products have been introduced (see Figure 4-1).

Today, the 10GE NIC market is predominately served with stand-alone adapter cards. These cards plug into the PCIe bus expansion slots of a server to provide 10GE connectivity.

Mezzanine form-factor NICs are appropriate for server blades that are installed into blade servers. In this case, there is not a standard PCIe slot. The mezzanine is a daughter card with a proprietary connector, size, and power consumption. While the connector is proprietary, the protocol spoken is always PCIe.

---

2   The authors thank Intel® for providing the text of the next few sections. The pictures are courtesy of Intel®.

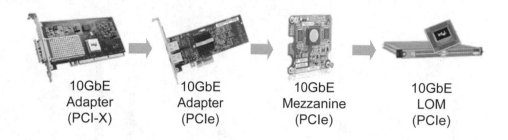

Figure 4-1 NIC evolution

In the next couple of years, OEMs will start providing 10GE LAN on Motherboard (LOM) solutions. LOM solutions implement LAN chipset integrated onto the PC motherboard thus freeing up valuable PCI slots. LOM implementations are less expensive than adapter or mezzanine cards and also implement effective management technologies that require signal transfer directly to the system board. With LOM implementation, 10GE will be pervasive; every server will ship with an on-board 10GE controller.

The tipping point for 10GE will come when data centers refresh their environment with the new Intel® Xeon® 5500 class of server products (formerly known by the codename Nehalem, see "Intel Microarchitectures" in Chapter 2, page 45).

Figure 4-2 shows that previous generation platforms were saturated at 2 ports 10GE throughput. The Intel® Nehalem platform is able to scale up to five 10GE ports and beyond and still have enough CPU headroom for other tasks.

Three specific Intel® 10GE adapters that can be used in the UCS are presented in the next sections, outlining advantages and peculiarities.

Intel® 82598 10 Gigabit Ethernet Controller (Oplin)

Intel® 82598 is a high-performing, PCIe 1/10 Gigabit Ethernet controller that is ideally suited for demanding enterprise applications and embedded system designs. It includes support for multi-core processors, it improves virtualized server performance, and it delivers efficient storage over Ethernet. The 82598 is an ideal candidate for server consolidation. It is a single chip dual port 10GE implementation in a 31x31mm package (see Figure 4-3) with industry leading power consumption of 4.8 Watts (typical).

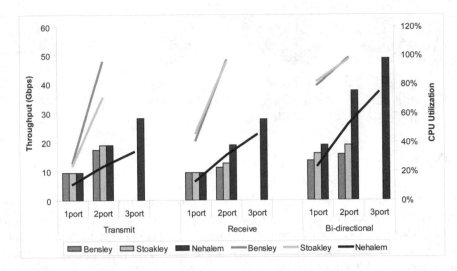

Figure 4-2   Performance comparison

Source: Intel® Labs 2008. Performance calculated based on 64k I/O IxChariot test with Intel® 82598 10 Gigabit Ethernet controller, with Linux 2.6.18 kernel on a Quad Core Intel® Xeon® Platform (formerly Bensley/Stoakley) and Intel® Next Generation (Nehalem). Actual performance may vary depending on test and system configuration.

UCS supports a mezzanine card named Cisco UCS 82598KR-CI that is based on the Intel® 82598.

Figure 4-4 shows a block diagram of the 82598 that integrates two 10GE Media Access Control (MAC) and XAUI ports. Each port supports CX4 (802.3ak) and KX4/KX (802.3ap) interfaces and contains a Serializer-Deserializer (SerDes) for backward compatibility with gigabit backplanes. The device is designed for high performance and low memory latency. Wide internal data paths eliminate performance bottlenecks by efficiently handling large address and data words. The controller includes advanced interrupt-handling features and uses efficient ring-buffer descriptor data structures, with up to 64 packet descriptors cached on a chip. A large on-chip packet buffer maintains superior performance. The communication to the Manageability Controller (MC) either is available through an on-board System Management BUS (SMBus) port or through the Distributed Management Task Force (DMTF) defined NC-SI. The 82598 also supports PXE and iSCSI boot.

Figure 4-3   The Intel® 82598 Oplin ASIC

The 82598 was designed to offer outstanding performance and power efficiency, while at the same time providing support for multi-core processors, virtualization, and unified I/O over a broad range of operating systems and virtualization hypervisors. It can be installed in PCIe form-factor cards, or in mezzanine cards or directly on the server motherboard (LOM).

Figure 4-5 shows the 82598 in mezzanine form factor for UCS B-Series.

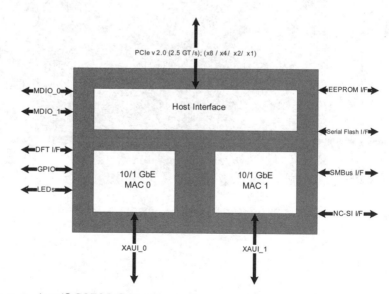

Figure 4-4   Intel® 82598 Oplin block diagram

Support for Multi-Core CPUs

The 82598 introduces new networking features to support multi-core processors. Supported features include:

- Message Signaled Interrupts-Extended (MSI-X) that distributes network controller interrupts to multiple CPUs and cores. By spreading out interrupts, the system responds to networking interrupts more efficiently, resulting in better CPU utilization and application performance.

- Multiple Tx/Rx queues: A hardware feature that segments network traffic into multiple streams that are then assigned to different CPUs and cores in the system. This enables the system to process the traffic in parallel for improved overall system throughput and utilization.

- Low latency enables the server adapter to run a variety of protocols while meeting the needs of the vast majority of applications in HPC clusters and grid computing.

- Intel® QuickData Technology, which enables data copy by the chipset instead of the CPU, and Direct Cache Access (DCA) that enables the CPU to pre-fetch data, thereby avoiding cache misses and improving application response times.

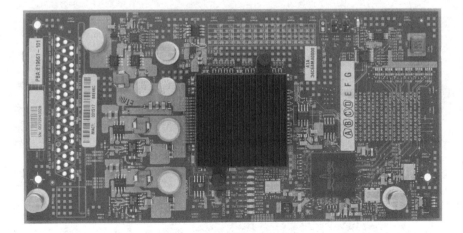

Figure 4-5   Cisco UCS 82598KR-CI using Intel® 82598

Hardware-Assisted Virtualization

Intel® has invested in hardware support for improving virtualization performance. These hardware enhancements have been implemented in the processors, in the chipsets and in the adapters. The 82598 includes support for the Intel® Virtualization Technology for Connectivity (Intel® VT-c), to reduce the need for compute-intensive software translations between the guest and host OSes. An important assist for virtualized environments is the Virtual Machine Data Queues (VMDq), which is described in "Intel® VT-c for Connectivity" in Chapter 2, page 65.

Advanced Features for Storage over Ethernet

The 82598 includes support for iSCSI acceleration and advanced features for unified storage connectivity. It supports native iSCSI storage with all major operating systems including Microsoft®, Linux®, and VMware®, as well as iSCSI remote boot.

An advantage of iSCSI compared to FC is cost: Since iSCSI can run over existing IP infrastructure (as oppose to a dedicated FC network), this can provide the storage features at a reduced price.

iSCSI remote boot offers a number of advantages and simplifications: Server Consolidation and Virtualization. Remote boot enables servers to boot from an OS image on the SAN. This is particularly advantageous for servers in high-density clusters as well as for server consolidation and virtualization.

With OS images stored on the SAN, provisioning new servers and applying upgrades and patches is easier to manage; when a server remotely boots from the SAN, it automatically acquires the latest upgrades and fixes.

Improved Disaster Recovery-All information stored on local SAN-including boot information, OS image, applications, and data can be duplicated on a remotely located SAN for quick and complete disaster recovery.

Intel® 82599 10 Gigabit Ethernet Controller (Niantic)

The 82599 is the second-generation PCIe Gen-2-based 10GE controller from Intel. The 82599 delivers enhanced performance by including advanced scalability features such as Receive Side Coalescing (RSC) and Intel® Flow Director Technology. The 82599 delivers virtualization capabilities implementing Single Route I/O virtualization (SR-IOV, see "SR-IOV" in Chapter 3, page 83). Finally, the 82599 delivers advanced capabilities for unified network including support for iSCSI, NAS, and FCoE.

Like the 82598, the 82599 is a single chip, dual port 10GE implementation in a 25x25mm package (see Figure 4-6). It also integrates serial 10GE PHYs and provides SFI and KR interfaces. With a power consumption of less than 6 Watts (typical[3]), a small footprint, and integrated PHYs, the 82599 is suited for LOM and Mezzanine card implementations. The advanced features of 82599 along with the Intel® Nehalem processor enables customers to scale servers to fully utilize to 10GE capacity.

Figure 4-7 shows a 82599 that integrates two 10 GE Media Access Control (MAC) and Multi-Speed Attachment Unit Interface (MAUI) ports that support IEEE 802.3ae (10Gbps) implementations as well as perform all of the functions called out in the standards for:

- XAUI
- IEEE 802.3ak and IEEE 802.3ap backplane Ethernet (KX, KX4, or KR)
- PICMG3.1 (BX only) implementations including an auto-negotiation layer and PCS layer synchronization
- SFP+ MSA (SFI)

Figure 4-8 shows the mezzanine card for the UCS B-series blades.

Figure 4-6   Intel® 82599 10 Gigabit Ethernet Controller

3   Note that these power consumption ranges are interface-dependent.

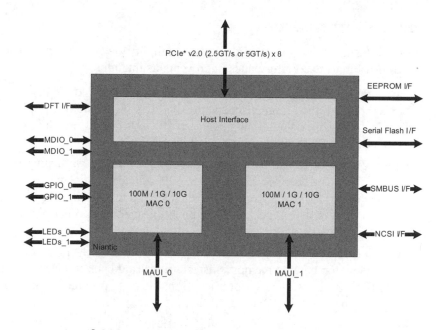

Figure 4-7   Intel® 82599 block diagram

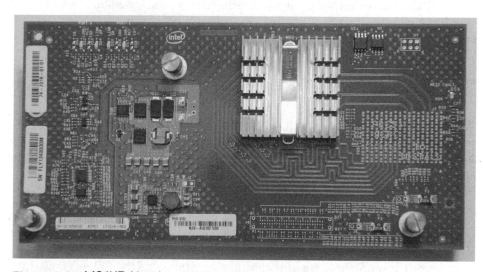

Figure 4-8   M61KR-I Intel converged network adapter

Improved Performance

The 82599 is designed with improved data throughput, lower memory latency, and new security features. Performance improvements include:

- **Throughput**—The 82599 provides wire speed dual-port 10 Gbps throughput. This is accomplished using the PCIe physical layer (PCIe Gen-2), by tuning the internal pipeline to 10 Gbps operation, and by enhancing the PCIe concurrency capabilities.

- **Latency**—Reduced end-to-end latency for high-priority traffic in presence of other traffic. Specifically, the 82599 reduces the delay caused by preceding TCP Segmentation Offload (TSO) packets. Unlike previous 10 GE products, a TSO packet might be interleaved with other packets going to the wire.

- **Tx Descriptor Write Back**—The 82599 improves the way Tx descriptors are written back to memory. Instead of writing back the Descriptor Done (DD) bit into the descriptor location, the head pointer is updated in system memory.

- **Receive Side Coalescing (RSC)**—RSC coalesces incoming TCP/IP (and potentially UDP/IP) packets into larger receive segments. It is the inverse operation to TSO on the transmit side. The 82599 can handle up to 32 flows per port at any given time.

- **PCIe v2.0**—Several changes are defined in the size of PCIe transactions to improve the performance in virtualization environment.

- **Rx/Tx Queues and Rx Filtering**—The 82599 Tx and Rx queues have increased in size to 128 Tx queues and 128 Rx queues. Additional filtering capabilities are provided based on L2 Ethertype, 5-tuples, SYN identification.

- **Flow Director**—A large number of flow affinity filters that direct receive packets by their flows to queues for classification, load balancing, and matching between flows and CPU cores.

- **Interrupts**—A new interrupt scheme is available in the 82599:
  - Control over the rate of Low Latency Interrupts (LLI)
  - Extensions to the filters that invoke LLIs
  - Additional MSI-X vectors

- **Packet Filtering and Replication**—The 82599 adds additional coverage for packet filtering for virtualization by supporting the following filtering modes:
  - Filtering by unicast Ethernet MAC address
  - Filtering by VLAN tag

    — Filtering of multicast Ethernet MAC address

    — Filtering of broadcast packets

- For each of the preceding categories, the 82599 can replicate packets to multiple Virtual Machines (VMs). Various mirroring modes are supported, including mirroring a VM, a Virtual LAN (VLAN), or all traffic into a specific VM.

- **Packet Switching**—The 82599 forwards transmit packets from a transmit queue to an Rx software queue to support VM-VM communication. Transmit packets are filtered to an Rx queue based on the same criteria as packets received from the wire.

- **Traffic Shaping**—Transmit bandwidth is allocated among the virtual interfaces to avoid unfair use of bandwidth by a single VM. Allocation is done separately per traffic class (see "Bandwidth Management" in Chapter 3, page 74) so that bandwidth assignment to each traffic class is partitioned among the VMs.

Hardware-Assisted Virtualization

The 82599 supports two modes of operation for virtualized environments:

1. Direct assignment of part of the port resources to different guest OSes using the PCI-SIG SR-IOV standard. Also known as Native mode or Pass Through mode.

2. Central management of the networking resources by an I/O Virtual Machine (IOVM) or by the Virtual Machine Monitor (VMM). Also known as software switch acceleration mode. This mode is referred to as VMDq mode.

The virtualization offload capabilities provided by 82599, apart from the replication of functions defined in the PCI-SIG IOV specification, are part of VMDq.

A hybrid model, where some of the VMs are assigned a dedicated share of the port and the rest are serviced by an IOVM, is also supported. However, in this case, the offloads provided to the software switch might be more limited. This model can be used when parts of the VMs run operating systems for which VF (Virtual Function, aka vNIC) drivers are available and thus can benefit from an IOV and others that run older operating systems for which VF drivers are not available and are serviced by an IOVM. In this case, the IOVM is assigned one VF and receives all the packets with Ethernet MAC addresses of the VMs behind it.

The 82599 also supports the PCI-SIG single-root I/O Virtualization Initiative (SR-IOV) including the following functionality:

- Replication of PCI configuration space
- Allocation of BAR (Base Address Register) space per virtual function
- Allocation of requester ID per virtual function
- Virtualization of interrupts

The 82599 provides the infrastructure for direct assignment architectures through a mailbox mechanism. Virtual Functions (VFs) might communicate with the Physical Function (PF) through the mailbox and the PF can allocate shared resources through the mailbox channel.

Support for DCB (Data Center Bridging)

DCB is a set of features that improve the capability of Ethernet to handle multiple traffic types (see "United Fabric" in Chapter 3, page 69).

The layer 2 features of DCB implemented in the 82599 are:

- **Multi-class priority arbitration and scheduling**—The 82599 implements an arbitration mechanism on its transmit data path. The arbitration mechanism allocates bandwidth between traffic classes (TC) in bandwidth groups (BWGs) and between Virtual Machines (VMs) or Virtual Functions (VFs) in a virtualization environment.

- **Class-based flow control (PFC—Priority Flow Control)**—Class-based flow control functionality is similar to the IEEE802.3X link flow control. It is applied separately to the different TCs.

- **DMA queuing per traffic type**—Implementation of the DCB transmit, minimization of software processing and delays require implementation of separate DMA queues for the different traffic types. The 82599 implements 128 descriptor queues in transmit and 128 descriptor queues in receive.

- **Multiple buffers**—The 82599 implements separate transmit and receive packet buffers per TC.

- **Rate-limiter per Tx queue**—Limiting the transmit data rate for each Tx queue.

Storage over Ethernet

Refer to the 82598 description for details in "Advanced Features for Storage over Ethernet" in Chapter 4, page 109.

Fibre Channel over Ethernet (FCoE)

Existing FC HBAs offload the SCSI protocol to maximize storage performance. In order to compete with this market, the 82599 offloads the main data path of SCSI Read and Write commands.

82599 offloads the FC CRC check, receive coalescing, and Direct Data placement (DDP) tasks from the CPU while processing FCoE receive traffic.

FC CRC calculation is one of the most CPU intensive tasks. The 82599 offloads the receive FC CRC integrity check while tracking the CRC bytes and FC padding bytes. The 82599 recognizes FCoE frames in the receive data path by their FCoE Ethernet type and the FCoE version in the FCoE header.

The 82599 can save a data copy by posting the received FC payload directly to the kernel storage cache or the user application space.

When the packet payloads are posted directly to user buffers their headers might be posted to the legacy receive queues. The 82599 saves CPU cycles by reducing the data copy and minimizes CPU processing by posting only the packet headers that are required for software.

Time Sync—IEEE 1588

The IEEE 1588 International Standard lets networked Ethernet equipment synchronize internal clocks according to a network master clock. The PTP (Precision Time Protocol) is implemented mostly in software, with the 82599 providing accurate time measurements of special Tx and Rx packets close to the Ethernet link. These packets measure the latency between the master clock and an endpoint clock in both link directions. The endpoint can then acquire an accurate estimate of the master time by compensating for link latency.

The 82599 provides the following support for the IEEE 1588 protocol:

- Detecting specific PTP Rx packets and capturing the time of arrival of such packets in dedicated CSRs (Control and Status Registers)
- Detecting specific PTP Tx packets and capturing the time of transmission of such packets in dedicated CSRs
- A software-visible reference clock for the above time captures

Double VLAN

The 82599 supports a mode where all received and sent packets have an extra VLAN tag in addition to the regular one. This mode is used for systems where the switches add an additional tag containing switching information.

When a port is configured to double VLAN, the 82599 assumes that all packets received or sent to this port have at least one VLAN. The only exception to this rule is flow control packets, which do not have a VLAN tag.

Security

The 82599 supports the IEEE P802.1AE LinkSec specification. It incorporates an inline packet crypto unit to support both privacy and integrity checks on a packet per packet basis. The transmit data path includes both encryption and signing engines. On the receive data path, the 82599 includes both decryption and integrity checkers. The crypto engines use the AES GCM algorithm, which is designed to support the 802.1AE protocol. Note that both host traffic and manageability controller management traffic might be subject to authentication and/ or encryption.

The 82599 supports IPsec offload for a given number of flows. It is the operating system's responsibility to submit (to hardware) the most loaded flows in order to take maximum benefits of the IPsec offload in terms of CPU utilization savings. Main features are:

- Offload IPsec for up to 1024 Security Associations (SA) for each of Tx and Rx
- AH and ESP protocols for authentication and encryption
- AES-128-GMAC and AES-128-GCM crypto engines
- Transport mode encapsulation
- IPv4 and IPv6 versions (no options or extension headers)

Intel's NetEffect™ iWARP Controller (NE020)

In Q4 of 2008, Intel acquired NetEffect, a networking startup company that has developed an iWARP controller for 10 GE. Intel offers the NE020 under the original NetEffect brand in the form of various PCIe adaptors and mezzanine cards.

The NE020 is a PCIe Gen-1-based controller that implements the iWARP protocol on top of hardware TCP engine, enabling an RDMA over Ethernet solution. iWARP/RDMA enables very low-latency communication for High Performance Computing (HPC) and other ultra-low-latency workloads.

The NE020 Adapters come in single-port and dual-port 10GE flavors and support three different 10 GE interfaces:

- CX4: 8-pair twinaxial copper
- SFP+ Direct Attach: Pluggable twinaxial copper
- SFP+ Optical: Pluggable short range fiber

A picture of the SFP+ adapter with the 35mm x 35mm NE020 controller is shown in Figure 4-9.

iWARP and RDMA

iWARP (Internet Wide Area RDMA Protocol) is a low-latency RDMA over TCP/IP solution. The specification defines how the RDMA (Remote Direct Memory Access) protocol runs over TCP/IP. iWARP delivers improved performance by:

- **Delivering a Kernel-bypass Solution:** Placing data directly in user space avoids kernel-to-user context switches which adds additional latency and consumes additional CPU cycles that could otherwise be used for application processing.

Figure 4-9   NE020 in PCI form factor

■ **Eliminating Intermediate Buffer Copies:** Data is placed directly in application buffers versus being copied multiple times to driver and network stack buffers, thus freeing up memory bandwidth and CPU compute cycles for the application.

■ **Accelerated TCP/IP (Transport) Processing:** TCP/IP processing is done in silicon/hardware versus in the operating system network stack software, thereby freeing up valuable CPU cycles for application compute processing.

Figure 4-10 shows a comparison of a standard network flow on the left vs. an accelerated iWARP network flow on the right. The short horizontal lines represent the buffer copies occurring at each stage in the flow. The illustration shows how buffer copies as well as context switches between kernel space and user space are averted.

The iWARP protocol was developed to perform within a TCP/IP infrastructure, and thus does not require any modifications to existing Ethernet networks or equipment. At the same time, iWARP's can take advantage of enhancements to Ethernet, such as Data Center Bridging (DCB, see "Terminology" in Chapter 3, page 72), low-latency switches, and IP security. By leveraging Ethernet, iWARP preserves key benefits, like:

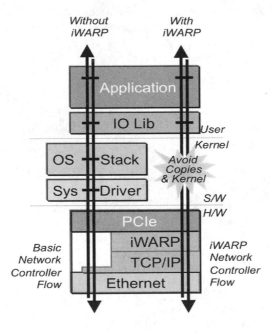

Figure 4-10   iWarp frame flow

- **Uses Existing Network Infrastructure:** Standard Ethernet switches and routers carry iWARP traffic over existing TCP/IP protocols. Because iWARP is layered over TCP, network equipment doesn't need to process the iWARP layer, nor does it require any special-purpose functionality.

- **Uses Existing Management Solutions:** Industry-accepted management consoles operate using existing IP management protocols. iWARP brings compatibility with TCP/IP.

- **Uses Existing Software Stacks:** Complete OS support and driver support is available today for Linux and Windows. The Open Fabrics Alliance (www.openfabrics.org) provides an open-source RDMA software stack that is hardware-agnostic and application-agnostic for iWARP solutions.

N2020 Architecture

Figure 4-11 shows the internal architecture of the NE020.

The NE020 supports the following features:

- **TCP Acceleration:** Complete offload of up to 256K simultaneous connections.

- **iWARP Protocol:** Direct data placement into user space memory.

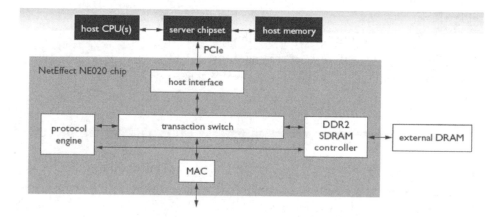

Figure 4-11   NE020 architecture

- **Low power:** 6.2W max. Adapters do not require heat sinks.
- **Advanced Configuration and Power Interface (ACPI):** Compliant power management support, including Wake-on-LAN.
- **VLAN:** IEEE 802.1Q VLAN tagging.
- **Pause:** Full link pause support.
- **Jumbo Frame:** 9K frame size support.

The NE020 supports the following interfaces:

- **PCIe Host Interface:** A PCIe Gen-1 x8 interface.
- **External DDR2 SDRAM Interface:** A side-band interface to a local DDR2 memory is used to store active connection. This interface supports external memories from 64MB to 2GB using various configurations and numbers of DDR2 components. For reliability, an additional DDR2 SDRAM is required to store an ECC code, allowing read bit errors to be corrected.
- **2x SFI Interfaces:** Two 10GE interfaces for SFP+ or CX4 connectivity.
- **EEPROM Interface:** For local configuration storage.
- **Flash Interface:** For firmware code and option ROM code storage.

When the NE020 is installed in the current adapter, the resulting implementation supports:

- **TCP Connections:** Maximum of 8K simultaneous off-loaded.
- **Memory:** 256MB of state storage memory + ECC.
- **PXE Boot:** Option ROM support for PXE network boot.

Performance

The NE020 does support a conventional state-less network interface, but its intended purpose is for iWARP operation. For that reason, only iWARP performance data is reported in the following.

The NE020 is capable of deliver <6µs latency for half-trip RDMA read and write operations for small numbers of active connections (see Figure 4-12 and Figure 4-13). As the connections scale, the latency increases, but at a very respectable rate, delivering <25µs latency for 64 active connections.

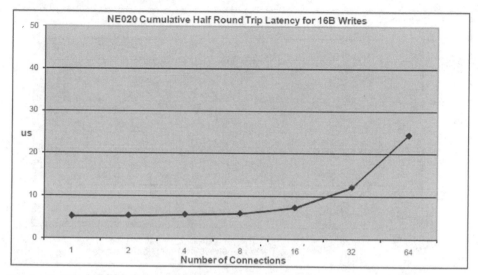

Figure 4-12   NE020 Cumulative Half Round Trip Latency

The NE020 is capable of saturating the 10GbE wire with bandwidth using RDMA at approximately 1KB message sizes. Moreover, bandwidth is used more effectively as more connections are off-loaded, as shown in Figure 4-14 and Figure 4-15.

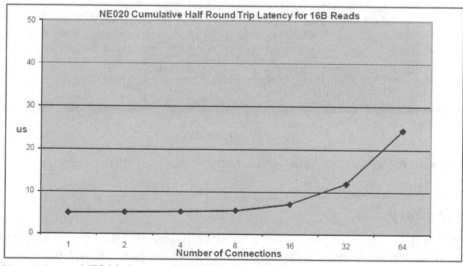

Figure 4-13   NE020 Cumulative Half Round Trip Latency

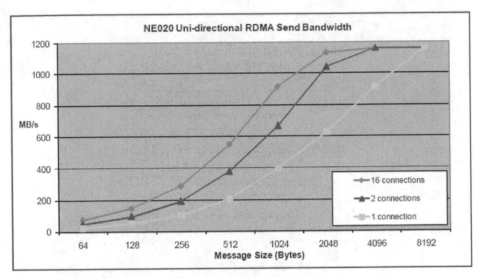

Figure 4-14   NE020 RDMA send bandwidth

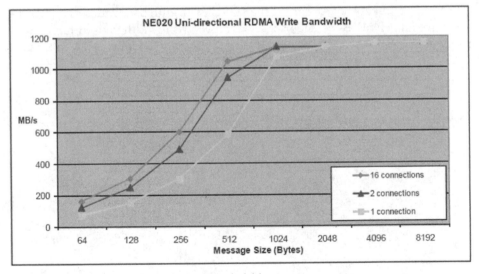

Figure 4-15   NE020 RDMA write bandwidth

Summary

The NE020 controller provides an iWARP dual-port 10 GE solution capable of delivering single digit μs half-trip latencies for applications and workloads that demand top performance. The iWARP protocol enables this by implementing RDMA over Ethernet, providing an OS/kernel-bypassed path for direct application-to-application communication. The NE020 provides the acceleration support on die to implement the iWARP and TCP protocols, thus providing a low-latency RDMA Ethernet solution.

Converged Network Adapters (CNAs)

Converged Network Adapters is a term used by some vendors to indicate a new-generation of consolidated I/O adapters that include features previously present in HBAs, NICs, and HCAs (see also "FCoE (Fibre Channel over Ethernet)" in Chapter 3, page 75).[4]

CNAs offer several key benefits over conventional application unique adapters, including the following:

- Fewer total adapters needed
- Less power consumption and cooling
- Reduced and simplified cabling

It is important to note that CNAs rely on two distinct device drivers at the OS level: one for the FC part, and one for the Ethernet part. This is exactly similar to the way physically separate FC and Ethernet adapters function. This key attribute allows the implementation of CNAs to be evolutionary in nature, while providing revolutionary advances.

CNAs are typically dual-port 10 GE, providing more than adequate bandwidth and high-availability to operate in a converged environment.

The first CNAs to appear on the market were PCIe standard form-factor adapters for industry standard servers, but the same consolidation benefits extend to blade servers using custom form-factor mezzanine cards provided by the server manufacturer.

PCIe form-factor CNAs are appropriate for industry standard servers (e.g., rack-mounted servers) that have PCIe slots that use standard PCIe connectors (see Figure 2-23). The PCIe standards define the size, connector, and power consumption of these adapters guaranteeing multi-vendor interoperability.

Mezzanine form-factor CNAs are appropriate for server blades that are installed into blade servers. A blade server that requires 10 or more dual-port Ethernet (LAN) mezzanine cards and 10 or more dual-port Fibre Channel (SAN) mezzanine cards (one each per processor blade) could reduce the hardware 50% by using 10 or more CNA mezzanine cards instead (one per processor blade). The use of

---

4   The authors are thankful to QLogic® Corporation for writing most of the text of this section.

CNAs in the blade server can also reduce the number of embedded switches or pass-through modules required by 50%. This will also significantly simplify backplane complexity and power/thermal burden for blade servers.

The minimum characteristics required for a CNA to operate optimally in a converged environment are listed below:

- Dual-port, full-bandwidth 10 Gbps per port maximum throughput for high bandwidth storage (SAN) and networking (LAN) traffic
- Hardware offload for FCoE protocol processing
- Support for de facto industry standard Fibre Channel software stacks
- Full support for TCP/IP and Ethernet performance enhancements such as priority-based flow control (802.1Qbb), Enhanced Transmission Selection (802.1Qaz), DCBX protocol (802.1Qaz), jumbo frames, checksum offloads, and segmentation offloads
- Boot from LAN / SAN: PXE boot, BIOS, UEFI, FCode, depending on OS
- PCIe 1.0 x8 or PCIe 2.0 x4 system bus support

Several different companies manufacture CNAs, including Broadcom®, Brocade®, Cisco®, Emulex®, Intel®, and QLogic®.

The next sections describes different mezzanine CNAs that can be used in the UCS B-Series, outlining advantages and peculiarities.

Cisco® Palo

Palo is a CNA developed by Cisco® Systems. It is currently supported only on the UCS.

It derives its name from the City of Palo Alto, California. Figure 4-16 shows a picture of the mezzanine board with Palo called Cisco UCS VIC M81KR Virtual Interface Card.

It is a single chip ASIC designed in 90 nm silicon technology with seven metal layers. The die is approximately 12x12 mm and it is mounted in a 31x31mm FC BGA (Ball Grid Array) package, with 900 balls.

Figure 4-16   Palo mezzanine board for UCS B-Series

The single ASIC design has major advantages in terms of space, cost, and power consumption. The Palo ASIC typically has a power consumption of 8 Watts and the overall mezzanine card of 18 Watts, well below the maximum of 25 Watts established by the PCIe standard.

Palo is compliant with PCIe version 1.1, it has 16 lanes for a total of 32 Gb/s of raw bandwidth, full duplex, more than enough to support the two 10 GE ports that provide the external connectivity.

Palo was designed from day one to be a CNA capable of providing hardware support for virtualization. It is capable of handling all traffic to and from the host, including network, storage, inter-processor communication, and management. Management agents run on embedded processors inside Palo, providing server, network, and storage management functions.

When used in conjunction with UCS servers, Palo provides several important system-level features:

- I/O consolidation and Unified Fabric
- DCB-compliant Ethernet interfaces
- Capability to support active/active and active/standby
- Capability to be fully configured through the network
- Capability to create I/O devices on demand to better support virtualization
- Capability to support kernel and hypervisor bypass

- Low latency and high bandwidth
- SRIOV compliant hardware
- Native support for VNTag
- Native support for FCoE

The logical diagram of Palo is reported in Figure 4-17, where the two DCB interfaces are 10 GE interfaces.

Palo has an internal switch and can also as Port Extender using VNTag (see "The IEEE Standard Effort" page 83 and "VNTag" page 86, both in Chapter 3).

The MCPU (management CPU) is in charge of the configuration of Palo and creates the vNIC that are seen by the OS or the hypervisor as regular PCI devices. Palo supports up to 128 vNICs and each vNIC may be either an Ethernet NIC or a FC HBA. Other types of vNICs are supported in hardware, but currently not used.

In the preferred way of operation, Palo assigns a VNTag to each vNIC and uses an external switch to switch between them. VNTag also provides traffic separation between the different VMs that share the same Palo adapter.

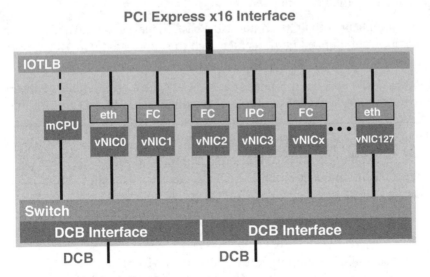

Figure 4-17   Palo logical diagram

This architecture is aligned with VN-Link Hardware and VN-Link in hardware with VMDirectPath (see "VNLink" in Chapter 3, page 90). In these architectures, each VM, for each Ethernet vNIC, gets a data plane interface into the adapter and performs I/O operation without going through the hypervisor. Of course, the pass-through interface is protected to prevent each VM from interfering with other VMs and with the hypervisor.

Figure 4-18 details this architecture and shows the strong capability of PCIe virtualization. In PCI terminology, a "PCIe device" can be either a traditional endpoint, such as a single NIC or HBA, or a switch used to build a PCIe topology. A PCIe device is typically associated with a host software driver; therefore, each Palo entity that requires a separate host driver is defined as a separate PCI device. Every PCIe device has an associated configuration space that allows the host software to:

- Detect PCIe devices after reset or hot plug events
- Identify the vendor and function of each PCIe device
- Discover and assign system resources to each PCIe device needs, such as memory address space and interrupts
- Enable or disable the PCIe device to respond to memory or I/O accesses
- Tell the PCIe device how to respond to error conditions
- Program the routing of PCIe device interrupts

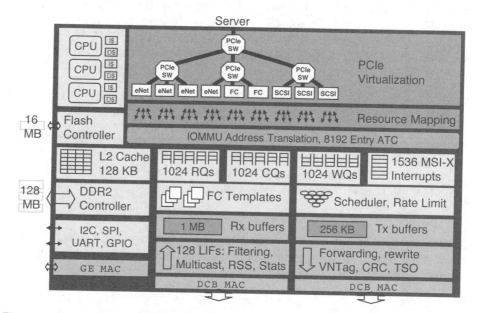

Figure 4-18 Palo detailed block diagram

Each PCIe device is either type 0 or type 1. Type 0 devices are endpoints, including vNICs. Type 1 devices include switches and bridges, and may contain additional functions beyond the ASIC bridge or switch function. For example, the IOMMU control interface is not an endpoint, but rather a function attached to the primary bridge in Palo.

The firmware and configuration of Palo are stored in an external Flash memory. At boot time, the management CPU loads the firmware and the configuration and builds a PCIe topology. This initial topology can be modified later by using the PCIe hot plug interface standard, wherein devices can be removed and added from a running system. The BIOS and the OS/hypervisor see any configured PCIe device on the PCIe bus. The OS/hypervisor for any PCIe device loads an appropriate driver.

Depending on the system configuration stored in flash and dynamically modified by UCS Manager (see "UCSM Overall Architecture" in Chapter 7, page 223), the embedded management CPU can create any legal PCIe topology and device combination and make it visible to the host. Palo is capable of a maximum of 64K PCIe devices, even if there are only 128 useful endpoints supported.

Palo is a data center class adapter, all internal and external memories for data and control are ECC protected, and it has diagnostics LEDs. As we have already discussed, it fully supports the DCB and FCoE standards, and it support virtualization through vNIC, PCIe topologies, and VNTag.

Focusing on the Ethernet vNIC aspect, Palo supports interrupt coalescing (MSI and MSI-X), Receive Side Scaling (RSS), stateless offload acceleration (checksum, LSO: Large Segment Offload), IEEE 802.1Q VLAN trunking, IEEE 802.1p priorities, jumbo frames (9KB), 32 multicast filters, promiscuous mode, and PXE.

The FC vNIC is depicted in Figure 4-19 that shows that the SCSI protocol is supported in HW by the eCPU (embedded CPU), but a path is also provided for sending raw FC frames (mainly for control and management protocols). Also data sequencing and FC frame generation is handled by dedicated hardware engines

Palo supports 2048 concurrent logins and 8192 active exchanges; it is capable to operate as a SCSI initiator or target; it supports multiple VSANs (Virtual SANs) and NPIV (N_Port Id Virtualization) over FCoE.

Some preliminary performance data are reported in the following.

At the hardware layer, it is possible to saturate both ports in both directions, but this is not a particularly interesting number, since the performance perceived by the user is at the application layer.

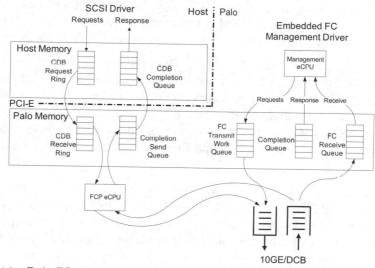

Figure 4-19   Palo FC vNIC

Using Linux netperf with 1,500 bytes MTU, enabling a single port, the throughput measured was 9.4 Gb/s at the application layer (10 Gb/s minus the overhead of the headers). This holds for both simplex and full-duplex traffic.

For FC, the preliminary performance measured is as follows:

- 512 byte reads: 590K IOPS
- 512 byte write: 500K IOPS

In term of latency, using two hosts with Palo connected back to back, Linux Net-PIPE latency is 9.8 usec (microseconds), measured at the application latency. The hardware latency of the two Palo connected back-to-back is 3 usec—i.e., approximately 2 usec for the sending Palo and 1 usec for the receiving Palo.

Palo is supported on all OSes and hypervisors that are supported in UCS.

Emulex

The Emulex[®5] OneConnect™ Universal Converged Network Adapter (UCNA) is a single-chip, high-performance 10 Gigabit Ethernet (10GbE) adapter that leverages Data Center Bridging (DCB) and Fibre Channel over Ethernet (FCoE) to consolidate network and storage I/O over a common infrastructure. This allows data

5   The authors are thankful to Emulex® Corporation for the information and the material provided to edit this section. Pictures are courtesy of Emulex®.

centers to reduce capital expense (CapEx) by deploying UCS blades with a converged OneConnect OCm10102-FC mezzanine adapter and reduce operational expense (OpEx) with corresponding savings for power, cooling, and management.

Although the network link is common, OneConnect adapters present separate NIC and FCoE adapters to the operating system (see Figure 4-20 and Figure 4-23). Using IEEE-approved standards for DCB, OneConnect enables IT administrators to provision guaranteed bandwidth for each traffic type using of traffic groups. This capability supports a "wire once" mode of deployment and allows bandwidth to be configured dynamically as workloads change on an individual server.

In additional to multiple protocol support, OneConnect provides hardware acceleration with full CPU offload for stateless TCP/IP, TCP Offload Engine (TOE), and FCoE. Protocol offloads optimize CPU and memory resources, which enables better performance for compute-intensive applications and deployment of more virtual machines on virtualized servers.

Emulex OneConnect OCm10102-FC

The OneConnect OCm10102-FC (Cisco part number 74-709-01, see Figure 4-21) is a multi-protocol CNA in mezzanine card format for Cisco UCS Blade Servers that supersedes the Emulex LP2105-CI. In addition to 10GbE connectivity for

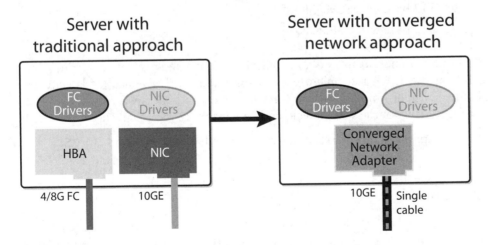

Figure 4-20 CNAs drivers

TCP/IP networks, the OCm10102-FC supports FCoE by encapsulating 2KB Fibre Channel frames into 2.5KB mini-jumbo Ethernet frames. When combined with the "lossless" capability of Priority-based Flow Control (PFC), transmissions are processed with the low latency required for Fibre Channel storage.

The OCm10102-FC is a dual-channel adapter that connects to the host bus through an 8-lane PCIe Gen 2 interface for both network and storage traffic. The Fibre Channel driver stack leverages ten generations of field-proven Emulex Fibre Channel technology and provides seamless integration with existing Fibre Channel storage infrastructures.

The Emulex OneCommand™ Manager application (see Figure 4-22) provides management of network and storage functions for OneConnect UCNAs. One Command Manager also supports Emulex LightPulse® HBAs that may be deployed on other severs in the data center.

OCm10102-FC hardware details:

- Connectivity: Two DCB ports that support 10GbE and FCoE
- Host Interface: PCIe Gen 2 (x8, 5GT/s)
- Back Plane Interconnect: 10G-Base-KR interface
- Mezzanine Form Factor: 3.65" x 7.25"

Figure 4-21   OneConnect OCm10102-FC

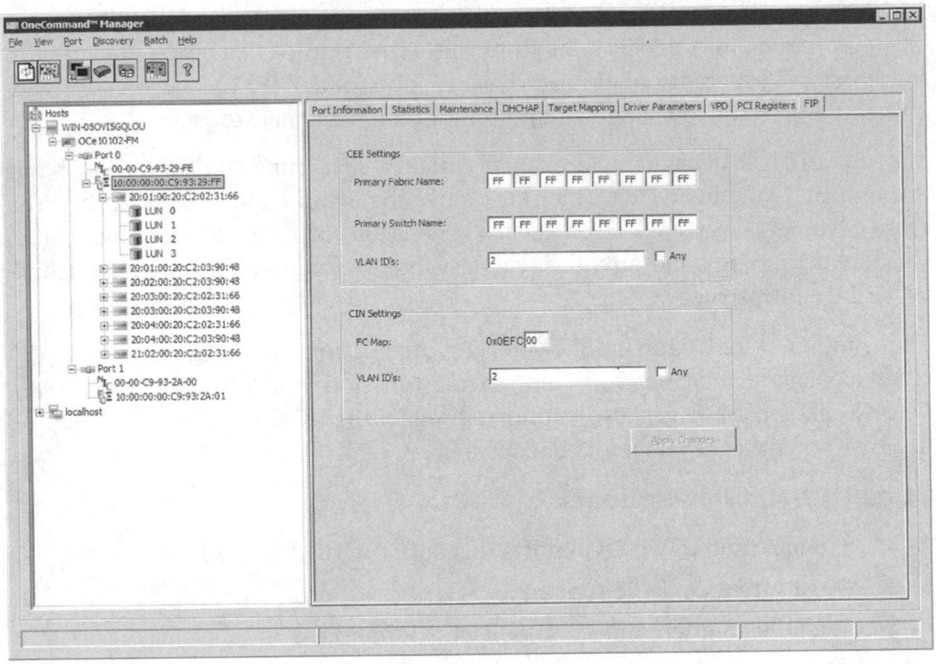

Figure 4-22 Emulex OneCommand™ Manager application

FCoE Features

The OCm10102-FC supports the following IEEE standards for DCB:

- Priority-based Flow Control (IEEE 802.1Qbb)
- Quality of Service (IEEE 802.1p)
- Enhanced Transmission Selection (IEEE 802.1Qaz)
- Data Center Bridging Capability Exchange (IEEE 802.1ab)

The OCm10102-FC also provides key Fibre Channel capabilities:

- Optimized performance with Fibre Channel protocol offload
- Support for Message Signaled Interrupts eXtended (MSI-X)
- Full-duplex throughput
- Comprehensive virtualization capabilities including support for N-Port ID Virtualization (NPIV) and Virtual Fabric
- Efficient administration with the Emulex OneCommand Manager application

Ethernet Features

The OCm10102-FC has the following Ethernet features:

- FCoE support using 2.5KB mini-jumbo Ethernet frames
- VLAN tagging (IEEE 802.1q)
- Advanced Error Reporting (AER)
- Receive Side Scaling (RSS)
- Large Send Offload, Large Receive Offload
- TCP Offload Engine (TOE)
- IP, TCP, UDP Checksum offload
- Tx TCP Segmentation offload
- Link Aggregation/Teaming (IEEE 802.3ad)
- Adaptive Load Balancing

Functional Architecture

The OCm10102-FC presents two separate PCI functions to the host operating system—a two-port network adapter and a two-port Fibre Channel adapter (see Figure 4-23). Host networking and storage drivers communicate with the corresponding PCI functions.

I/O operations are processed by the respective functionality of the OCm10102-FC CNA (see Figure 4-24). For outbound traffic, network I/O is processed at the lossless Media Access Control (MAC) sub-layer of the level 2 Data Link Layer for delivery to the converged fabric. Fibre Channel frames are sent to the OneConnect encapsulation engine and then transferred to the lossless MAC sub-layer for delivery to the converged fabric.

Received I/O uses the reverse of the same process. Incoming traffic is processed by the lossless MAC sub-layer. FCoE traffic is de-capsulated by the FCoE engine and forwarded to the Fibre Channel HBA device for further processing by the Emulex HBA device driver. Non-FCoE traffic is forwarded to the NIC device for further processing by the Emulex NIC device driver.

Deployment in UCS

The Emulex OCm10102-FC connects to the mid-plane using the 10G-KR interfaces that provides connectivity to the UCS fabric (see Figure 4-25).

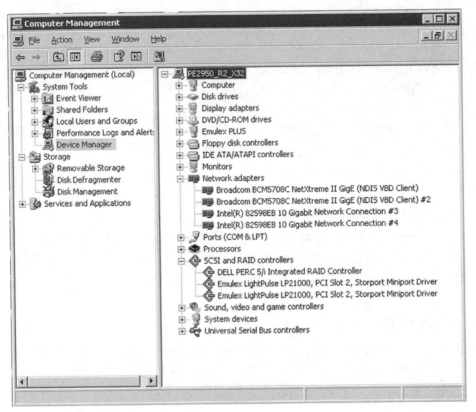

Figure 4-23   CNA drivers for Windows

Management of OneConnect UCNAs

Emulex management applications provide additional OpEx savings by minimizing the time spent managing OneConnect OCm10102-FC adapters. An extensive collection of management software and utilities facilitate the deployment and management of OneConnect UCNAs throughout the data center.

Management begins with the installation. In addition to streamlined interactive installations, scripting capabilities allow the driver installation process to be automated for deployments throughout the SAN.

The OneCommand Manager application provides comprehensive management for NIC and FCoE functions from a single console. NIC and FCoE adapters are displayed for each OneConnect port and appropriate management options are provided for each function (see Figure 4-22 and Figure 4-26).

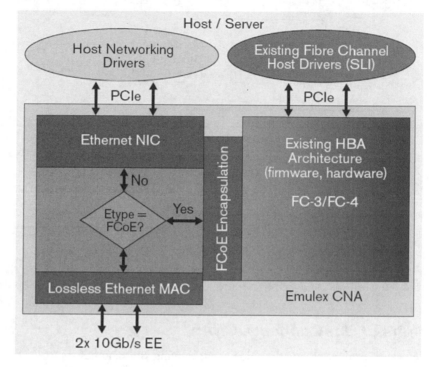

Figure 4-24   Frame processing

OneCommand Manager uses industry standard HBA APIs for FCoE management which facilitates upward integration with element manager applications. This level of integration greatly simplifies deployment and management of UCS servers with converged network connectivity.

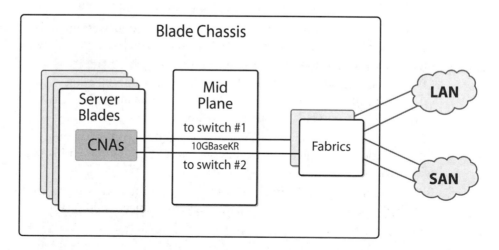

Figure 4-25   Emulex® CNA inside UCS B-Series

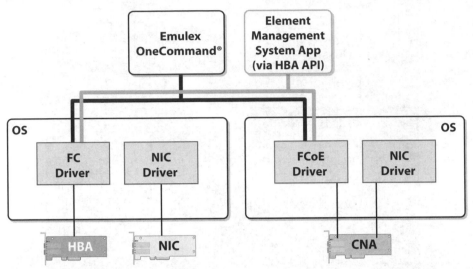

Figure 4-26   HBA and CNA management

Benefits of OneConnect UCNAs

Emulex OneConnect UCNAs provide the following key benefits:

- Field-proven Fibre Channel driver and management stack. Emulex One-Connect UCNAs and LightPulse® HBAs use a common driver model for all adapters enabling simplified driver qualification and management for greater scalability.

- Extensive interoperability. OneConnect UCNAs leverage ten generations of Emulex testing to protect investments that have been made in Fibre Channel switches, directors, and storage arrays.

- Support for all major operating systems. OneConnect drivers are qualified and supported for all major operating systems including Windows, Linux, VMware, and Solaris.

- Effective management. The OneCommand Manager application is highly intuitive and provides a single window to manage Emulex UCNAs, CNAs, and HBAs (see Figure 4-26).

- Multipathing. OneConnect UCNAs are certified to work with multipathing solutions from all of the leading server, storage, and operating system suppliers.

- Boot from SAN. OneConnect UCNAs support Boot from SAN to enable efficient management of operating system images and server migration.

QLogic®

QLogic® Corporation is a market leader in SAN Fibre Channel adapters and iSCSI / Ethernet adapters for both standard discrete servers and the mezzanine form-factor for blade servers. Since 2004, QLogic® has held the number-one market share position for Fibre Channel adapters.[6]

QLogic has also established itself as a leader in the Converged Network Adapter (CNA) market by launching the world's first CNA in 2008 (QLogic's 8000 series CNA), followed by the world's first single-chip CNA in 2009 (QLogic's 8100 series CNA).

The ideal CNA needs to combine all the features, capabilities, and performance of a best-in-class Ethernet NIC and best-in-class Fibre Channel SAN Host Bus Adapter (HBA) into a highly-reliable, low-power, cost-effective converged network adapter. However, in order for the benefits to be fully realized, neither the Ethernet NIC functionality, nor the FC HBA functionality can be substandard or compromised in any way. Customers have grown accustomed to OEM-hardened LAN / SAN software stacks, broad operating system driver support, and interoperability, which are now baseline requirements for any enterprise operation.

QLogic's family of converged network adapters draws upon the intellectual property of two successful families of QLogic® products. One is the highly successful iSCSI/Ethernet product family, in use today by multiple OEM server providers in both discrete and blade server form factor. The other is the market share leading Fibre Channel SAN adapter family, in use today by every server and storage OEM server provider, in both discrete and blade server form factor.

8000 Series—First Generation CNA

QLogic's first generation CNA, the 8000 series, is a multichip solution that includes a PCIe switch, a QLogic 4Gbps Fibre Channel controller (ISP2432), an Intel Ethernet controller (Intel 82598, aka Oplin), a "framer" ASIC that merges Fibre Channel traffic onto the shared 10GE Ethernet link (Cisco "Menlo"), and Broadcom PHY's that connect to SFP+ cages (see Figure 4-27).

The 8000 Series CNA's have a PCIe Gen-1 x8 bus and two 10GE ports that transport both FCoE and NIC traffic over shared Ethernet links. The adapters support both optical (Short Reach (SR) 850nm, multimode fibre, 300m max distance) and copper (direct attach Twinax, 5m max distance) connections with SFP+ pluggable

---

6   The authors are thankful to QLogic® Corporation for the information and the material provided to write this section.

modules. Due to the multichip implementation, the 8000 series CNA's are full-height, full-length and consume 27 watts under nominal conditions. The adapters support priority flow control to ensure lossless operation. The adapters leverage QLogic's proven and battle-hardened Fibre Channel driver stack and support 150,000 FCoE IOps per port will full FCoE hardware offload.

Cisco's M71KR-Q (see Figure 4-28) is a mezzanine adapter for Cisco's UCS blade servers that is based on the 8000 series CNA design. It, too, combines QLogic's 4Gbps Fibre Channel controller with an Intels 82598 10GE controller onto a single adapter. The design fits onto Cisco's UCS mezzanine form factor (7.25" x 3.65") and consumes 21 watts under nominal conditions. The mezzanine card routes Ethernet traffic over the UCS backplane using 10Gbase-KR signaling.

8100 Series—Second Generation CNA

QLogic's second generation CNA, the 8100 series, is a single chip design that increases performance, slashes power consumption, and fits into denser form factors compared to existing CNAs in the market.

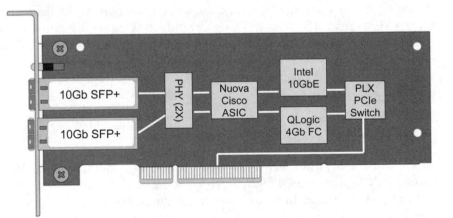

Figure 4-27   QLogic first generation CNA

Figure 4-28 M72KR-Q Qlogic converged network adapter

The 8100 series is based on QLogic's network plus architecture, a single chip design that incorporates a Fibre Channel controller and an Ethernet controller into a monolithic piece of Silicon in a single package (see Figure 4-29). This ASIC (aka ISP8112) fits into a 29x29 mm rohs-6 compliant package with 783 pins. Power consumption is a miniscule 3 watts under nominal conditions. The design includes two FCoE and two NIC PCI functions—four PCI functions total. Communication with the server travels over either PCIe Gen-1 x8 or PCIe Gen-2 x4 links, and MSI-X interrupts are supported to reduce CPU overhead. Two ports of 10GE can be connected through XAUI, 10Gbase-KX4, XFI, or 10Gbase-KR signaling. In addition, a baseboard management port supports both System Management Bus (SMBus) and Reduced Media Independent Interface (RMII) signaling over Network Controller Sideband Interface (NC-SI).

This single chip design fits onto a variety of adapter form factors including low profile PCIe (see Figure 4-30) and custom mezzanine adapters. QLogic offers both single and dual port low profile PCIe adapters with options to connect using either optical fibre (Short Reach (SR), 850nm, multi-mode fibre, 300m max distance) or copper (direct attach Twinax, 5m max distance). Power consumption is significantly lower than competing solutions—as low as 5.1 watts for a single port adapter and 7.4 watts for a dual port adapter (nominal conditions).

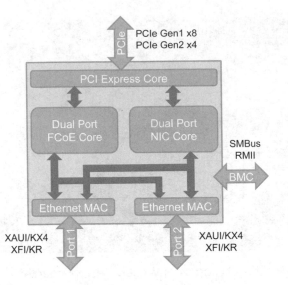

Figure 4-29   QLogic 8100 block diagram

At the time of writing (February 2010), QLogic is designing and qualifying multiple adapters for the Cisco UCS platform based on their 8100 series CNA design. This includes standard, low-profile PCIe adapters for Cisco's UCS rack-mount servers, as well as custom mezzanine adapters for Cisco's UCS blade servers. The standard low-profile adapters started shipping in the second half of 2009 and the mezzanine adapters for Cisco's UCS blade servers will become generally available in the first half of 2010.

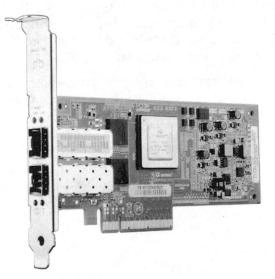

Figure 4-30   QLogic 8100 in PCIe form factor

High Performance

QLogic® 8100 series CNAs boost system performance with 10GE speed and full hardware offload for FCoE protocol processing. Leading-edge 10GE bandwidth eliminates performance bottlenecks in the I/O path with a 10X data rate improvement versus existing 1GE solutions. Additionally, full hardware offload for FCoE protocol processing reduces system CPU utilization for I/O operations, which leads to faster application performance and higher levels of consolidation in virtualized systems. Benchmark tests have shown these adapters are capable of 250,000 FCoE I/O per second and greater than 2,000 MB/s FCoE throughput on a single port! Table 4-1 summarizes the high performance demonstrated by the 8100 series CNAs.

Table 4-1   QLogic CNA: High Performance

Feature	Function	Benefit
Single or Dual 10GE Ports	Maximizes throughput between the 8100 Series and the attached Ethernet devices	Increases throughput to support high bandwidth applications (i.e., video, streaming, voice, and broadcast)
PCI Express 2.0 Host Bus Interface	PCI Express 2.0 enables maximum throughput of up to 4GBps (x4 Gen-2)	Improves server scalability and performance.
250,000 FC I/O per second per port	Provides high I/O data transfer rates for storage traffic	Delivers high performance and response time for read and write transfers
Stateless NIC Offloads: (TCP/UDP/IP checksum offloads, Large/Giant Send Offloads, Receive Side Scaling, Header-Data split)	Allows for real performance benefit through acceleration of the TCP protocol	Reduces CPU overhead on processing of the TCP/IP stack
Data Center Bridging (DCB) previously known as Enhanced Ethernet, Datacenter Ethernet, Lossless Ethernet	Eliminates dropped Ethernet frames in congested Ethernet networks	Increases storage networking performance by eliminating retries/resends due to dropped frames in congested fabrics
Jumbo Frames	Transfer of up to 9 KB data block sizes	Allows higher volume of data to be transferred in a short time
MSI/MSI-X Interrupts	Data is sent with the interrupt event	CPU spends less time processing interrupts

Investment Protection

QLogic® 8100 Series CNAs are designed to preserve existing investment in Fibre Channel storage and core Ethernet switches and routers for data networking. They leverage the same software and driver stacks that have been deployed and battle-hardened in millions of previous installations.

Table 4-2   QLogic CNA: Investment Protection

Feature	Function	Benefit
Compatibility with existing FC drivers	Utilizes battle-proven drivers that have been used in over 7 million installations	Reduces risk inherent in using unproven drivers
Compatibility with existing FC storage	FCoE protocol still carries FC traffic	Eliminates need to "forklift" the data center and replace existing storage
Compatibility with existing Ethernet infrastructure	Uses industry standard Ethernet protocol for data networking	Eliminates need to "forklift" the data center and replace existing routers and core Ethernet switches

Lower Total Cost of Ownership (TCO)

QLogic® 8100 series CNAs reduce data center costs through convergence. Now, one CNA can do the work of a discrete FC Host Bus Adapter (HBA) and Ethernet NIC. This convergence also means fewer cables, fewer switches, less power consumption, reduced cooling, and easier LAN and SAN management. They preserve familiar FC concepts such as WWNs, FC-IDs, LUN masking, and zoning, thereby eliminating training costs that would be required for a new storage technology.

Table 4-3   QLogic CNA: Lower TCO

Feature	Function	Benefit
Data and storage (FC) networking traffic travel on the same Ethernet link	Single CNA replaces separate FC HBA and Ethernet NIC	Reduced hardware, cabling, power, and cooling costs
Preservation of familiar FC storage concepts	WWN, zoning, LUN masking, etc. are still used so new training requirements are minimal	Reduces training costs for data center personnel
Unified management tool	Manage LAN & SAN networking functions from a single unified management utility	Simplifies CNA management by providing an identical LAN & SAN management interface across multiple OS platforms

Full FCoE Hardware Offload

QLogic 8100 series CNAs feature full hardware offload for FCoE protocol processing. This means the adapter is responsible for building FCoE frames for transmission and processing FCoE frames upon receipt. This contrasts the operation of many competing FCoE adapter solutions whereby they server CPU is responsible for building outgoing FCoE frames before passing to the adapter and interpreting incoming FCoE frames upon receipt from the adapter. The benefit of QLogic's off-loaded approach is that it frees up the server CPU to perform other tasks. This results in faster application performance and higher levels of server virtualization in virtualized environments.

Proven FCoE Drivers and Pervasive Operating System Support

QLogic CNA's leverage QLogic's proven and bulletproof Fibre Channel driver stack that has been deployed in nearly 7 million ports worldwide. This makes QLogic's CNA's the most reliable FCoE adapters in the industry. While QLogic's 8000 series CNA's leverage networking drivers form Intel, the 8100 series adapters are built with QLogic technology and use QLogic networking drivers. This is possible due to QLogic's existing expertise in Ethernet and networking based on our iSCSI product line. QLogic offers support for all major operating Systems (Windows, Linux, VMware, Solaris, AIX), hypervisors, and hardware platforms (Intel, AMD, SPARC, PowerPC).

Broadcom®

Broadcom[7] is shipping its fifth generation (GbE) and fourth generation (10GbE) of Converged NIC (C-NIC) solutions. The Broadcom NetXtreme II™ C-NIC family offers comprehensive convergence by supporting lossless LAN (DCB), Storage (Block or File), Manageability, and HPC (IPC) traffic types within a high performance, low latency architecture, single firmware image, common driver framework, and an industry standard NC-SI management interface. The Broadcom C-NIC family architecture also includes advanced hardware offload facilities for L3-L5. Hardware offload enables workloads such as iSCSI, FCoE, TOE (TCP Offload Engine), and RDMA. Hardware offload has proven to dramatically improve CPU utilization, significantly lower system level power, and enhance performance.

Broadcom C-NIC's offer new economics from a single-chip solution deployable across Ethernet Network Card Adapters (NIC), Converged Network Host Bus Adapter (CNA), or LAN on Motherboard (LOM) form factors within Rack, Tower, and/or Blade servers.

BCM57711 Dual-Port 10GbE Controller

The Broadcom® NetXtreme II™ 10-Gbit dual-port Ethernet Controller, BCM57711, provides a fully integrated OSI layer 4 and layer 5 solution that enables convergence of data networking, storage networking, and high-performance computing, and management. It is a fourth-generation CNIC (Converged NIC) product with hardware capabilities offering unprecedented functionality: TCP/IP, RDMA, and iSCSI to a network controller for increased performance at lower system power consumption points. A block diagram is shown in Figure 4-31.

Other features include:

- PCI Express version 2.0 for high host bus data throughput
- MSI and MSI-X for flexible interrupt routing
- Receive Side Scaling for IPv6 and IPv4 for optimized traffic steering to different CPU cores and/or memory
- TCP/IPv6 and IPv4 Checksum Offload acceleration for layer-2 Ethernet traffic

---

7   The authors are thankful to Broadcom® Corporation for the information and the material provided to write this section.

- Large Segment Offload or Giant Send Offload
- IEEE 802.1Q VLAN Tagging
- IEEE 802.3x Flow Control
- Jumbo Frames up to 9,600B
- Teaming for Layer-2, 4, and 5 applications
- Pre-Boot Execution Environment (PXE) v2.1 for remote boot
- iSCSI boot

Advanced Integration

Broadcom integrates advanced PCIe, SerDes, and PHY technology directly into the controllers. Integration using in-house portfolio improves efficiency, performance, power, cost, and reliability. The BCM57711 has integrated PCIe™ x8 v2.0-compliant bus interface for supporting two 10 Gbps ports, dual SerDes devices supporting SGMII, 1000/2500 Base-X, 10GBase-CX4, 10GBase-KX4, and XAUI™ network interfaces, dual IEEE 802.3-compliant MAC devices supporting 1-/2.5-/10-Gbps speeds. Networking interfaces support autonegotiation between 10G, 1G, and slower speeds permitting link with network partners of varying speeds.

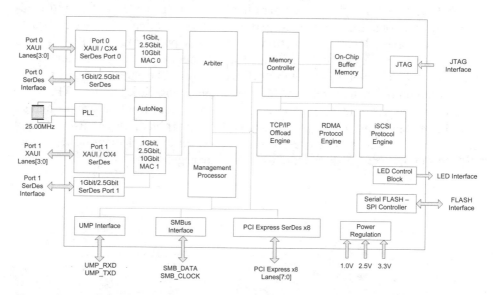

Figure 4-31   Broadcom 57711 NetXtreme II™ block diagram

Controller supports advanced protocol processing capabilities for on-chip iSCSI and TCP Chimney. Protocol processing engines accomplish this task without requiring power consuming external buffer packet memory enabling end user with higher efficiency and lower system power Ethernet and storage networking.

High-Performance Hardware Offload

TOE (TCP Offload Engine)

The TCP protocol is used to provide transport (L4) services for a wide range of applications. File transfer protocols like CIFS and NFS, to name a few, utilize the services of TCP/IP. For a long time, this protocol suite was run on the host CPU consuming a very high percentage of its resources and leaving little resources for the applications themselves. When TCP/IP has reached unprecedented ubiquity and maturity, it can be ported to hardware. In the last few years, several partial offloads have been implemented, for example: checksum and large send offload (or TCP segmentation) have provided some relief to the host CPU utilization.

The Broadcom NetXtreme II provides an industry-first TCP offload that is carefully architected for integration with the operating system, unlike many of the standalone TCP offloads, see Figure 4-32. In basic terms, the Broadcom NetXtreme II architecture allows the operating system to provide control and management functions (e.g., connection setup, prevention of denial-of-service attack, system resource allocation, selection of the most promising TCP/IP flows for offload, error and exception handling). The Broadcom NetXtreme II fully owns the data processing of TCP/IP flows off-loaded to it. The Broadcom NetXtreme II is fully compliant with relevant Internet Engineering Task Force (IETF) RFCs and fully supports modern TCP options like time stamp, window scaling, and so on. The implementation also provides flexibility and robustness against potential changes to TCP algorithms like congestion control by implementing this functionality in firmware, making changes easy to manage.

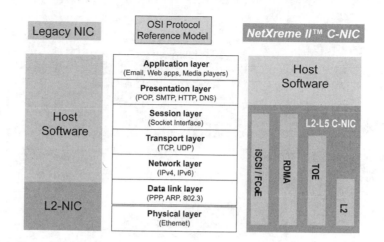

Figure 4-32   Broadcom NetXtreme II™ C-NIC

iSCSI

For iSCSI, the BCM57711 provides hardware offload for the most host CPU-intensive tasks. The BCM57711 has multiple modes for iSCSI support. In one of the modes, the BCM57711 copies the transmit data directly from the iSCSI buffers, adds framing support (Fixed Interval Marker [FIM]), if used, and calculates the header and data CRC. On the receive data path, the BCM57711 strips the framing headers (if present), checks header and data CRC, then stores the data in the designated iSCSI buffers (see Figure 4-33). iSCSI boot for diskless environments is also supported.

FCoE

FCoE maps Fibre Channel natively over Ethernet. The FCoE protocol specification replaces the FC0 and FC1 layers of the Fibre Channel stack with Ethernet. Many data centers use Ethernet for TCP/IP networks and Fibre Channel for storage area networks (SANs). With FCoE, Fibre Channel becomes another network protocol running on Ethernet, alongside traditional Internet Protocol (IP) traffic.

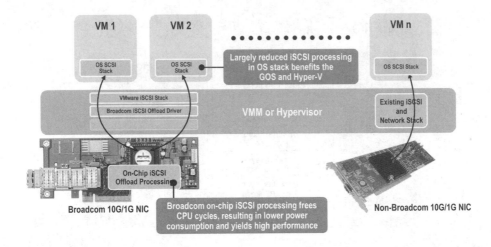

Figure 4-33   iSCSI hardware offload and virtualization

Broadcom leverages five generations of hardened SCSI protocol layer hardening used by its iSCSI offering to deliver the Fibre Channel over Ethernet (FCoE) storage protocol for data center convergence. The hardened SCSI layer coupled with the latest IEEE standards Data Center Bridging (DCB) standards support provide highest level of reliability and performance including:

- FC-BB-5: Fibre Channel Back bone defines mappings for transporting Fibre Channel over different network technologies
- PFC: Priority-based flow control to enable per traffic type lossless Ethernet network
- QCN: Congestion notification for source rate reduction when congestion is detected
- DCBX: Data Center Bridging Capability Exchange Protocol to coordinate the DCB parameters with the link peer
- ETS: Enhanced transmission selection for bandwidth sharing between traffic types

RDMA

For RDMA, the BCM57711 provides for direct data movement to/from user or kernel space (for example, iSER) and from/to the wire. The BCM57711 is RDMA Consortium (RDMAC) 1.0-compliant. The BCM57711 also adds the RDMA headers and CRC for transmitted data. For receive data, the BCM57711 processes the RDMA headers, verifies the CRC and strips out the header information, and then stores the data in the designated upper layer protocol (ULP) buffers.

Virtualization

The Broadcom NetXtreme II C-NIC family has superior support for I/O and Network Virtualization within the architecture with comprehensive industry software support from VMware and Microsoft.

Broadcom C-NIC's support the following levels of I/O and Network virtualization.

Multiple Queues (NetQueues and VMQ)

Broadcom NetXtreme II controllers with Netqueue support on VMware ESX or VMQ for Microsoft Hyper-V provide extended performance benefits that meet the demands of bandwidth-intensive applications requiring high-performance block storage I/O by removing single queue bottleneck between hypervisor and the network controller. By utilizing the hardware queues provided by the Broadcom network controllers (see Figure 4-34), VMware and Microsoft have eliminated single thread limitations and have optimized the hypervisors for multiple hardware threads.

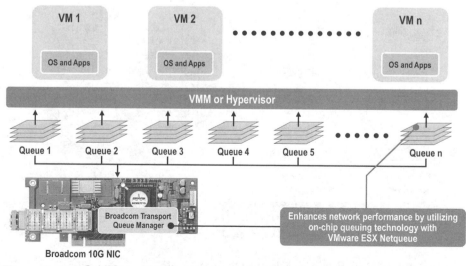

Figure 4-34   C-NIC multiple queue overview

Static VMDirectPath

Static VMDirectPath provide the Broadcom NetXtreme II controllers to be physically assigned to a VM / Guest Operating System (GOS) (see Figure 4-35). The on chip TCP Offload Engine (TOE) accelerates networking performance in a virtualized environment. The TOE provides additional benefits such as lower system power and improved CPU utilization since the Hypervisor no longer needs to process each I/O request.

SR-IOV / VEB

PCI Express (PCIe) specification forms the basis for SR-IOV implementation of Broadcom SR-IOV capable Ethernet network controllers (see Figure 4-36). A VF with Hypervisor support can be directly assigned to a VM. This will yield native performance and eliminate additional I/O copy in the Hypervisor with added advantage of being able to support all virtualization features including live migration (VMotion). The direct assignment of PCI devices to VM's enables virtualization to address new market segments, such as I/O high performance/low latency applications or virtual I/O appliances. Fine-grained I/O virtualization and sharing will enable interoperability between VMs, VFs, chipsets, switches, end points, and bridges. Broadcom C-NIC has a built-in Virtual Embedded Bridge (VEB) enabling Ethernet L2 switching between VMs or VF to VF and to or from an external port. This can be used for vSwitch performance acceleration or for local policy enforcement with hardware-based ACLs.

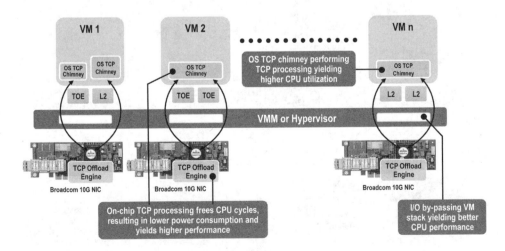

Figure 4-35 C-NIC Static VMDirectPath Overview

VNTag

Broadcom NetXtreme II controllers support network virtualization with the first hop switch through the implementation of Cisco VNTag. VNTag provides traffic separation and port extension for the VM's within the local vSwitch enabling the external switch to perform the switching and policy enforcement. The blade or rack server is effectively a line card for the first hop switch.

Broadcom and UCS

The UCS C-Series Rack Servers can use the Broadcom NetXtreme II™ C-NIC in standard PCIe form factor.

The UCS B-Series Blade Servers can use the mezzanine card shown in Figure 4-37.

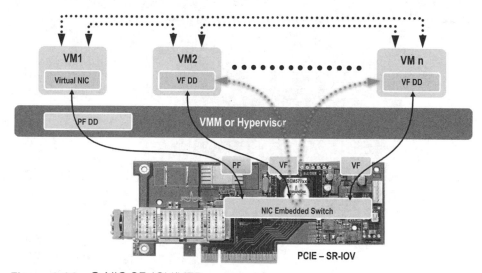

Figure 4-36   C-NIC SR-IOV/VEB overview

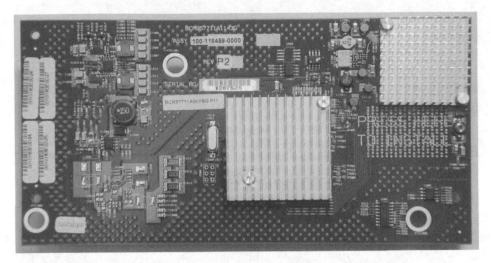

Figure 4-37   M51KR-B Broadcom BCM57711 network adapter

Chapter 5

UCS B-Series Blade Servers

The Cisco® Unified Computing System (UCS) is a data center server architecture that unifies network virtualization, storage virtualization, and server virtualization, within open industry standard technologies and with the network as the platform.

This chapter will first give a brief overview of the various components and then describe them in detail.

Components Overview

Figure 5-1 shows the components of a UCS, with the exception of the UCS Manager that is a software element.

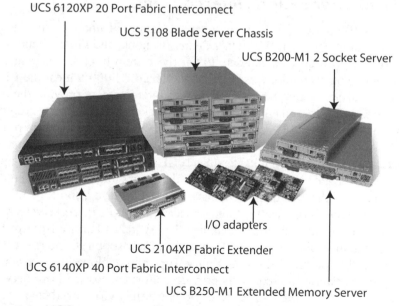

UCS 6120XP 20 Port Fabric Interconnect

UCS 5108 Blade Server Chassis

UCS B200-M1 2 Socket Server

I/O adapters

UCS 2104XP Fabric Extender

UCS 6140XP 40 Port Fabric Interconnect

UCS B250-M1 Extended Memory Server

Figure 5-1 UCS components

UCS Manager

The Cisco® UCS Manager (UCSM) software integrates the components of a Cisco® Unified Computing System into a single, seamless entity. It manages all the server blades and rack-mounted servers of a UCS as a single logical domain using an intuitive GUI with both CLI and XML API options, enabling near real time configuration and reconfiguration of resources (see Chapter 7, "UCS Manager," on page 223). Tasks that once required multiple administrators (server, network, and storage) and days or hours now can be accomplished in minutes, with reduced risk for human errors. The software's role-based design supports existing best practices, allowing server, network, and storage administrators to contribute their specific subject matter expertise to a system design. Any user's role may be limited to a subset of the system's resources using organizations and locales, so that a Cisco® Unified Computing System can be partitioned and shared between organizations. For organizations implementing Information Technology Infrastructure Library (ITIL)-based processes, the Cisco® UCS Manager helps to codify and enforce best practices. It maintains and conducts all operations based on an internal configuration database that can be exported to populate CMDBs (Configuration Management Data Bases) and integrate with higher-level software provisioning tools; see Chapter 8.

UCS 6100 Series Fabric Interconnects

Cisco's UCS 6100 Series Fabric Interconnects, a family of line-rate, low-latency, lossless 10 Gigabit Ethernet, IEEE Data Center Bridging, and Fiber Channel over Ethernet (FCoE) switches, consolidate I/O at the system level. Leveraging upon the same switching technology as the Cisco® Nexus™ 5000 Series, the Cisco® Unified Computing System Series 6100 Fabric Interconnects provide the additional features and management capabilities that make up the central nervous system of the Cisco® Unified Computing System. The Fabric Interconnects provide a unified network fabric that connects every server resource in the system via wire once 10GE/FCoE downlinks, flexible 10GE uplinks, and 2/4/8 GFC uplink modules. Out of band management, switch redundancy, and console-based diagnostics are enabled through dedicated management, clustering, and RS-232 ports. A single UCS 6100 Series Fabric Interconnect unites up to 320 servers within a single system domain for large scalability. The switches feature front to back cooling, redundant front hot-pluggable fans and power supplies, and rear cabling enabling efficient cooling and serviceability. Typically deployed in active-active redundant pairs, Fabric Interconnects provide uniform access to both networks and storage, eliminating the barriers to deploying a fully virtualized environment based on a flexible, programmable pool of resources.

UCS 6120XP 20 Port Fabric Interconnect

The Cisco® UCS U6120XP Fabric Interconnect features twenty 10GE/FCoE ports in one RU height. Additional ports are available via an Expansion Module. At the time of writing, the following uplink modules exist:

- 6 ports 10 GE with DCB/FCoE support
- 4 ports 10 GE with DCB/FCoE support and 4 ports Fibre Channel 1/2/4 Gbps
- 8 ports Fibre Channel 1/2/4 Gbps
- 6 ports Fibre Channel 2/4/8 Gbps

With Cisco's UCS Manager embedded, this Fabric Interconnect can support up to 160 blade servers in a single domain.

UCS 6140XP 40 Port Fabric Interconnect

The Cisco® UCS U6140XP Fabric Interconnect features 40 10GE/FCoE ports in two RU height. Additional expansion is available via two Expansion Modules (the same used in the 6120XP). With Cisco's UCS Manager embedded, this Fabric Interconnect can support up to 320 servers in a single domain.

UCS 2100 Series Fabric Extenders

At the time of writing, there is a single fabric extender, the UCS 2104XP.

UCS 2104XP Fabric Extender

The Cisco® UCS U2104XP Fabric Extender extends the I/O fabric into the blade server enclosure providing one to four 10GE connections between the blade enclosure and the Fabric Interconnect, simplifying diagnostics, cabling, and management.

The Fabric Extender multiplexes and forwards all traffic using a cut-through architecture to the Fabric Interconnect where the Fabric Interconnect manages network profiles efficiently and effectively. Each Fabric Extender has eight 10GBASE-KR connections to the blade enclosure mid-plane, one connection per each half slot. This gives each half-slot blade server access to two 10GE unified-fabric links offering maximum throughput and redundancy. The Cisco® UCS U2104XP Fabric Extender features an integrated Chassis Management Controller (CMC) for the blade enclosure physical components, including power supplies, fans, and temperature sensors. The fabric extender also connects to each blade's management port for management, monitoring, and firmware updates.

UCS 5100 Series Blade Server Chassis

At the time of writing, there is a single blade server chassis, the UCS 5108, shown in Figure 5-2.

UCS 5108 Blade Server Chassis

The Cisco® UCS U5108 Blade Server Enclosure physically houses blade servers and up to two fabric extenders. The enclosure is 6RU high, allowing for up to 7 enclosures and 56 servers per rack. Compared to complex traditional blade enclosures, the U5108 Blade Server Enclosure is dramatically simpler in its design. It supports up to eight half slot or four full slot blade servers with four power supplies, and eight cooling fans. Both power supplies and fans are redundant and hot swappable. Featuring 90%+ efficient power supplies, front to rear cooling, and airflow optimized mid-plane, the Cisco® UCS U5108 is optimized for energy efficiency and reliability.

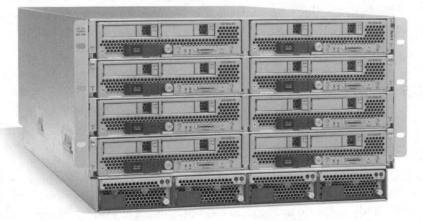

Figure 5-2   UCS 5108

UCS B-Series Blade Servers

The Cisco® UCS B-Series Blade Servers are designed for compatibility, performance, energy efficiency, large memory footprints, manageability, and unified I/O connectivity. Based on Intel® Xeon® 5500, 5600, and 7500 series processors, B-Series Blade Servers adapt to application demands, intelligently scale energy use, and offer best in class virtualization. Each Cisco® UCS B-Series Blade Server utilizes converged network adapters for consolidated access to the unified fabric with various levels of transparency to the operating system. This design reduces the number of adapters, cables, and access-layer switches for LAN and SAN connectivity at the rack level. This Cisco® innovation significantly reduces capital and operational expenses, including administrative overhead, power, and cooling.

UCS B200 Two-Socket Server

The Cisco® UCS B200 two-socket blade server is a half-slot, two-socket blade server (Figure 5-1 shows it with the metal sheet; Figure 5-3 shows just the board). The system features two Intel® Xeon® 5500/5600 Series processors, up to 12 DDR3 DIMMs (96 GB with 8 GB DIMMs), two optional small form factor SAS disk drives, and a dual-port converged network adapter mezzanine slot for up to 20 Gbps of I/O throughput. The B200 balances simplicity, performance, and density for mainstream virtualization and other data center workload performance.

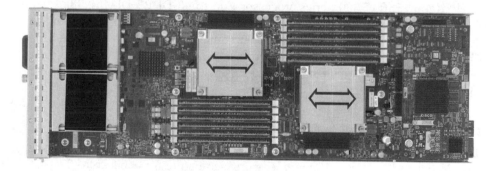

Figure 5-3   UCS B200 two-socket server

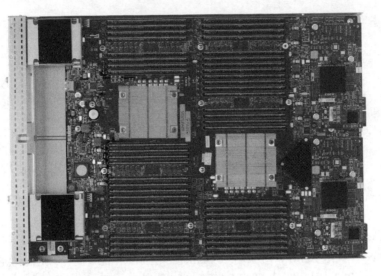

Figure 5-4   UCS B250 extended memory server

UCS B250 Extended Memory Server

The Cisco® UCS B250 two-socket blade server is a full-slot, two-socket blade server featuring Cisco® Extended Memory Technology (Figure 5-1 shows it with the metal sheet; Figure 5-4 shows just the board). The system features two Intel® Xeon® 5500/5600 Series processors, up to 48 DDR3 DIMMs (384 GB if 8 GB DIMMs are used), two optional small form factor SAS disk drives, and two dual-port converged network adapter mezzanine slots for up to 40 Gbps of I/O throughput. The B250 maximizes performance and capacity for demanding virtualization and memory intensive workloads, with greater memory capacity and throughput.

UCS B440 Four-Socket Server

The Cisco® UCS B440 four-socket blade server is a full-slot, blade server featuring four Nehalem-EX (Xeon 7500) processors (see Figure 5-5) and up to 32 DDR3 DIMMs (256 GB if 8 GB DIMMs are used), four optional small form factor SAS/ SATA disk drives, and two dual-port converged network adapter mezzanine slots for up to 40 Gbps of I/O throughput.

The UCS B440 increases the numbers of core with respect to the UCS B250 thus further improving performance and capacity for demanding CPU and memory intensive workloads.

A UCS 5108 chassis with four UCS B440 has up to 128 cores, 2 TB of RAM (16 GB DIMMs), 16 disks, and 80 Gbps of I/O.

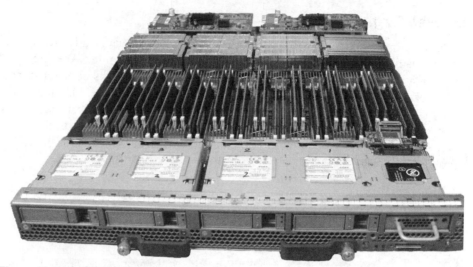

Figure 5-5   UCS B440 front view

I/O Adapters

The following I/O adapters are available at the time of writing:

- UCS NIC M51KR-B Broadcom BCM57711 Network Adapter (see "Broadcom®" in Chapter 4 on page 144)

- UCS CNA M61KR-I Intel Converged Network Adapter (see "Intel® 82599 10 Gigabit Ethernet Controller (Niantic)" in Chapter 4 on page 109)

- UCS CNA M72KR-E Emulex Converged Network Adapter (see "Cisco Palo®" in Chapter 4 on page 124)

- UCS CNA M72KR-Q Qlogic Converged Network Adapter (see "QLogic®" in Chapter 4 on page 137)

- UCS 82598KR-CI—Cisco® Converged Network Adapter (see "Intel® 82598 10 Gigabit Ethernet Controller (Oplin)" in Chapter 4 on page 105)

- Cisco® UCS VIC M81KR—Virtual Interface Card (see "Cisco® Palo" in Chapter 4 on page 124)

- UCS CNA M71KR-E—Emulex® Converged Network Adapter

- UCS CNA M71KR-Q—QLogic® Converged Network Adapter

Overall Organization

A UCS is organized as shown in Figure 5-6. There is one or typically two fabric interconnects that have uplinks to the LAN, SANs (two separate SANs are supported), and to the management network. The 10GE downlinks connect to the blade server chassis: any number of chassis from 1 to 40 is supported. Each blade server chassis contains one or typically two fabric extenders; the fabric extenders connect to the I/O adapters and to the management processors on each server blade (the connections are point to point, but are shown in Figure 5-6 as buses for graphic simplicity).

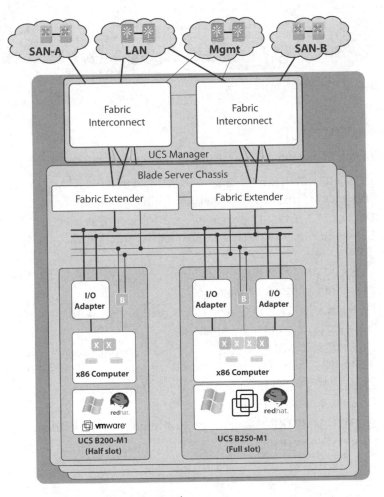

Figure 5-6   Component interconnection

A UCS 5108 Blade Server Chassis has eight half-slots. Each pair of half-slots can be converted into a full slot by removing a metal sheet separator. This allows the installation of either:

- 8 half-slot server blades, or
- 6 half-slot server blades and 1 full-slot server blade, or
- 4 half-slot server blades and 2 full-slot server blades, or
- 2 half-slot server blades and 3 full-slot server blades, or
- 4 full-slot server blades

UCS C-Series Rack Servers

The Cisco® UCS C-Series Rack Servers are part of the UCS family and can be either used as stand-alone servers, or interconnected in a UCS, with hybrid configuration (blade and rack) supported. They are described in Chapter 6.

Detailed Description

The next few sections will add detail to the previous descriptions.

UCS 6100 Series Fabric Interconnects

The UCS 6100 Fabric Interconnects are depicted in Figure 5-7. On top is the 6120XP and on the bottom the 6140XP. The 6120XP has twenty 10GE ports that support DCB (Data Center Bridging, see "10 Gigabit Ethernet" in Chapter 3 on page 71) and FCoE (see "FCoE (Fiber Channel over Ethernet)" in Chapter 3 on page 75), and one Expansion module. The 6140XP has double the ports and performance of the 6120XP. Detailed physical data can be found in "Physical Sizing Environmental Requirement" in Chapter 9 on page 357.

Figure 5-7   UCS 6120XP and UCS 6140XP

Different Expansion modules are available to provide additional Ethernet and Fibre Channel connectivity. All the Ethernet ports (not only those in the expansion module) can be used as uplinks toward a network backbone or as downlinks toward the Fabric Extenders. The Fibre Channel ports can only be used as uplink toward Fibre Channel fabrics.

Ethernet Connectivity

In the definition of UCS (see "Unified Computing System (UCS)" in Chapter 1, page 18), it became clear that the system is network centric. As such, it can be configured to behave on the Ethernet uplinks either as a group of hosts or as a switch.

The UCS 6100 Fabric Interconnects are derived from the hardware of the Nexus 5000 and as such, they can support a variety of network protocols and are capable of acting as Ethernet switches. To explain how Ethernet connectivity works refer to Figure 5-8.

FI1 and FI2 are two UCS 6100 (the number of ports does not matter) and SW1 and SW2 are two data center switches like the Nexus 5000 or the Nexus 7000.

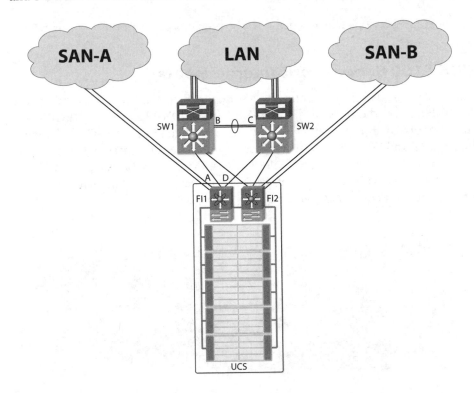

Figure 5-8   UCS external connectivity

Spanning Tree

The first possibility is to configure FI1 and FI2 as Ethernet switches (see Figure 5-8). In this case, the spanning tree protocol needs to be enabled and it detects a loop FI1 – A – SW1 – B – C – SW2 – D– FI1. Spanning tree needs to prune any loop into a tree and probably it blocks either port A or port D (the root of the spanning tree is typically either in SW1 or SW2). This is a suboptimal solution; although it provides high availability, uplink bandwidth is wasted as half the uplinks are not used by traffic as they are in blocking state.

To solve this issue, several different techniques can be used.

EtherChannel

The first possibility is to connect FI1 to a single switch (e.g., SW1), thus avoiding any loop. The connection itself can be made highly available using multiple links in parallel with EtherChannel.

EtherChannel is a port aggregation technology primarily introduced by Cisco® in 1994 and standardized by IEEE in 2000 in the project IEEE 802.3ad. EtherChannel allows aggregating several physical Ethernet links to create one logical Ethernet link with a bandwidth equal to the sum of the bandwidths of the aggregated links. EtherChannel can aggregate from 2 to 16 links and all higher-level protocols see these multiple links as a single connection. This is beneficial for providing fault-tolerance and high-speed links between Fabric Interconnects and the LAN backbone, without blocking any port and therefore using all the links. A limitation of EtherChannel is that all the physical ports in the aggregation group must be between one Fabric Interconnect and one LAN switch. For this reason, the next solutions—VSS, vPC, L2MP, and Ethernet Host Virtualizer—were developed.

VSS

VSS (Virtual Switching System) is the first of two Cisco® technologies that allows using EtherChannel from a Fabric Interconnect to two LAN switches avoiding any blocked port. VSS accomplishes this by clustering the two LAN switches SW1 and SW2 into a single, managed, and logical entity. The individual chassis become indistinguishable and therefore each Fabric Interconnect believes the upstream LAN switches to be a single STP (Spanning Tree Protocol) bridge, and EtherChannel can be deployed unmodified on the Fabric Interconnect. VSS has also other advantages; since it improves high availability, scalability, management, and maintenance, see [17] for more details. Today VSS is deployed on the Catalyst 6500 switches.

vPC

vPC (virtual Port Channel), aka MCEC (Multi-Chassis EtherChannel), achieves a result similar to VSS without requiring the clustering of the two LAN switches.

From the Fabric interconnect perspective, nothing changes: It continues to use an unmodified EtherChannel, and it sees the vPC switches as a single LAN switch.

The two LAN switches coordinate who is in charge of delivering each frame to the Fabric Interconnect, fully utilizing both links. The key challenge in vPC (common also to VSS) is to deliver each frame exactly once, avoiding frame duplication and loops. This must also be guaranteed when some Fabric Interconnect that are connected to both LAN switches and some that are connected to only one (because, for example, one uplink has failed), without using Spanning Tree.

L2MP

Layer 2 Multi-Path (L2MP) is a technology developed by Cisco and standardized by IETF in the TRILL working group [18]. IS-IS replaces Spanning Tree protocol as the loop-free mechanism and all the links are actively forwarding traffic. At the time of writing, the TRILL support is planned on the Nexus switches.

Ethernet Host Virtualizer

VSS and vPC are techniques implemented on the LAN switches to allow the Fabric Interconnects to keep using EtherChannel in a traditional manner.

In addition, the same problem can also be solved on the Fabric Interconnect by a technique called Ethernet Host Virtualizer (aka End Host Mode).

With reference to Figure 5-8, the Fabric Interconnect implements Ethernet Host Virtualizer while the LAN switches continue to run the classical Spanning Tree Protocol.

A Fabric Interconnect running Ethernet Host Virtualizer divides its ports into two groups: host ports and network ports. Both types of ports can be a single interface or an EtherChannel. The switch then associates each host port with a network port. This process is called "pinning". The same host port always uses the same network port, unless it fails. In this case, the Fabric Interconnect moves the pinning to another network port (dynamic pinning).

In the example of Figure 5-9, MAC-A is always presented on the left network port and MAC-B is always presented on the right network port.

The Fabric Interconnect assign each host port to a network port. It does this according either to manual configuration or to network port load. This assignment remains stable unless the host port or the network port loses connectivity.

When this happens, the associated host ports are redistributed to the remaining set of active network ports. Particular attention must be paid to multicast and broadcast frames to avoid loops and frame duplications. Typically Fabric Interconnects act as follows:

■ They never retransmit a frame received from a network port to another network port.

■ They divide the multicast/broadcast traffic according to multicast groups and they assign each multicast group to a single network port. Only one network port may transmit and receive a given multicast group.

The Ethernet Host Virtualizer is the default configuration at UCS first customer shipment, since it can plug in any LAN network, without requiring any modification.

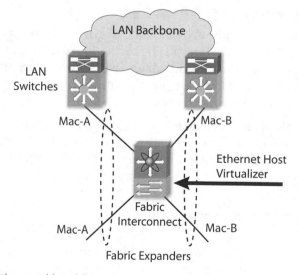

Figure 5-9   Ethernet Host Virtualizer and pinning

Fibre Channel Connectivity

The Fibre Channel connectivity has historically used a different high availability mode than the Ethernet connectivity. Most Fibre Channel Installations use two separate SANs (normally called SAN-A and SAN-B) built with two different sets of Fibre Channel switches. Each host and storage array connects to both SANs using two separate HBAs. High Availability is achieved at the application level by running multipathing software that balances the traffic across the two SANs using either an active/active or active/standby mode.

A UCS supports this model by having two separate Fabric Interconnects, two separate Fabric Extenders and dual-port CNAs on the blades. One Fabric Interconnect with all the Fabric Extenders connected to it belongs to SAN-A and the other Fabric Interconnect with all the Fabric Extenders connected to it belongs to SAN-B. The two SANs are kept fully separated as in the classical Fibre Channel model.

As in the case of Ethernet, each Fabric Interconnect is capable of presenting itself as a FC switch or as a FC host (NPV mode).

Fabric Interconnect as FC Switch

This is on the software roadmap at the time of writing (February 2010) and it is standards compliant. It consists of running the FC switching software on the Fabric Interconnect and using E_Ports (Inter Switch Links) to connect to the FC backbones. With reference to Figure 5-8, the links between FI1 and SAN-A and FI2 and SAN-B are E_Port on both ends.

Unfortunately, this implies assigning a FC domain_ID to each UCS and since the number of domain_IDs is typically limited to 64, it is not a scalable solution. Some storage manufacturers support a number of domain that is much smaller than 64 and this further limits the applicability of this solution.

Fabric Interconnect as a Host

This solution is based on a concept that has recently been added to the FC standard and it is known as NPIV (N_Port ID Virtualization): a Fibre Channel facility allowing multiple N_Port IDs (aka FC_IDs) to share a single physical N_Port. The term NPIV is used when this feature is implemented on the host—for example, to allow multiple virtual machines to share the same FC connection. The term NPV

(N_Port Virtualization) is used when this feature is implemented in an external switch that aggregates multiple N_Ports into one or more uplinks. A NPV box behaves as an NPIV-based HBA to the core Fibre Channel switches. According to these definitions, each Fabric Interconnect can be configured in NPV mode, i.e.:

- Each Fabric Interconnect presents itself to the FC network as a host, i.e., it uses an N_Port (Node Port).
- The N_Port on the Fabric Interconnect is connected to an F_Port (Fabric Port) on the Fibre Channel Network.
- The Fabric Interconnect performs the first FLOGI to bring up the link between the N_Port and the F_Port.
- The FLOGIs received by the Fabric Interconnect from the server's adapter are translated to FDISCs according to the NPIV standard.

This eliminates the scalability issue, since it does not assign a FC domain_ID to each Fabric Interconnect. It also greatly simplifies interoperability, since multivendor interoperability is much better in FC between N_Port and F_Port as opposed to E_Port and E_Port. Finally, it guarantees the same high availability present today in a pure FC installation by fully preserving the dual fabric model.

With reference to Figure 5-8, the links between FI1 and SAN-A and FI2 and SAN-B are N_Ports on the Fabric Interconnect side and F_Ports on the SAN side.

Value added features that can be used in NPV mode are F_Port Trunking and F_Port Channeling:

- F_Port Channeling is similar to EtherChannel, but it applies to FC. It is the bundling of multiple physical interfaces into one logical high-bandwidth link. F_Port Channeling provides higher bandwidth, increased link redundancy, and load balancing between a Fabric Interconnect and a FC switch.
- F_Port Trunking allows a single F_Port to carry the traffic of multiple VSANs, according to the FC standards.

All Cisco MDS9000 switches with 8G FC ports make a perfect fit, since they support NPIV, F Port Trunking, and F Port Channeling features.

UCS 2104XP Fabric Extender

The Cisco® UCS 2104XP Fabric Extender (aka FEX, see Figure 5-10) is a special blade that plugs in the rear of a UCS 5108 chassis (see Figure 5-13).

Its block diagram is shown in Figure 5-11. The UCS 2104XP Fabric Extender has three subsystems inside:

- The Redwood IO_MUX
- The Chassis Management Controller (CMC)
- The Chassis Management Switch (CMS).

Each of these subsystems is designed to perform a specific task in the UCS.

Redwood IO_MUX

The Redwood IO_MUX is used as a bridge between the server blades and the Fabric Interconnect. Redwood is the ASIC that implements the data plane of the Fabric Extender. It provides:

- Eight 10GE external downlink ports to connect the server blades
- Four 10GE external uplink ports to connect to the fabric interconnect
- One 1GE internal port to connect the CMS
- One 100Mbps internal port toward the CMC

Figure 5-10   UCS 2104XP Fabric Extender

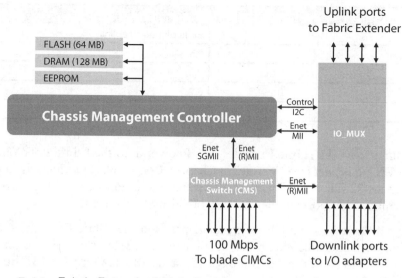

Figure 5-11 Fabric Extender block diagram

By default, mezzanine adapters installed on server blades are pinned to uplinks in a pre-determined fashion. This method makes it easy to understand which blade uses which uplink. Each half-slot supports one adapter. The UCS B200 blade fits into a half-slot and therefore supports a single adapter, but the UCS B250 takes a full-slot and can have two adapters.

Future blade offerings could even increase the number of slots that a single blade can use. Table 5-1 gives an understanding of the server pinning to the uplinks in different scenarios.

In future firmware releases, the configuration of slot pinning to an uplink will be a user configurable feature.

Table 5-1 Uplink Pinning

Number of Links from Fabric Extender to Fabric Interconnect = 1	
Uplink	Slots pinned to uplink
1	1,2,3,4,5,6,7,8
Number of Links from Fabric Extender to Fabric Interconnect = 2	
Uplink	Slots pinned to uplink
1	1,3,5,7
2	2,4,6,8

continues

Number of Links from Fabric Extender to Fabric Interconnect = 4	
Uplink	Slots pinned to uplink
1	1,5
2	2,6
3	3,7
4	4,8

The uplinks from the Fabric Extender (i.e., Redwood) to the Fabric Interconnect use the VNTag header (see "VNTag" in Chapter 3, page 86). A particularly important field inside the VNTag is the VIF (Virtual Interface) that is used to identify the downlink port (ports in the case of a broadcast/multicast frame).

VNTag may also be used between the adapter and the Fabric Extender on the downlink ports, but this requires an adapter that is VNTag capable, like the one based on Menlo (see "Emulex" on page 129 and "Qlogic®"on page 137, both in Chapter 4) or Palo (see "Cisco® Palo" in Chapter 4 on page 124).

Frame Flow in Redwood—Host to Network

With reference to Figure 5-11:

- The frame arrives at the downlink port from the mezzanine card.
- The destination uplink port is selected as a function off the port on which the frame was received.
- The frame is stored in a receiver buffer and queued to an uplink port (virtual output queuing):
    - Virtual output queues are per output, per CoS (Class of Service).
- The appropriate VNTag is added to the frame.
- The frame is transmitted on the selected Uplink port:
    - Frame transmit arbitration is per destination Uplink port; it is based on a round-robin algorithm for CoS and in order delivery inside each CoS.
- Any given frame is forwarded on a single uplink.

Frame Flow in Redwood—Network to Host

With reference to Figure 5-11:

- The frame arrives at the uplink port from the Fabric Interconnect.
- The destination downlink port is selected according to the VNTag header:
    - The decision is based on the destination VIF.

- The frame is stored in the receiver buffer and queued at the downlink port:
  - Separate resources are available for different CoS values.
- A single frame can be forwarded to multiple destinations (e.g., broadcast/multicast frames).

It is important to understand that there is no local switching function in the Redwood ASIC. A frame coming from a downlink port cannot be forwarded to another downlink port. The multicast/broadcast replication is done only from an uplink port toward downlink ports, not vice-versa.

Chassis Management Controller—CMC

The Chassis Management Controller (CMC) is a processor embedded in the Fabric Extender. The CMC interacts with the UCS Manager and the Cisco Integrated Management Controller (CIMC), aka BMC (Board Management Controller), present on the server blades. The administrator does not interact directly with the CMC, but only through the UCSM. The CMC main function is to provide overall chassis discovery and management and to report the result to the UCS manager. It also provides platform services for the Redwood management software.

The CMC implements seven main functions:

- It controls the chassis fans.
- It monitors and logs fan speed.
- It monitors and logs ingress and egress temperatures.
- It controls location indication and chassis fault indications.
- It powers up/powers down power supplies, monitoring and logging voltages, currents, and temperatures inside the chassis.
- It detects presence, insertion, and removal of UCS blades.
- It reads the IDs of the chassis, UCS blades, and Fabric Extenders.

It is important to understand that CMC does not manage UCS blades.

If two UCS2104XP Fabric Extenders are installed in a chassis, the two CMC processors automatically form a cluster and only one of them will be active at a given time. A high-availability algorithm between the two CMCs defines the active CMC. A serial interface is used for heartbeats between the two CMCs. Failover is triggered either by loss of heartbeat, or if the active CMC is unplugged for any reason. The UCS Manager can also force a fail-over. The information about the active CMC is stored into a SEEPROM (Serial EPROM) and the CMC must read it before accessing shared resources.

Chassis Management Switch (CMS)

The Chassis Management Switch (CMS) provides connectivity to the Cisco Integrated Management Controller (CIMC) present on each server blade. There are eight 100Mbps Ethernet connections and one 1Gb Ethernet connection available in the CMS. Each slot has its own 100Mbps-dedicated Ethernet Interface connected to the blade CIMC. The 1GbE interface is used to connect the CMS to the Redwood IO_MUX. The CMS is an unmanaged switch that requires no configuration.

UCS 5108 Blade Server Chassis

The UCS 5108 Blade Server Chassis is depicted in Figure 5-2, Figure 5-12, and Figure 5-13. The physical dimensions are reported in "Physical Sizing and Environmental Requirements" in Chapter 9, page 357. On the front of the chassis are the eight half-slots for the server blades and the four slots for the power supplies. On the back of the chassis are the slots for the eight fans, the two Fabric Extenders and the power entry module. The airflow is front-to-back and the cooling is extremely efficient due to a chassis midplane that is widely open and facilitates the airflow.

Figure 5-14 shows the chassis midplane that is installed vertically in the middle of the chassis, approximately 3/4 toward the back of the chassis (see Figure 5-12).

Two-Socket Blade Architecture

The two-socket UCS blades are based on Intel® reference architecture for dual-socket Nehalem-EP and Westmere-EP servers (see "Intel Microarchitectures" in Chapter 2, page 45). These blades have multiple components in them and Figure 5-15 helps identifying each of them.

Figure 5-16 shows how the different components are interconnected.

The CPUs

The two-socket UCS blades use the Intel® Xeon® 5500/5600 series CPUs. Different CPU models can be installed on these blades. The Xeon 5500 CPUs (Nehalem-EP) have 4 cores (see Table 5-2) and the Xeon 5600 (Westmere-EP) up to six cores (see Table 5-3).

Hyper-Threading (see "Intel® Hyper-Threading Technology" in Chapter 2, page 27) and TurboBoost (see "CPU Architecture" in Chapter 2, page 49) capabilities are supported. Both type of CPUs are compliant with the Intel® Nehalem architecture described in detail in "Intel Microarchitectures" in Chapter 2, page 45.

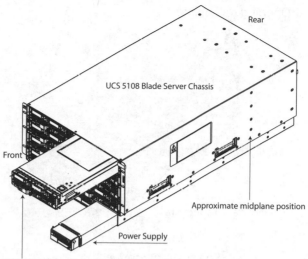

Figure 5-12   UCS 5108 front isometric view

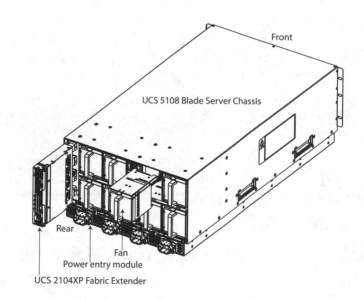

Figure 5-13   UCS 5108 rear isometric view

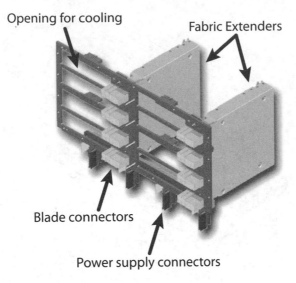

Opening for cooling

Fabric Extenders

Blade connectors

Power supply connectors

Figure 5-14   UCS 5108 mid-plane

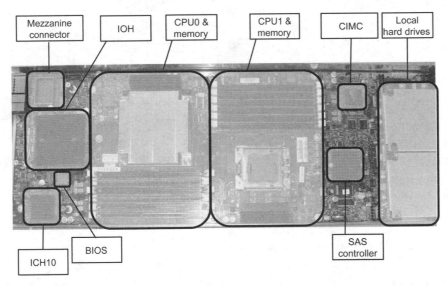

Mezzanine connector

IOH

CPU0 & memory

CPU1 & memory

CIMC

Local hard drives

ICH10

BIOS

SAS controller

Figure 5-15   Blade components

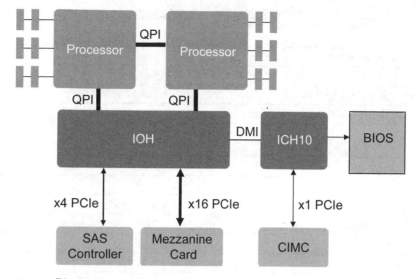

Figure 5-16   Blade block diagram

Table 5-2   Intel® Nehalem-EP Processors

Intel® Xeon® L5520	
CPU Speed	2.26 GHz
Power Consumption	60W
QPI Speed	5.87 GT/s
Memory and Maximum Speed	DDR3@1066 MHz
TurboBoost Bin Upside (133 MHz Increments)	1/1/2/2

Intel® Xeon® E5520	
CPU Speed	2.26 GHz
Power Consumption	80W
QPI Speed	5.87 GT/s
Memory and Maximum Speed	DDR3@1066 MHz
Turbo Boost Bin Upside (133 MHz Increments)	1/1/2/2

Intel® Xeon® E5540	
CPU Speed	2.53 GHz
Power Consumption	80W
QPI Speed	5.87 GT/s
Memory and Maximum Speed	DDR3@1066 MHz
Turbo Boost Bin Upside (133 MHz Increments)	1/1/2/2

continues

Intel® Xeon® X5570	
CPU Speed	2.93 GHz
Power Consumption	95W
QPI Speed	6.4 GT/s
Memory and Maximum Speed	DDR3@1333 MHz
Turbo Boost Bin Upside (133 MHz Increments)	2/2/3/3

Intel® Xeon® X5550	
CPU Core Speed	2.66 GHz
Number of Cores	4
Power Consumption	95 Watts
Memory and Maximum Speed	DDR3@1333 MHz
L3 Cache	8 MB
QPI Speed	6.4 GT/s
Turbo Boost Bin Upside (4C/2C Active)	2/3

Intel® Xeon® E5504	
CPU Core Speed	2 GHz
Number of Cores	4
Power Consumption	80 Watts
Memory and Maximum Speed	DDR3@800 MHz
L3 Cache	8 MB
QPI Speed	4.8 GT/s
Turbo Boost Bin Upside	None

Table 5-3   Intel Westmere-EP Processors

Intel® Xeon® X5680	
CPU Core Speed	3.33 GHz
Number of Cores	6
Power Consumption	130 Watts
Memory and Maximum Speed	DDR3@1333 MHz
L3 Cache	12 MB
QPI Speed	6.4 GT/s
Turbo Boost Bin Upside (6C/4C/2C Active)	1/1/2

Intel® Xeon® X5670

CPU Core Speed	2.93 GHz
Number of Cores	6
Power Consumption	95 Watts
Memory and Maximum Speed	DDR3@1333 MHz
L3 Cache	12 MB
QPI Speed	6.4 GT/s
Turbo Boost Bin Upside (6C/4C/2C Active)	2/2/3

Intel® Xeon® X5650

CPU Core Speed	2.66 GHz
Number of Cores	6
Power Consumption	95 Watts
Memory and Maximum Speed	DDR3@1333 MHz
L3 Cache	12 MB
QPI Speed	6.4 GT/s
Turbo Boost Bin Upside (6C/4C/2C Active)	2/2/3

Intel® Xeon® E5640

CPU Core Speed	2.66 GHz
Number of Cores	4
Power Consumption	80 Watts
Memory and Maximum Speed	DDR3@1066 MHz
L3 Cache	12 MB
QPI Speed	5.86 GT/s
Turbo Boost Bin Upside (4C/2C Active)	1/2

Intel® Xeon® E5620

CPU Core Speed	2.4 GHz
Number of Cores	4
Power Consumption	80 Watts
Memory and Maximum Speed	DDR3@1066 MHz
L3 Cache	12 MB
QPI Speed	5.86 GT/s
Turbo Boost Bin Upside (4C/2C Active)	1/2

The I/O Hub (IOH)

Both UCS blades use the Intel® X58 chip as an I/O Hub. This chip is connected to the CPUs with the Intel® QuickPath Interconnect (see "Intel® QuickPath Interconnect" in Chapter 2, page 31). The connectivity to the I/O Controller Hub is based on the Intel® Direct Media Interface (DMI). The Direct Media Interface is a point-to-point interconnection between the I/O Hub and the I/O Controller Hub. In previous Intel® architectures, it was used as a link between the Northbridge and the Southbridge.

The X58 chip supports 36 PCIe lanes. In the UCS blades, these lanes are arranged in:

- One PCIe x4 link used for the SAS Controller
- One PCIe x16 links used for the first mezzanine cards
- One PCIe x16 links used for the second mezzanine cards (only on the UCS B250)

The X58 PCIe ports support PCIe2.0 and are capable of running up to 0.5GB/s per lane. That gives maximum bandwidth for 8GB/s (64 Gbps) for each UCS blade mezzanine connector.

There are two QuickPath interfaces in a X58 chip and each of them is capable of running at speeds of 12.8GT/s. Each QuickPath Interface is connected to one CPU.

The I/O Controller Hub

UCS Blades use the Intel® ICH10 I/O Controller Hub. This chip is sometimes referred to as "Southbridge" (old name). The ICH is used to connect various "low-speed" peripherals, like USB devices, and it also provides connectivity for the Cisco Integrated Management Controller (CIMC), aka BMC (Board Management Controller), chip.

The Cisco Integrated Management Controller (CIMC)

In the UCS blades, the CIMC is used to provide pre-OS management access to blade servers and KVM (Keyboard Video and Mouse) access. It also functions as an aggregation point for the blade hardware.

The CIMC used is a single chip, IP-based, server management solution. It provides the following functionality:

- General Inventory
- Blade Thermal, Power, and Health monitoring
- KVM access to blade
- Front panel video/USB access
- Serial over LAN
- Provide IPMI 2.0 interface to manage blade

The CIMC has two integrated 100Mb Ethernet connections that are connected in a redundant manner to the Chassis Management Switches inside the Fabric Extenders. The CIMC connects to the ICH10 via a PCIe connection.

To provide the KVM function and the front panel video access, the CIMC has an integrated graphics engine that is Matrox G200e compatible.

The SAS Controller

The UCS blades use the LSI Logic 1064e storage processor. It supports 1.5 and 3GB/s SAS and SATA transfer rates. It has integrated mirroring and striping functions to provide different RAID availability levels for internal disks in blades.

The Storage Controller is connected to the processing complex by x4 PCIe Gen1 connection to IOH module. Both UCS blades use Small Form Factor (SFF) drives. Normal SAS and SATA drives will be supported as well as SSD drives.

UCS B200 Two-Socket Server

The UCS B200 Two-Socket Server (see Figure 5-17 and Figure 5-3) has all the features described in "Two-Socket Blade Architecture" on page 172 in Chapter 5, as well as the following memory and mezzanine card configuration.

Memory

The UCS B200 blade supports up to 12 DDR3 DIMMs. Two DIMM slots are connected to each of the six memory channels. The supported memory speeds are 800, 1066 and 1333 MHz. Not all speeds are available in all memory configurations. Table 5-4 lists the supported memory configurations (i.e., number of ranks and number of DIMMs per memory channel) and the resulting maximum memory speed.

Table 5-4   Supported Memory Configurations

Number of ranks	800 MHz	1066 MHz	1333 MHz
Single rank	2 DIMMs per channel	2 DIMMs per channel	1 DIMMs per channel
Dual rank	2 DIMMs per channel	2 DIMMs per channel	1 DIMMs per channel
Quad rank	2 DIMMs per channel	1 DIMMs per channel	Not supported

For example:

- Twelve 8 GB quad rank DIMMs can operate only at 800 MHz speed, even if they are rated at 1066 MHz.

- Six of the same DIMMs (one DIMMs per memory channel) can operate at 1066 MHz.

To achieve the fastest possible speed (1333 MHz), only six DIMMs can be used (this reduces the load on the memory channel allowing higher speed). They have to be placed one per memory channel. If there is more than one DIMM in a memory channel, the 1333 MHz DIMMs are lowered to 1066 MHz.

If different DIMM are mixed in a single blade, all the DIMMs will default to the same speed—i.e., the one of the lowest-speed DIMM.

Mezzanine Cards

The UCS B200 blade has one mezzanine card slot available for one I/O Adapter. Available mezzanine cards are explained in detail in Chapter 4.

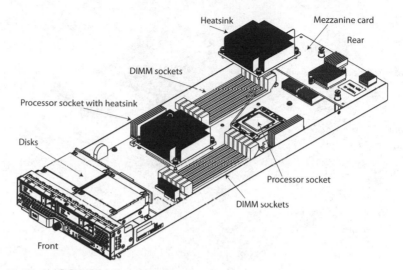

Figure 5-17   UCS B200 isometric view

UCS B250 Extended Memory Server

The UCS B250 Extended Memory Server (see Figure 5-4 and Figure 5-18) has all the features described in "Two-Socket Blade Architecture" on page 172 in Chapter 5, as well as the following memory and mezzanine card configuration.

Memory

The UCS B250 blade has the Cisco® specific memory extension architecture described in "Memory Expansion" in Chapter 3, page 93. It is based on Cisco® ASICs that allows the UCS B250 blade to address up to four times the memory of a standard Nehalem processor.

The UCS B250 blade has 48 DIMM slots that can be fully populated and still operate at 1066 MHz speed. From the BIOS, CPU, or OS point of view, these 48 DIMMs still look like 12 DIMMs and there is no need to modify or insert specific drivers in the Operating Systems or Applications. In fact, this technology is very transparent to the Operating Systems and Applications.

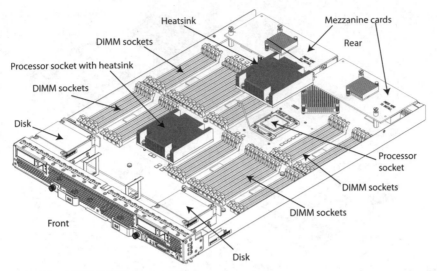

Figure 5-18   UCS B250 isometric view

Mezzanine Card

The UCS B250 blade has two mezzanine card slots available for I/O adapters. Available mezzanine cards are explained in detail in Chapter 4.

Four-Socket Blade Architecture

The four-socket UCS blades are based on Intel® reference architecture for four-socket Nehalem-EX servers (see "The Processor Evolution" in Chapter 2, page 24). These blades have multiple components in them and Figure 5-19 helps identifying each of them.

Figure 5-20 shows how the different components are interconnected.

The CPUs

The four-socket UCS blades use the Intel® Xeon® 7500 series CPUs. At the time of the first customer shipment, four different CPU models can be installed on UCS. Table 5-5 illustrates the differences between them.

CPUs have up to eight cores and Hyper-Threading (see "Intel® Hyper-Threading Technology" in Chapter 2, page 27) and TurboBoost (see "CPU Architecture" in Chapter 2, page 49) capabilities. Intel® Nehalem architecture is described in detail in "Intel Microarchitectures" in Chapter 2, page 45.

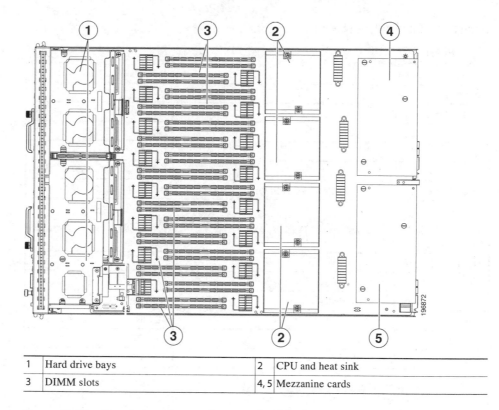

| 1 | Hard drive bays | 2 | CPU and heat sink |
| 3 | DIMM slots | 4, 5 | Mezzanine cards |

Figure 5-19   Components on a four-socket blade

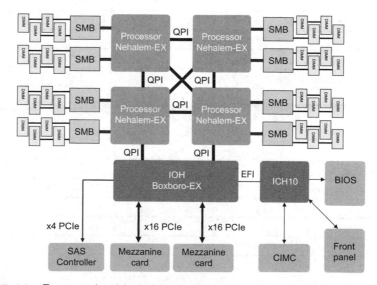

Figure 5-20   Four-socket blade block diagram

Table 5-5   Intel Nehalem-EX Processors

Intel® Xeon® X7560	
CPU Core Speed	2.26 GHz
Number of Cores	8
Power Consumption	130 Watts
Memory and Maximum Speed	DDR3@1066 MHz
L3 Cache	24 MB
QPI Speed	6.4 GT/s
Turbo Boost Bin Upside (8C/6C/4C/2C Active)	1/2/3/3

Intel® Xeon® X7550	
CPU Core Speed	2 GHz
Number of Cores	8
Power Consumption	130 Watts
Memory and Maximum Speed	DDR3@1066 MHz
L3 Cache	18 MB
QPI Speed	6.4 GT/s
Turbo Boost Bin Upside (8C/6C/4C/2C Active)	1/2/3/3

Intel® Xeon® L7555	
CPU Core Speed	1.86 GHz
Number of Cores	8
Power Consumption	95 Watts
Memory and Maximum Speed	DDR3@976 MHz
L3 Cache	24 MB
QPI Speed	5.86 GT/s
Turbo Boost Bin Upside (8C/6C/4C/2C Active)	1/2/4/5

Intel® Xeon® E7540	
CPU Core Speed	2 GHz
Number of Cores	6
Power Consumption	105 Watts
Memory and Maximum Speed	DDR3@1066 MHz
L3 Cache	18 MB
QPI Speed	5.86 GT/s
Turbo Boost Bin Upside (8C/6C/4C/2C Active)	0/1/1/2

Intel® Xeon® E7520	
CPU Core Speed	1.86 GHz
Number of Cores	4
Power Consumption	95 Watts
Memory and Maximum Speed	DDR3@800 MHz
L3 Cache	18 MB
QPI Speed	4.8 GT/s
Turbo Boost Bin Upside (8C/6C/4C/2C Active)	None

The four sockets are fully interconnected with Intel's QuickPath Interconnect (QPI) links. Two of the CPU sockets are also connected directly to the Boxboro IOH with QPI links. The remaining two CPU sockets access the IOH, through CPU-to-CPU QPI links. Attached to each CPU are four Mill Brook memory buffers (aka SMBs: Serial Memory Buffers), using Serial Memory Interface (SMI) links. Two DDR3 DIMM sockets per Mill Brook provide 32 DIMMs.

The I/O Hub (IOH)

The two main I/O paths toward the two mezzanine CNAs are provided through the Boxboro IOH PCIe ports. Two 16x PCIe Gen2 ports from the IOH support two PCIe mezzanine card options. These cards provide dual-ported 10Gbase-KR Ethernet links to the two UCS 2104XP fabric extenders.

An embedded 6G SAS RAID controller is connected to the IOH through a 4x PCIe Gen2 port. This controller connects to the four disks on the board.

The I/O Controller Hub (IOC)

An I/O Controller Hub, ICH10R, is also linked to the IOH by means of an EFI bus. The ICH10R provides connections to the Cisco Integrated Management Controller (CIMC), aka BMC (Board Management Controller), the card Front-Panel, and an optional embedded USB module.

The Cisco Integrated Management Controller (CIMC)

The Cisco Integrated Management Controller (CIMC) is used for service functions. It proves OS independent and Pre-OS load management for the card. It is run on standby power and connects to both Chassis Management Controller in each UCS 2104XP with dual 100Mbit Ethernet links and I2C buses (see Figure 5-11). A more detailed description of the CIMC can be found in "UCS B-Series Blade Servers" in Chapter 5, page 157.

UCS B440 Four-Socket Server

The UCS B440 four-socket server (see Figure 5-21) is the first UCS blade server using Nehalem-EX (Xeon 7500) processors. It is a full-size blade and therefore four UCS B440 can be hosted in a UCS 5108 chassis.

Key characteristics of the UCS B440 are:

- Four Nehalem-EX sockets (96 MB Total on-chip cache)
- Fully Cross-Connected Socket to Socket Intel 6.4 G/Ts QPI Links
- 32 DIMM slots for up to 512 GB of memory
- Support for 2, 4, 8, 16 GB DIMMs, with Mirroring, ECC, Chipkill
- Two mezzanine PCIe slots capable of hosting two CNAs

Figure 5-21   B440 isometric view

- The Cisco Integrated Management Controller (CIMC)
- LSI Liberator RAID controller with RAID 0, 1, 5, 6, and Nested RAID
  - Battery backed cache
  - 4 x 2.5" SAS, SATA HDD, and SSD drives
  - Supports 6G SAS
- 4G Byte internal eUSB module
- Front-panel USB 2.0 ports

The power consumption of this blade is up to 1,100 W, of which 520W are just for the processors.

Description of Communication Flows

The UCS leverages consolidated I/O to communicate between different components in the system and it divides the traffic into three different categories: management, IP, and FC. The management traffic is out-of-band and leverages two pre allocated classes, dedicated for internal traffic. Separating the management traffic from other traffic ensures that management traffic is always available and communication is possible between the different components. Table 5-6 lists the different traffic types with reference to the connections highlighted on the UCS block diagram of Figure 5-22 (FEX is the Fabric Extender).

The Boot Sequences

The UCS components boot up when power is restored. During the boot phase the component is not responsive. Depending on the components, the boot sequence goes through different steps.

POST

POST (Power-On Self-Test) runs when power is turned on.

It is a diagnostic testing sequence that a component (processor) runs to determine if the hardware is working correctly.

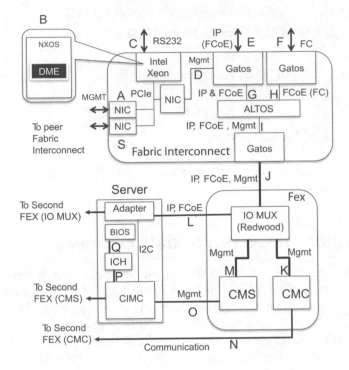

Figure 5-22 UCS block diagram

Boot Loader

Boot Loader is a bootstrapping process.

The boot sequence is the initial set of operations that a computer performs when it is switched on, which loads and starts an operating system when the power is turned on.

Table 5-6 Traffic Types

Description	Connection	Type
CLI (SSH, Telnet), GUI , KVM, XML API <-> DME	A, B	Mgmt
Console	C, B	Serial RS232
DME <-> Peer Fabric Interconnect	B, S	Cluster/Mgmt/Data
DME <-> IO_MUX	B, D, G, I, J	Mgmt
DME <-> CMC	B, D, G, I, J, K	Mgmt

Description	Connection	Type
DME <-> Adapter (Palo, Menlo)	B, D, G, I, J, L	Mgmt
DME <-> CMS	B, D, G, I, J, M	Mgmt
DME <-> CIMC	B, D, G, I, J, M, O	Mgmt
DME <-> BIOS	B, D, G, I, J, M, O, P, Q	Mgmt
Adapter <-> Uplink Ether Port's (IP & FCoE)	L, J, I, G, E	Ethernet
Adapter <-> Uplink FC Ports (FC)	L, J, I, H, F	Fibre Channel
FEX <-> to peer FEX	N	Serial RS232

Boot Errors

All components in the UCS that have two firmware banks will always try to boot from backup bank (Backup version) in case of a boot failure.

Fabric Interconnect and UCSM

The Fabric Interconnect has two different firmware images that need to be booted: Kernel and System. The boot process is as follows:

1. POST (Power On Self Tests)
   — Low-level diagnostics
2. Boot Loader loads
   — Boot Loader reads the boot pointer from flash memory and boots starting version (startup version defined by administrator) of Kernel
3. Kernel loads and starts
   — Kernel components for NX-OS
4. System loads and starts
   — System components (Port manager, etc.)
   — System plug-in UCSM
   — Self diagnostics
5. Complete

UCS Manager

The UCS manager (UCSM) is a plug-in to NX-OS. At boot time, the NX-OS starts daemons and services; one of them is UCSM. The firmware repository is located on each Fabric Interconnect. If more versions of UCSM are available, only one can be started at a time; NX-OS will start the version the administrator chooses as the startup version.

Fabric Extender

The Fabric Extender (FEX) has two slots or banks with firmware, and a boot pointer. The boot pointer determines which of the two banks is the startup; the other one is declared the backup.

The boot process is as follows:

1. POST (Power On Self Tests)
   — Low-level diagnostics
2. Boot Loader loads
   — Boot Loader reads the boot pointer from memory and boots the firmware from the startup bank/slot (starting version)
3. Firmware loads and starts
   — Internal system components start
4. Self diagnostics
5. Complete

Baseboard Management Controller

The CIMC has two slots or banks with firmware, and a boot pointer, just like the FEX.

The boot pointer determines which of the two banks is the startup; the other one is declared the backup.

The boot process is as follows:

1. POST (Power On Self Tests)
   — Low-level diagnostics
2. Boot Loader loads
   — Boot Loader reads the boot pointer from memory and boots the firmware from the startup bank/slot (starting version)

3. Firmware loads and starts
    — Internal system components start
4. Self diagnostics
5. Complete

Chapter 6

UCS C-Series Rack Servers

Cisco® UCS C-Series Rack Servers extend unified computing innovations to an industry-standard form factor. These servers operate in both standalone environments and as part of the Cisco Unified Computing System.

The C-Series incorporates all the key technological innovations of the B-Series like standards-based unified network fabric, Cisco VN-Link virtualization support, and Cisco Extended Memory Technology. They can be mixed and matched with the B-Series servers.

They support an incremental deployment model and protect customer investments with a future migration path to unified computing. Today, Rack Servers are the majority of data center servers and are better in terms of I/O expansion slots and capacity to host local disk

Rack-mounted servers are robust, versatile, and cost effective. Most of the servers are two socket platforms for increasingly demanding infrastructure workloads. Table 6-1 lists the current members of the UCS C-Series family.

Table 6-1   The UCS C-Series Family

Item	CPU	Size	Memory	Disks	I/O
UCS C200	Intel® Xeon® 5500 or 5600	1RU	12 DIMM 96 GB	4 x 3.5" SAS/ SATA Drives	2 PCIe
UCS C210	Intel® Xeon® 5500 or 5600	2RU	12 DIMM 96 GB	16 SFF SAS/ SATA Drives	5 PCIe
UCS C250	Intel® Xeon® 5500 or 5600	2RU	48 DIMM 384 GB	8 SFF SAS/ SATA Drives	5 PCIe
UCS C460	Intel® Xeon® 7500	4RU	64 DIMM 512 GB	12 SFF SAS/ SATA Drives	10 PCIe

UCS C200

The Cisco UCS C200 is a one RU (Rack Unit) server with two Westmere-EP/Nehalem-EP sockets. It is a high-density server with balanced compute performance and I/O flexibility.

Figure 6-1 shows the front view of the C200. On the top left, there is the DVD-RW unit. On the top right, there are:

- The power button and LED
- The UID (Unit IDentification) button and LED
- The status LEDs (PSU, Mem, CPU, and NIC)
- The reset button
- The same console dongle connector used on the B-Series servers.

On the bottom, there are the four bays for the 3.5" SAS-2 and SATA-2 drives that are hot swappable from the front of chassis. Supported drives include:

- 15,000 RPM SAS drives for highest performance
- 7,200 RPM SAS drive for high capacity and performance
- 7,200 RPM SATA II drives for high capacity and value

Figure 6-2 shows the rear view of the C200. On the left, there are the two hot swappable power supplies, 650W each. They load balance when both are running and they are hot swappable from rear of chassis. In term of power supply efficiency, they are Energy Star 80+ Gold (88% eff. @ 20% load, 92% eff. @ 50% load).

To the right of the power supplies are:

- The UID LED
- Two USB v2.0 ports
- A 10/100BaseT Out-of-Band management interface
- A DB15 video port
- A DB9 serial port

Figure 6-1   UCS C200 front view

Figure 6-2   UCS C200 rear view

- Two 10/100/1000BaseT LOM (LAN ON Motherboard) interfaces based on Intel 82576 NIC
- Two half-length PCIe form factor add-in slots.

One PCIe slot is standard high, half-length slot (x16 PCIe Gen 2 interface, x16 connector); the other is a low-profile half-length PCIe Slot (x8 PCIe Gen 2 interface, x8 connector). In Figure 6-2, one of the two expansion slots is populated with a two-port 1 GE Ethernet adapter available as an option.

Figure 6-3 shows the inside of the chassis, where there are two Westmere-EP/Nehalem-EP processors with one Tylersburg 36D IOH (I/O Hub) with 36 lines PCI express, two system buses Intel QuickPath, and ICH10R Southbridge. Each socket can host processors up to 95 W.

If all twelve DDR3 DIMM sockets are populated with 8 GB DIMMs, then the chassis will hold 96 GB of memory. These chassis support ECC and ChipKill™ as well as a mirroring option.

Also inside the chassis are a USB Key slot intended for hypervisor boot, light guided diagnostics (one LED at each FRU: CPUs, DIMMs, drives, and fans), and the Cisco Integrated Management Controller (CIMC), aka BMC.

There are three HDD Controller options:

- Integrated: ICH-based SATA Controller
- Optional low-cost SAS and SATA: LSI 1064-based mezzanine card, RAID 0 & 1
- Optional high performance SAS and SATA Controller: LSI 6G Mega-RAID 9260-4i add-on card, 512 MB write cache with battery backup, RAID 0, 1, 5, 6, 10

UCS C210

The Cisco UCS C210 is a two RU high-capacity server with two Westmere-EP/Nehalem-EP sockets. It is a general-purpose server for workloads requiring economical, high-capacity, internal storage.

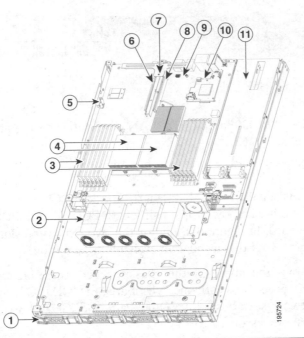

1	Hard drives (up to four, accessible through front bays)	2	Fan tray
3	DIMM slots (up to 12)	4	CPUs and heatsinks (up to two)
5	Motherboard CMOS battery	6	PCIe card slot for riser card (with chassis opening for standard-profile card)
7	Riser card assembly	8	PCIe card slot for riser card (with chassis opening for low-profile card)
9	Socket for trusted platform module (TPM)	10	Socket for LSI mezzanine card
11	Power supplies (up to two, accessible through rear bays)		

Figure 6-3   UCS C200 isometric view

Figure 6-4 shows the front view of the C210. On the top left, there is:

- The optional DVD-RW unit
- The power button (it acts also as reset) and LED
- The UID (Unit IDentification) button and LED
- The status LEDs (PSU, Mem, CPU, and NIC)
- The same console dongle connector used on the B-Series servers.

On the bottom, there are the sixteen bays for the 2.5" SAS-2 and SATA-2 drives that are hot swappable from the front of chassis. Supported drives include:

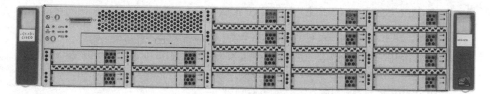

Figure 6-4 UCS C210 front view

- 15,000 RPM SAS drives for highest performance
- 10,000 RPM SAS drives for high performance and value
- 7,200 RPM SATA drives for high capacity and value

Figure 6-5 shows the rear view of the C210. On the left, there are the two hot swappable power supplies, 650W each. They load balance when both are running and they are hot swappable from rear of chassis. In terms of power supply efficiency, they are Energy Star 80+ Gold (88% eff. @ 20% load, 92% eff. @ 50% load).

To the right of the power supplies are:

- The UID LED
- Two USB v2.0 ports
- A 10/100BaseT Out-of-Band management interface
- A DB15 video port
- A DB9 serial port
- Two 10/100/1000BaseT LOM (LAN ON Motherboard) interfaces based on Intel 82576 NIC
- Five standard high PCIe Slots two full-length slots, three half-length slots. All the slots have x8 PCIe Gen 2 interface, with x16 connectors

Figure 6-5 UCS C210 rear view

The PCIe lane configuration in the C210 is as shown in Figure 6-6:

- On full-length slots, each slot gets eight lanes each.
- On half-length slots, the top-most slot gets eight dedicated lanes and the remaining two slots are connected to a PCIe switch that shares the remaining eight lanes between them.

Figure 6-7 shows the inside of the chassis, where there are two Westmere-EP/Nehalem-EP processors with one Tylersburg 36D IOH (I/O Hub) with 36 lines PCI express, two system buses Intel QuickPath, and ICH10R Southbridge. Each socket can host processors up to 95W.

If all twelve DDR3 DIMM sockets are populated with 8GB DIMMs, then the chassis will hold 96 GB of memory. These chassis support ECC and ChipKill™ as well as a mirroring option.

Also inside the chassis are a USB Key slot intended for hypervisor boot, light guided diagnostics (one LED at each FRU: CPUs, DIMMs, drives, and fans), and the Cisco Integrated Management Controller (CIMC), aka BMC.

There are three HDD Controller options:

- Integrated: ICH-based SATA controller, four drives maximum.
- Optional: Low cost SAS and SATA LSI 1064-based mezzanine card, RAID 0 and 1, four drives maximum.
- Optional: High-performance SAS and SATA Controller, LSI 6G Mega-RAID PCIe add-on card, 512 MB write cache with battery backup, RAID 0, 1, 5, 6, 10, 50, 60.

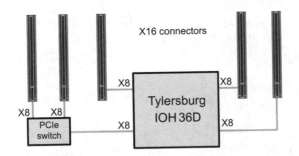

Figure 6-6   C210: PCIe connectors

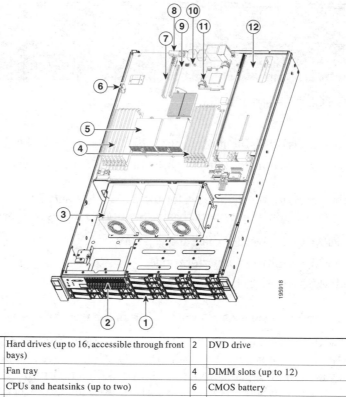

1	Hard drives (up to 16, accessible through front bays)	2	DVD drive
3	Fan tray	4	DIMM slots (up to 12)
5	CPUs and heatsinks (up to two)	6	CMOS battery
7	PCIe card slot for riser card (with chassis openings for three standard-profile cards)	8	Riser card assembly
9	PCIe card slot for riser card (with chassis openings for two standard-profile cards)	10	Socket for trusted platform module (TPM)
11	Socket for LSI mezzanine card	12	Power supplies (up to two, accessible through rear bays)

Figure 6-7   C210: Isometric view

UCS C250

The Cisco UCS C250 is a two RU large memory server with two Westmere-EP/Nehalem-EP sockets. It is a high-performance, memory-intensive server for virtualized and large data-set workloads.

Figure 6-8 shows the front view of the C250. On the top left, there are:

■ The DVD-RW unit

■ The power button (it acts also as reset) and LED

■ The UID (Unit IDentification) button and LED

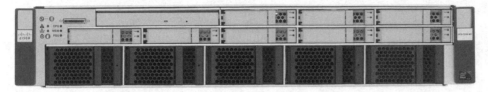

Figure 6-8 UCS C250—front view

■ The status LEDs (PSU, Mem, CPU, and NIC)

■ The same console dongle connector used on the B-Series servers.

On the top-right, there are the eight bays for the 2.5" SAS-2 and SATA-2 drives that are hot swappable from the front of chassis. Supported drives include:

■ 10,000 RPM SAS drives for value and capacity

■ 15,000 RPM SAS drives for performance

■ 7,200 RPM SATA drives for high capacity and performance

On the bottom, there are five fans hot swappable from the front of chassis.

Figure 6-9 shows the rear view of the C250. On the top-right, there are the two hot swappable power supplies, 750W each. They load balance when both are running and they are hot swappable from rear of chassis. In term of power supply efficiency, they are Energy Star 80+ Gold (88% eff. @ 20% load, 92% eff. @ 50% load).

To the bottom of the power supplies, from left to right, are:

■ Replication of front panel indicators

  — UID button and LED

  — Status indicators for System Activity, Health, Fault LEDs for Processors and Memory

Figure 6-9 UCS C250 rear view

- One DB9 serial port
- One DB15 video port
- Two USB 2.0 ports
- Four 10/100/1000BaseT LOM interfaces based on Broadcom BCM5709
- Two 10/100BaseT Out-of-Band management interfaces

To the left are five PCIe Gen 2 Slots:

- Three low-profile, half-length x8, with x16 connectors
- Two full-height, half-length x16, with x16 connectors

The PCIe lane configuration in the C250 is as shown in Figure 6-10:

- One of the full-height slots has dedicated 16 PCIe 2.0 lanes.
- The other one shares 8 lanes with one of the low-profile, half-length through a PCIe switch.
- The remaining two low-profile, half-length x8 slots share 8 lanes through a PCIe switch.

Figure 6-11 shows the inside of the chassis, where there are two Nehalem-EP processors with one Tylersburg 36D IOH (I/O Hub) with 36 lines PCI express, two system buses Intel QuickPath, and ICH10R Southbridge. Each socket can host processors up to 95W.

If all 48 DDR3 DIMM sockets are populated with 8 GB DIMMs, then the chassis will hold 384 GB of memory. Another cost-effective alternative is 192 GB of main memory with 4 GB DIMMs. These chassis support ECC and ChipKill™ as well as a mirroring option.

Also inside the chassis are a USB Key slot intended for hypervisor boot, light-guided diagnostics (one LED at each FRU: CPUs, DIMMs, drives, and fans), and the Cisco Integrated Management Controller (CIMC), aka BMC.

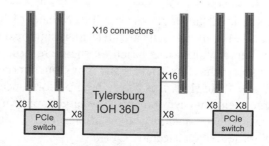

Figure 6-10   C250: PCIe connectors

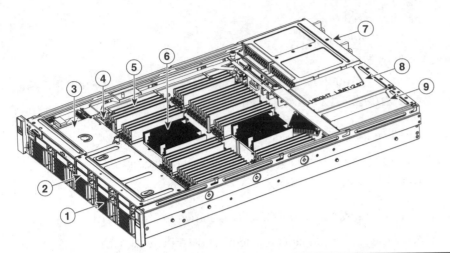

1	Fan modules (five), accessed through the front panel	2	Hard drives (up to eight), accessed through the front panel
3	DVD drive	4	Motherboard CMOS battery
5	DIMM slots (48)	6	CPUs and heatsinks (up to two)
7	Power supplies (up to two), accessed through the rear panel	8	PCIe riser card assembly (with chassis slots for two standard-profile cards)
9	PCIe riser card assembly (with chassis slots for three low-profile cards)		

Figure 6-11   UCS C250 isometric view

There is one HDD Controller option:

■   Optional: Low-cost SAS and SATA LSI SAS3081E-R PCIe add-on card, RAID 0 and 1

UCS C460

The Cisco UCS C460 is a four RU server with four Nehalem-EX sockets and two Boxboro-EX IOH (see Figure 6-12). Its architecture is significantly different from the three previous servers, since it is based on the more powerful Nehalem-EX (Xeon 7500) processor; it has four sockets and it has much more expendability in terms of memory and PCIe slots. It is a very high-performance server for multi-processor and large memory environments. The target applications are high-end virtualization, large data-set memory applications, ERP (Enterprise Resource Planning), and database like Oracle and SQL.

Figure 6-13 shows the front view of the C460. On the top, there is a ventilation grid, below it from left to right:

- Network activity LEDs
- The UID (Unit IDentification) button and LED
- The power button (it acts also as reset) and LED
- The status LEDs (PSU, Mem, CPU, and fans)
- One DB15 video port
- Three USB 2.0 ports

On the bottom are:

- The DVD-RW unit
- The twelve bays for the 2.5" SAS-2 and SATA-2 drives that are hot swappable from the front of chassis. Supported drives include:
    - 15,000 RPM SAS drives for highest performance
    - 10,000 RPM SAS drives for high performance and value

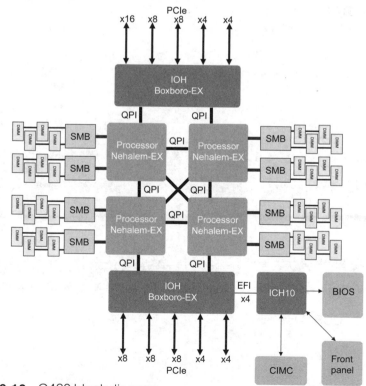

Figure 6-12   C460 block diagram

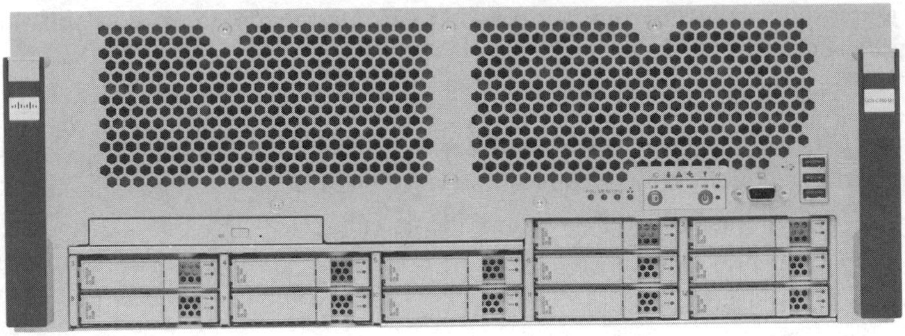

Figure 6-13   UCS C460 front view

Figure 6-14 shows the rear view of the C460. On the left, there are:

■ Replication of front panel indicators

— UID button and LED

— Status indicators for System Activity, Health, Fault LEDs for Processors and Memory

■ One DB9 serial port

■ Two 10/100/1000 LOM ports

■ Two 1/10 GE LOM ports

■ Two 10/100 Mbps managements ports

Figure 6-14   UCS C460 rear view

On the top-right, there are the 10 PCIe expansion slots, four of which are hot swappable with the following configuration:

- Four x8 Gen2
- One x16 Gen2
- Three x4 Gen2
- Two x4 Gen1

On the bottom are four hot swappable power supplies, 850W each. They are arranged in a 2 + 2 configuration and they are hot swappable from rear of chassis. In term of power supply efficiency, they are Energy Star 80+ Gold (88% eff. @ 20% load, 92% eff. @ 50% load).

Figure 6-15 shows the inside of the chassis where it is possible to notice:

- The I/O riser module that includes a Cisco Integrated Management Controller (CIMC), aka BMC, two 1 GE ports, two 10 GE ports, and two 10/100 Ethernet ports (see Figure 6-16).
- The SAS Riser slot, which holds an optional array controller card.

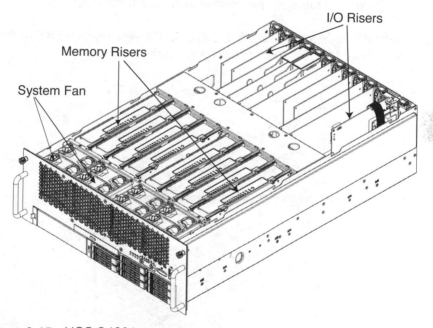

Figure 6-15   UCS C460 isometric view

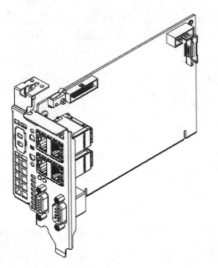

Figure 6-16   C460 I/O riser

- The eight memory boards, each hosting 8 DIMMs for a total of 64 DIMMs (see Figure 6-17).
- The frontal fan modules that are redundant and hot swappable.

In the middle of the box, there are four Nehalem-EX processors with two Box-boro-EXs, and two ICH10R Southbridges (see Figure 6-18).

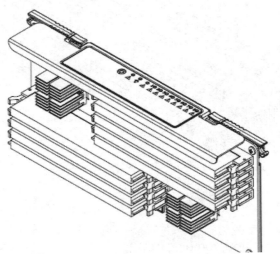

Figure 6-17   Memory riser

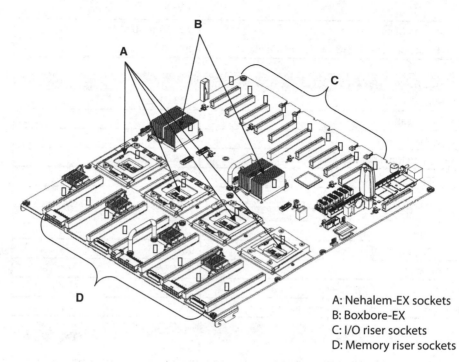

A: Nehalem-EX sockets
B: Boxbore-EX
C: I/O riser sockets
D: Memory riser sockets

Figure 6-18 C460 baseboard

Processors

The C200, C210, and C250 use the Nehalem-EP (see Table 6-2) and Westmere-EP (see Table 6-3) Intel processors.

Table 6-2 Intel® Nehalem-EP Processors

Intel® Xeon® L5520	
CPU Speed	2.26 GHz
Power Consumption	60W
QPI Speed	5.87 GT/s
Memory and Maximum Speed	DDR3@1066 MHz
Turbo Boost Bin Upside (133 MHz Increments)	1/1/2/2

Intel® Xeon® E5520	
CPU Speed	2.26 GHz
Power Consumption	80W
QPI Speed	5.87 GT/s

continues

Memory and Maximum Speed	DDR3@1066 MHz
Turbo Boost Bin Upside (133 MHz Increments)	1/1/2/2

Intel® Xeon® E5540	
CPU Speed	2.53 GHz
Power Consumption	80W
QPI Speed	5.87 GT/s
Memory and Maximum Speed	DDR3@1066 MHz
Turbo Boost Bin Upside (133 MHz Increments)	1/1/2/2

Intel® Xeon® X5570	
CPU Speed	2.93 GHz
Power Consumption	95W
QPI Speed	6.4 GT/s
Memory and Maximum Speed	DDR3@1333 MHz
Turbo Boost Bin Upside (133 MHz Increments)	2/2/3/3

Intel® Xeon® X5550	
CPU Core Speed	2.66 GHz
Number of Cores	4
Power Consumption	95 Watts
Memory and Maximum Speed	DDR3@1333 MHz
L3 Cache	8 MB
QPI Speed	6.4 GT/s
Turbo Boost Bin Upside (4C/2C Active)	2/3

Intel® Xeon® E5504	
CPU Core Speed	2 GHz
Number of Cores	4
Power Consumption	80 Watts
Memory and Maximum Speed	DDR3@800 MHz
L3 Cache	8 MB
QPI Speed	4.8 GT/s
Turbo Boost Bin Upside	None

Table 6-3   Intel® Nehalem-EP processors

Intel® Xeon® X5680	
CPU Core Speed	3.33 GHz
Number of Cores	6
Power Consumption	130 Watts
Memory and Maximum Speed	DDR3@1333 MHz
L3 Cache	12 MB
QPI Speed	6.4 GT/s
Turbo Boost Bin Upside (6C/4C/2C Active)	1/1/2

The X5680 is supported only on the C250; it is not supported on the C200 and C210.

Intel® Xeon® X5670	
CPU Core Speed	2.93 GHz
Number of Cores	6
Power Consumption	95 Watts
Memory and Maximum Speed	DDR3@1333 MHz
L3 Cache	12 MB
QPI Speed	6.4 GT/s
Turbo Boost Bin Upside (6C/4C/2C Active)	2/2/3

Intel® Xeon® X5650	
CPU Core Speed	2.66 GHz
Number of Cores	6
Power Consumption	95 Watts
Memory and Maximum Speed	DDR3@1333 MHz
L3 Cache	12 MB
QPI Speed	6.4 GT/s
Turbo Boost Bin Upside (6C/4C/2C Active)	2/2/3

Intel® Xeon® E5640	
CPU Core Speed	2.66 GHz
Number of Cores	4
Power Consumption	80 Watts
Memory and Maximum Speed	DDR3@1066 MHz
L3 Cache	12 MB
QPI Speed	5.86 GT/s
Turbo Boost Bin Upside (4C/2C Active)	1/2

continues

Intel® Xeon® L5640	
CPU Core Speed	2.26 GHz
Number of Cores	6
Power Consumption	60 Watts
Memory and Maximum Speed	DDR3@1066 MHz
L3 Cache	12 MB
QPI Speed	5.86 GT/s
Turbo Boost Bin Upside (6C/4C/2C Active)	2/3/4

Intel® Xeon® E5620	
CPU Core Speed	2.4 GHz
Number of Cores	4
Power Consumption	80 Watts
Memory and Maximum Speed	DDR3@1066 MHz
L3 Cache	12 MB
QPI Speed	5.86 GT/s
Turbo Boost Bin Upside (4C/2C Active)	1/2

Intel® Xeon® E6506	
CPU Core Speed	2.13 GHz
Number of Cores	4
Power Consumption	80 Watts
Memory and Maximum Speed	DDR3@800 MHz
L3 Cache	4 MB
QPI Speed	4.8 GT/s
Turbo Boost Bin Upside	None

The C460 supports the Nehalem-EX processors (see Table 6-4).

Table 6-4   Intel Nehalem-EX Processors

Intel® Xeon® X7560	
CPU Core Speed	2.26 GHz
Number of Cores	8
Power Consumption	130 Watts
Memory and Maximum Speed	DDR3@1066 MHz
L3 Cache	24 MB

QPI Speed	6.4 GT/s
Turbo Boost Bin Upside (8C/6C/4C/2C Active)	1/2/3/3

Intel® Xeon® X7550	
CPU Core Speed	2 GHz
Number of Cores	8
Power Consumption	130 Watts
Memory and Maximum Speed	DDR3@1066 MHz
L3 Cache	18 MB
QPI Speed	6.4GT/s
Turbo Boost Bin Upside (8C/6C/4C/2C Active)	1/2/3/3

Intel® Xeon® L7555	
CPU Core Speed	1.86 GHz
Number of Cores	8
Power Consumption	95 Watts
Memory and Maximum Speed	DDR3@976 MHz
L3 Cache	24 MB
QPI Speed	5.86 GT/s
Turbo Boost Bin Upside (8C/6C/4C/2C Active)	1/2/4/5

Intel® Xeon® E7540	
CPU Core Speed	2 GHz
Number of Cores	6
Power Consumption	105 Watts
Memory and Maximum Speed	DDR3@1066 MHz
L3 Cache	18 MB
QPI Speed	5.86 GT/s
Turbo Boost Bin Upside (8C/6C/4C/2C Active)	0/1/1/2

Intel® Xeon® E7520	
CPU Core Speed	1.86 GHz
Number of Cores	4
Power Consumption	95 Watts
Memory and Maximum Speed	DDR3@800 MHz
L3 Cache	18 MB
QPI Speed	4.8 GT/s
Turbo Boost Bin Upside (8C/6C/4C/2C Active)	None

Adapters

This section lists the most common adapters that can be installed on the C-Series servers. Not all the adapters are appropriate for all the configurations, and this list will become obsolete quickly:

- QLogic QLE8152 Dual Port 10-Gbps Converged Network Adapter (CNA) (two ports, copper)

- Broadcom NetXtreme II 5709 Quad Port Ethernet PCIe Adapter Card with TOE and iSCSI HBA

- Broadcom NetXtreme II 57711 Dual Port 10 Gigabit Ethernet PCIe Adapter Card with TOE and iSCSI HBA

- Emulex LightPulse LPe11002 4-Gbps Fibre Channel PCI Express Dual Channel Host Bus Adapter

- QLogic SANblade QLE2462 Dual Port 4-Gbps Fibre Channel Host Bus Adapter (HBA)

- Broadcom NetXtreme II 5709 Quad Port Ethernet PCIe Adapter Card with TOE and iSCSI HBA

- Emulex OneConnect OCe10102-F FCoE CNA

- Intel Quad port GbE

- Intel 10GbE 2port Niantec Controller with Copper and SFP+

- Logic QLE8152 Dual Port 10-Gbps Ethernet-to-PCIe Converged Network Adapter (CNA) (two ports, copper)

- QLogic SANblade QLE2462 Dual Port 4-Gbps Fibre Channel-to-PCI Express Host Bus Adapter (HBA)

- LSI 6G MegaRAID 9260-4i PCIe RAID Controller (SAS/SATA RAID 0, 1, 5, 6, 10) with 512 MB write cache (C200 only)

- LSI 6G MegaRAID 9261-8i PCIe RAID Controller (SAS/SATA RAID 0,1,5,6,10,50,60, eight ports) with 512 MB write cache (C210 and C250 only)

- LSI LSISAS3041E-R PCIe RAID Controller (C250 only)

- LSI 1064 Controller-Based Mezzanine Card (4-port SAS/SATA 3.0G RAID 0, 1, 1E controller) (C200 and C210 only)

Hard Disk

This section lists the most common disks that can be installed on the C-Series servers. Not all the disks are appropriate for all the configurations, and this list will become obsolete quickly.

The UCS C200 uses the following 3.5-inch SAS or SATA drives:

- 500 GB SATA; 7,200 RPM
- 1 TB SATA; 7,200 RPM
- 2 TB SATA; 7,200 RPM
- 300 GB SAS; 15,000 RPM
- 450 GB SAS; 15,000 RPM

The UCS C210, C250, and C460 use the following SFF 2.5-inch SAS or SATA drives:

- 73 GB SAS; 6G, 15,000 RPM
- 146 GB SAS; 6G, 10,000 RPM
- 300 GB SAS; 6G, 10,000 RPM
- 500 GB SATA; 7,200 RPM

SSD (Solid State Disk) options are also available.

Management

All Cisco UCS C-Series Rack Servers are equipped with a Cisco Integrated Management Controller (CIMC). The CIMC is Cisco's version of the Baseboard Management Controller (BMC), a Service Processor, and it is the primary component responsible for the remote management of the server. The CIMC was designed with UCS Manager in mind: It provides the same look and feel as UCS Manager, without breaking any rack server management processes currently in place in customer datacenters. Therefore, the CIMC provides multiple ways to perform an operation.

Depending on the model, the UCS C-Series Servers have one (C200 and C210) or two (C250 and C460) management ports connected to the CIMC. Multiple management interfaces allow for redundant management traffic paths, which reduce the risk of losing connectivity to the CIMC and the management capabilities in case of a failure.

The CIMC is compliant with standards-based Intelligent Platform Management Interface (IPMI) Specification v2.0. Any third-party products or custom-built solutions that support IPMI v.2.0 can both monitor and manage the C-Series.

The CIMC also provides additional functionality and interfaces like KVM (Keyboard, Video, Mouse, and Virtual Media), web-based User Interface, CLI (SMASH), SoL, and SNMP.

The C-Series also provides physical ports for connection of local Keyboard, Video, and Mouse.

The CIMC provides a comprehensive web-based user interface for management of the server. The CIMC user interface has the same look and feel as the UCS Manager user interface; the administration and actions performed on a C-Series are very similar to the B-Series. Figure 6-19 illustrates this CIMC web-based interface. It shows a UCS C250 Server Summary view, including health, and possible actions such as power on/off, launch KVM, etc.

The CIMC provides inventory information, health monitoring, sensor information, and event logs through the web-based user interface or the CLI in real time. The CIMC CPU GUI Inventory View shows key information like CPU details on a UCS C210 (see Figure 6-20).

The CLI provides the same information and capabilities as the web-based user interface, for example, Figure 6-21 shows the same CPU inventory information as the web-based user interface.

Just like the UCS Manager, the CIMC has an Admin tab, for administration and configuration of Network, IPMI, and SNMP settings, as well as User and Firmware management.

The CIMC incorporates a similar firmware management concept as the UCS Manager (see Figure 6-22), with two images, one active and one backup (Ready). The new firmware image is always uploaded to the non-active image. There are two different ways to upload firmware: One is the more traditional way through the web browser, and the other way is very similar to how it is implemented on UCS Manager (via a TFTP server).

Once the firmware has been uploaded to the non-Active image bank, it needs to be activated, just as in UCS Manager.

The CIMC in the C-Series provides multiple standard interfaces for easy integration and incorporation into existing management tools and environments. A common implementation is to use both out-of-band and in-band monitoring and management. Figure 6-23 shows a third-party tool using both in-band and out-of-band management. To give a better perspective, the figure also shows the C-Series native GUI and CLI interfaces.

In this example, the third-party management system has its own agent to perform OS and application management. It uses a standard SNMP agent for OS monitoring (these are marked as in-band). For hardware monitoring and management, it uses CIMC, SNMP, and IPMI (out-of-band). To add another variable to this example, the third-party management software also uses the SoL interface. The SoL interface is used to provide the administrator with native serial console access to the OS. Most likely the third-party tool would also allow OS console access through OS services, like SSH and Telnet.

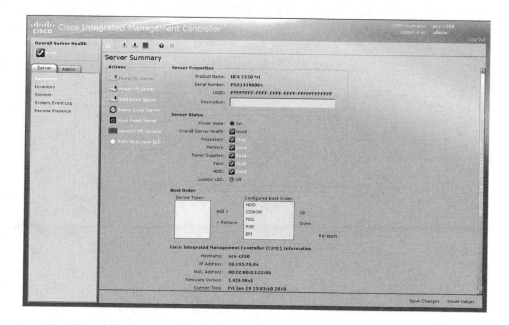

Figure 6-19   UCS C250 CIMC web-based Server Summary view

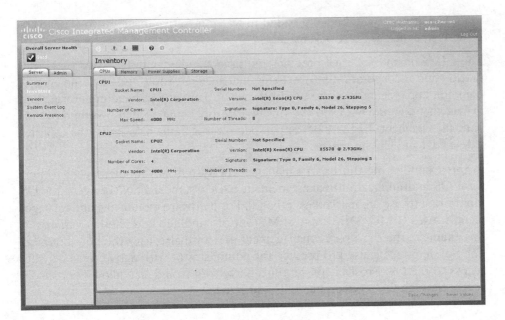

Figure 6-20   UCS C210 GUI CPU Inventory view

```
ucs-c2xx-m1#
ucs-c2xx-m1# scope chassis
ucs-c2xx-m1 /chassis # show cpu
Name          Cores    Version
------------  -------  --------------------------------------------------
CPU1            4        Intel(R) Xeon(R) CPU           X5570  @ 2.93GHz
CPU2            4        Intel(R) Xeon(R) CPU           X5570  @ 2.93GHz
ucs-c2xx-m1 /chassis # show cpu detail
Name CPU1:
    Manufacturer: Intel(R) Corporation
    Family: Xeon
    Thread Count : 8
    Cores : 4
    Serial No.: Not Specified
    Version: Intel(R) Xeon(R) CPU           X5570  @ 2.93GHz
    Speed (Mhz) : 2933
    Max. Speed (Mhz) : 4000
    Signature: "Signature: Type 0, Family 6, Model 26, Stepping 5
    Status: Enabled
Name CPU2:
    Manufacturer: Intel(R) Corporation
    Family: Xeon
    Thread Count : 8
    Cores : 4
    Serial No.: Not Specified
    Version: Intel(R) Xeon(R) CPU           X5570  @ 2.93GHz
    Speed (Mhz) : 2933
    Max. Speed (Mhz) : 4000
    Signature: "Signature: Type 0, Family 6, Model 26, Stepping 5
    Status: Enabled
ucs-c2xx-m1 /chassis # ucs-c2xx-m1#
```

Figure 6-21   UCS C210 CLI CPU Inventory view

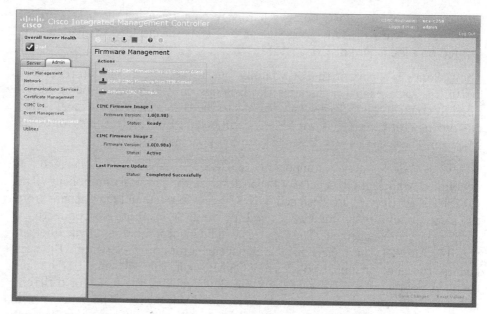

Figure 6-22   UCS C250 CIMC Firmware Management view

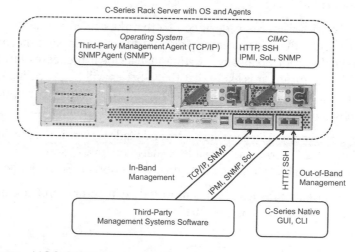

Figure 6-23   UCS C250 third-party integration example

Please note that the CIMC box is a hardware component on the baseboard of the C-Series, while the Operating System box is a user-installed OS with agents located on a local hard disk or a SAN LUN.

The C-Series is a part of the UCS family, but at the time of writing (February 2010), the UCS Manager manages the B-Series only. Software is being developed to connect the C-Series Rack Servers to the UCS Manager. The goal is that customers with C-Series and/or B-Series will benefit from all features from UCS Manager. The C-Series was designed with this goal in mind.

Today all B-Series server components in UCS are stateless, and managed via decoupled Managed Objects (MOs) that describe the physical components. The C-Series Rack Servers are designed with stateless in mind and may benefit from the same policy-driven framework used for the B-Series, both for connectivity and for device management. The C-Series will be incorporated as full members in the object model. This means that the management for both C-Series and B-Series can use the same or similar policies in UCS Manager. This will simplify the management for the rack servers, at the same time reducing the need for different processes in the data center for rack server and blade servers. The C-Series will be managed via service profiles just like the B-Series, and the service profiles will be able to be associated and disassociated between different C-Series compute resources. The current object model used by UCS Manager is very flexible and extensible and, for example, it would be little to no effort to make service profiles compatible between both B-Series and C-Series servers (assuming hardware compatible components).

The current C-Series firmware is designed so that the server can be managed as any other rack server in the data center. This was done to make sure that any UCS C-Series server does not break any existing management processes in place for rack servers. In the future, it is likely that the C-Series will be providing multiple firmware options, one for traditional rack server behavior (currently shipping) and one for complete integration into the UCS Management framework.

The obvious difference between rack servers and blade servers is the physical connectivity. Figure 6-24 shows one possible scenario on how C-Series Rack Servers can be connected to a UCS Manager that already supports B-Series Blade Servers.

Details on the actual implementation, supported architectures and combinations will be defined in the second part of 2010.

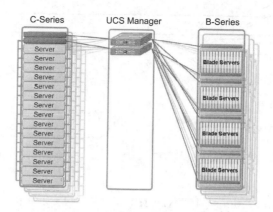

Figure 6-24 UCS Manager with both C-Series and B-Series

Software

The UCS C-Series servers run the most common operating systems and virtualization software available on the market. Table 6-5 lists the operating systems and virtualization software supported in the first half of 2010.

Table 6-5 OSes and Hypervisors

Microsoft	Windows Server 2003 R2 – 32bit
VMware	ESX 3.5 U4
Microsoft	Windows Server 2008 with Hyper-V - Standard and Enterprise Edition - 64 bit
VMware	vSphere 4
Red Hat	RHEL 5.4– 64 bit
VMware	vSphere 4i
Novell	SLES 11 - 64 bit
Red Hat	RHat 4.8 - 64 bit
Novell	SLES 10 SP3 64 bit
Red Hat	RHEL 5.4 with KVM 64 bit
Sun	Solaris x86 10.x - 64 bit
VMware	vSphere 4 U1
VMware	vSphere 4i U1
Oracle	OVM 2.1.2/2.2
Oracle	Oracle Enterprise Linux
Citrix	XenServer

continues

Novell	SLES 11 with XEN - 64 bit
Red Hat	RHEV-H (KVM) - 64 bit

Physical Parameters

C200

- Physical dimensions (HxWxD) 1RU: 1.7 x 16.9 x 27.8 in. (4.32 x 42.93 x 70.61 cm)
- Temperature: Operating 50°F to 95°F (10°C to 35°C)
- Temperature: Nonoperating −40°F to 149°F (−40°C to 65°C)
- Humidity: Operating 5% to 93% noncondensing
- Humidity: Nonoperating 5% to 93% noncondensing
- Altitude: Operating 0 to 10,000 ft (0 to 3000m)

C210

- Physical dimensions (HxWxD) 2RU: 3.45 x 17.2 x 28.4 in. (8.76 x 43.69 x 72.14 cm)
- Temperature: Operating 50°F to 95°F (10°C to 35°C)
- Temperature: Nonoperating -40°F to 149°F (-40°C to 65°C)
- Humidity: Operating 5% to 93% noncondensing
- Humidity: Nonoperating 5% to 93% noncondensing
- Altitude: Operating 0 to 10,000 ft (0 to 3000m)

C250

- Physical dimensions (HxWxD) 2RU: 3.39 x 17.5 x 28 in. (8.61 x 44.45 x 71.12 cm)
- Temperature: Operating 50°F to 95°F (10°C to 35°C)
- Temperature: Nonoperating −40°F to 149°F (−40°C to 65°C)
- Humidity: Operating 5% to 93% noncondensing

- Humidity: Nonoperating 5% to 93% noncondensing
- Altitude: Operating 0 to 10,000 ft (0 to 3000m)

C460

- Physical dimensions (HxWxD) 2RU: 6.8 x 16.7 x 27.7 in. (17.4 x 42.4 x 70.4)
- Temperature: Operating 50°F to 95°F (10°C to 35°C)
- Temperature: Non-operating -40°F to 1 58°F (-40°C to 70°C)
- Humidity: Operating 5% to 93% noncondensing
- Humidity: Nonoperating 5% to 95% noncondensing
- Altitude: Operating -100 to 5,000 ft (-30 to 1,500 m)

Weights

Table 6-6 Rack Server Weights

	Base Chassis	Fully Loaded Server
C200	21 lbs	33 lbs
C210	36 lbs	48 lbs
C250	50 lbs	65 lbs
C460	42 lbs	110 lbs

Chapter 7

UCS Manager

The UCS Manager (UCSM) provides a single point of management for a UCS.[1] An embedded policy-driven software manages all devices in a UCS as a single logical entity.

UCSM Overall Architecture

System Components

The architecture of UCSM consists of multiple layers with well-defined boundaries (see Figure 7-1). External interfaces provide communication with the outside world. The Data Management Engine (DME) is the central service that manages the components of a UCS. Application gateways act as a hardware abstraction layer between the DME and the managed End-Points (EPs). The EPs are the actual devices or entities that are managed by UCSM, but they are not considered as part of the UCSM itself.

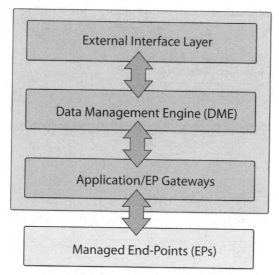

Figure 7-1 UCSM components

---

1   The authors thank Mike Dvorkin for his contribution to this chapter.

External Interface Layer

The External Interface Layer consists of multiple interface components, for outside world communication (e.g., SMASH-CLP, CIM-XML, and the UCSM-CLI), see Figure 7-2. The interface components are modular and well defined within UCSM. This design facilitates development of new interface components (to support new standards) or to enhance an existing interface component (to accommodate new features in currently-supported standards). All interface components are stateless in nature and their internal communication terminates on the DME.

Data Management Engine

The Data Management Engine (DME) is the central component in UCSM and consists of multiple internal services (see Figure 7-3). The DME is the only component in a UCS that stores and maintains states for the managed devices and elements. The DME is the authoritative source of configuration information. It is responsible for propagating configuration changes to the devices and endpoints in the UCS. The DME manages all devices and elements and represents their state in the form of managed objects (MOs). MOs contain the desired configuration and the current state of a corresponding endpoint.

Administrators make changes to MOs. These changes are validated by the DME and propagated to the specific endpoint. For example, suppose an operator initiates a server "power on" request through the GUI. When the DME receives the request, it validates it and, if valid, the DME makes the corresponding state change on the server object in the Model Information Tree (MIT). This state change is then propagated to the server via the appropriate Application Gateway (AG).

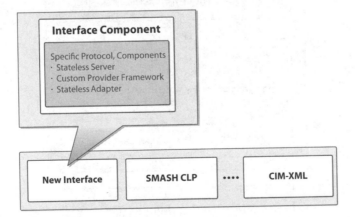

Figure 7-2   External interface layer

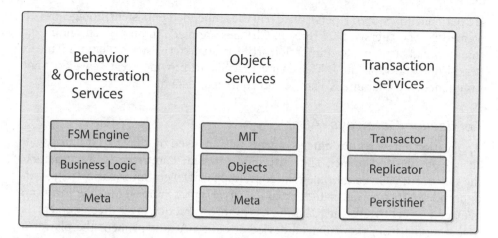

Figure 7-3 Data Management Engine layer

Object Services

Hardware components, such as network interface cards, ports, servers, and processors, are represented as MOs. Statistics, faults, and events are also represented as MOs. All MOs are hierarchically organized and contained in the MIT. The object services are driven by a meta-model that validates object properties, containments (objects that contain other objects), and relationships. They also handle the object life cycle.

Behavior and Orchestration Services

Behavior and orchestration services are driven by a meta-model. They handle the behavior and rules regarding the objects. Each object contains meta-information that describes such things as the object properties, object type, parsing, rendering rules, inheritance, and also how to invoke any business logic (product feature) specific to that object. Managed objects have their own Finite State Machine (FSM) in the form of a child object that is responsible for scheduling and performing tasks for the object. For example, a hardware inventory of a server is orchestrated by the FSM on the corresponding server object.

Transaction Services

Transaction services are responsible for the actual data mutations (configuration and state changes) of the objects (as performed by the "transactor" thread), and replication of state change to the secondary UCSM instance in a HA-environment (as performed by the "replicator" thread). It also verifies that the changes are permanently stored ("persistified") in the embedded persistent storage (as performed by the "persistifier" thread). Changes are made in an asynchronous and transactional fashion. No transaction artifacts are externally visible until data are persistified and replicated. This enables UCSM to provide great scalability and simultaneously guarantees a stable and consistent data model.

Application Gateways (AGs)

Application gateways are stateless agents that are used by the DME to propagate changes to the end-points. They also report system state from the endpoints to the DME. An AG is a module that converts management information (e.g., configuration, statistics, and faults) from its native representation into the form of a managed object (MO). The AG is the hardware abstraction layer that abstracts the object model from the managed device or entity. AGs implement the platform-specific details of each of the managed endpoints. In UCSM, the AGs are implemented for the NX-OS, chassis, blades, ports, host agents, and NICs (see Figure 7-4).

- **Host AG.** The host Agent AG is responsible for server inventory and configuration. It interacts with the server via the UCS Utility OS. This AG is responsible for BIOS firmware updates, local RAID controllers, third-party adapter option ROMs, and the RAID configuration of any local disks. It also ensures that the server becomes anonymous again by performing local disk scrubbing.

- **NIC AG.** The NIC AG monitors and manages the adapters, performs configurations changes, updates firmware, manages identifiers like MAC and WWPN, and manages the existence and Quality of Service settings for the Ethernet and Storage adapters.

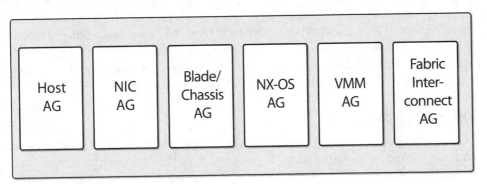

Figure 7-4   Application Gateway Layer

- **Blade/Chassis AG.** The Blade/Chassis AG monitors and manages the chassis management controller (CMC) inside the fabric extender (FEX, also known as I/O module) and the Cisco Integrated Management Controller (CIMC) located on the motherboard of each server. It performs firmware updates and configuration changes on the CMC and CIMC, including UUID and BIOS settings. It also performs server-related operations like powering on and off the blades.

- **Fabric Interconnect AG.** The Fabric Interconnect AG monitors and manages the Fabric Interconnect. It performs actions such as configuring server-facing ports and Ethernet uplink ports. It is also responsible for VLANs port channels, trunks, and uplink connectivity for vNICs and vHBAs from the servers.

- **NX-OS AG.** The NX-OS AG upgrades firmware on the Fabric Interconnect, monitors health and statistics of the FI, including flash memory and the running UCSM services.

- **VMM AG.** The VMM AG interacts with VMware vCenter to configure port profiles and discover the VMs running in the ESX.

Managed Endpoints

Managed endpoints are resources within a UCS that are managed by UCSM. The DME inside UCSM interacts with the endpoints via AGs. These resources are LAN, SAN, and server related (see Figure 7-5).

UCSM Is a Model-Driven Framework

UCSM uses a model-driven framework approach (see Figure 7-6) where system functionality is described in a generic, platform-independent Information Model (IM). "Content" is automatically generated by the NGEN (Nuova Generator, a program developed by Nuova Systems, now part of Cisco) from the Information Model (IM) and the manually coded "Business Logic", which extends and feeds into the Platform Definition Model (PDM). The two are then automatically translated to a Platform-Specific Model (PSM), described in C++. This generated code is then compiled and run inside the Fabric Interconnect and known as UCSM. About 70–75% of UCSM is automatically generated by code-generating robotics. Approximately 25–30% is written by developers. It mainly consists of Business Logic and the specific product features.

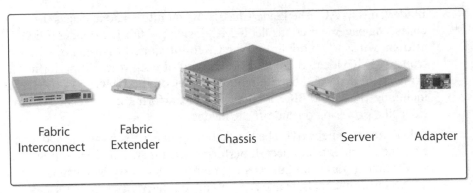

Figure 7-5 Managed end-points

When an operator initiates an administrative change to a UCS component (for example, a boot request of a server) through one of the management interfaces, the DME first applies the change to the corresponding MO in the information model and then subsequently (and indirectly) the change is propagated and applied to the actual managed endpoint. The separation of business logic from platform implementation in a model-driven framework is useful for many reasons. One of them is the ability to develop the business logic independently from the platform implementation (and vice versa).

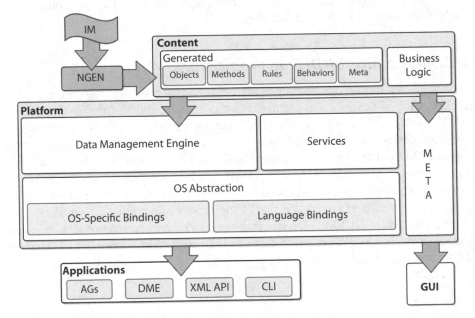

Figure 7-6 Model-driven framework

In UCSM, when the operator performs an action, the operator will get a response immediately, indicating that the DME has successfully received and accepted the change request. The immediate response is a success (if it is possible to satisfy the request) or a failure (if the request is impossible to satisfy). However, at this time, the End-Point may still not have yet received the request from the AG. For example, an operator can monitor the progress of a boot request by monitoring the operational "Power State". The "Power State" will change from "down" to "up" once the server is powered on.

Figure 7-7 and Table 7-1 contain an example of a server boot request.

Table 7-1   Example of a Server Boot Request

Step	Command / Process	Administrative Power State of MO (Server)	Operational Power State of MO (Server)
1.0	CMD Request: Boot Server	Down	Down
2.0	Request gets Queued	Down	Down
3.0	State Change in Model Information Tree	Up	Down
4.0	Transaction Complete	Up	Down
5.0	Pass change info and boot request stimuli	Up	Down
6.0	Persistify the state change of MO to local store	Up	Down
6.1	Send state change information to peer DME	Up	Down
6.2	Persistify the state of MO to peer's local store	Up	Down
6.3	Reply with success (replication and persistification)	Up	Down
7.0	CMD: Response & External Notification	Up	Down
8.0	Apply reboot stimuli	Up	Down
9.0	Instruct CIMC to power on server	Up	Down
10.0	Reply from CIMC, server power on success	Up	Up
11.0	Reply, reboot stimuli success; pass new Power state information	Up	Up

UCSM Lives in the Fabric Interconnect

UCSM is an NX-OS module and is therefore supervised, monitored, and controlled by the NX-OS (see Figure 7-8). UCSM can be upgraded or restarted (just like any other module) without affecting I/O to and from the servers in the UCS. The management functionality is unavailable during the period the UCSM is down.

UCSM in a Highly Available Configuration

UCSM can run in a highly available configuration. This is achieved by connecting two Fabric Interconnect devices together via two cluster ports on each Fabric Interconnect (see Figure 7-9). A Fabric Interconnect always runs an instance of the UCSM, independently of the configuration. In a non-HA configuration, the UCSM runs a standalone manager and controls all components of the UCS. While the UCS management plane runs in an active-standby configuration, the data plane is active-active. Both Fabric Interconnects are actively sending and receiving LAN and SAN traffic, even though only one of them is running the active UCSM instance.

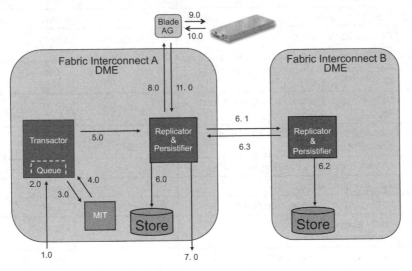

Figure 7-7   Sample flow of server boot request

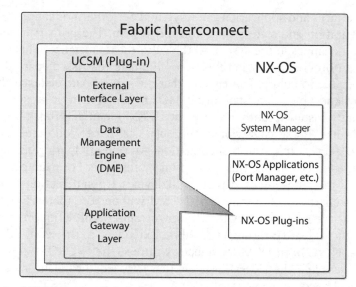

Figure 7-8   UCSM in the Fabric Interconnect

The UCSM contains cluster components similar (but not identical) to a traditional active-passive application cluster. When two instances of UCSM are connected, they work together to achieve HA. There is an election after which one UCSM is promoted to "primary" and the other UCSM is demoted to "subordinate". The primary UCSM instance is the owner of a virtual IP address to which all-external management connections are made. The primary instance handles all requests

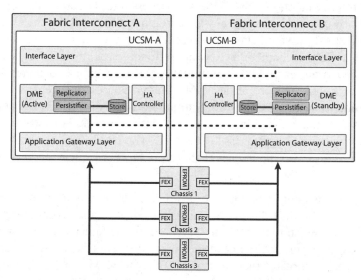

Figure 7-9   UCSM high availability

from all interfaces and application gateways, and performs model transformations (like configuration and state changes) in the system. The primary instance also replicates all changes in the system to the subordinate instance. This replication is done in an ordered and stateful way to eliminate the risk of partial information updates due to failure. This ensures that the subordinate instance always has a consistent and up-to-date state of all MOs in the system, in case of a failure of the primary instance. Both instances of UCSM are monitoring each other via the cluster links. If the cluster links fail a classical cluster quorum algorithm is used to avoid a possible split-brain situation. An odd number of chassis is used as quorum resources to determine the primary instance. For example, in a UCS with four chassis, three are used as quorum devices. Upon detection of a possible split-brain scenario, both instances of UCSM will demote themselves to subordinate and at the same time try to claim ownership of all the quorum resources by writing their identity, through the Fabric Extenders, to the serial EEPROM of the chassis. Next, both UCSM instances will read the EEPROM content of all quorum chassis and the UCSM instance that succeeded to claim most quorum resources will become the primary.

Management Information Model

As previously discussed, the Information Model or the UCS Management Information Model (MIM) is a tree structure where each node in the tree is a managed object (MO) (see Figure 7-10). Managed objects are abstractions of real-world resources—they represent the physical and logical components of the UCS, such as Fabric Interconnect, chassis, servers, adapters, etc. Certain MOs are implicit and cannot be created by users, they are automatically crated by the UCSM when a new device is discovered such as power supplies and fan modules. The properties in the MOs are characterized as operational via administrative settings. At MO creation time, each MO is assigned a DN (distinguished name) based on the value of its naming properties. DN's lifecycles are consistent with the MO that they identify; that is, they are immutable once the MO is created. A DN is a slash "/" delineated sequence of Rns (Relative names). For example, the DN for a compute blade is "sys/chassis-1/blade-1". The DN is used to unambiguously identify MOs and MO hierarchies that are the target of query and configuration operations.

Figure 7-10 shows containment relationships of MOs and how they are related in the MIM. Note that this is a small subset of the tree structure. Also, note that fault MOs and statistic MOs are parented by the faulty and monitored MOs, respectively. Later this chapter describes other concepts like policies, service profiles, pools, and templates that are also MOs in the MIM.

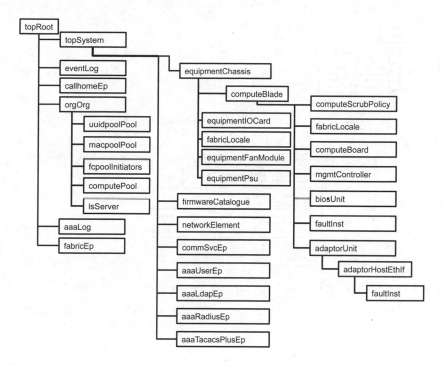

Figure 7-10   Managed objects

UCSM allows users to query the state of MOs using DNs. It also supports hierarchical queries. A hierarchical query returns all the MOs in the MIT subtree rooted at the identified MO.

Figure 7-11 depicts an MO (in this example, a host Ethernet interface) in the MIM. The MO DN is: "sys/chassis-3/blade-1/adaptor-1/host-eth-1."

Available Integration Points

Interfaces

All standard interfaces (see Figure 7-12) cover applicable subsets of the UCSM information model. The standard protocols that connect directly (cut-through) to a CIMC (Cisco Integrated Management Controller) via a unique external IP address bypassing the UCSM. All other interfaces terminate on the UCSM. Each request is queued, interpreted, de-duplicated, checked against the requestors' privileges, and executed by the UCSM.

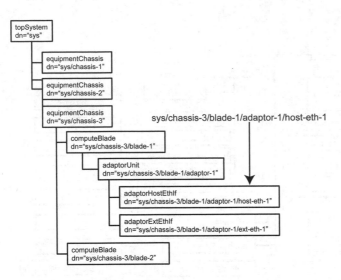

sys/chassis-3/blade-1/adaptor-1/host-eth-1

Figure 7-11   Information model

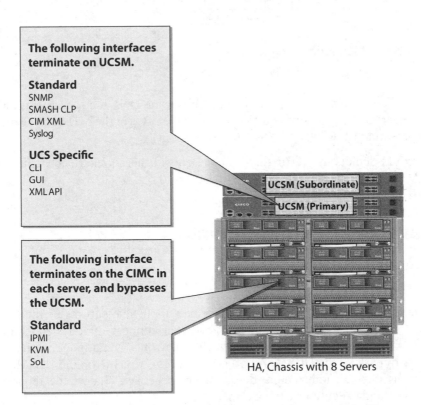

Figure 7-12   System interfaces

Standard (Cut-Through) Interfaces in a UCS

A cut-through interface provides direct access to a single server's CICMC. The advantage with a cut-through interface like IPMI, is that it allows for existing software that already leverage such interfaces to interact with the servers with no modifications or updates necessary. The disadvantage of using a cut-through interface is that it bypasses the DME. To alleviate this disadvantage, the DME is always in discovery mode, and it will detect any changes made through a cut-through interface, like a reboot. However, if an operator performs a task on a server (via DME, GUI, CLI, XML, API, etc.) and a different operator uses a cut-through interface and performs a contrasting action at same time on the same server, the DME initiated task will always win and complete the request (due to the transactional nature of the DME). The UCS provides a unique external management IP address to each CIMC for external management. This external management IP address for each CIMC must be within the same network as the Fabric Interconnect management ports and UCSM virtual IP.

IPMI (Intelligent Platform Management Interface)

IPMI is a protocol for monitoring and managing single server hardware information such as voltage, CPU, statistics, and ambient temperature. Data collected from sensors are captured and available at the CIMC. This interface is commonly used by management software to perform server management out-of-band, including reboot, power-on, and power-off. In a UCS, these capabilities are a small subset of all the capabilities provided natively by UCSM via the XML API.

SoL (Serial-over-LAN)

SoL enables an administrator to connect remotely to a single server and to get full keyboard and text access to the server console.

KVM (Keyboard-Video-Mouse)

KVM enables an administrator to obtain remotely keyboard, video, and mouse access to a single server, but also to the server administrative tasks, like power on/off, local storage management, policy association, etc. The KVM console is also commonly used to install a single server OS and to troubleshoot OS-related issues (see Figure 7-13 and Figure 7-14).

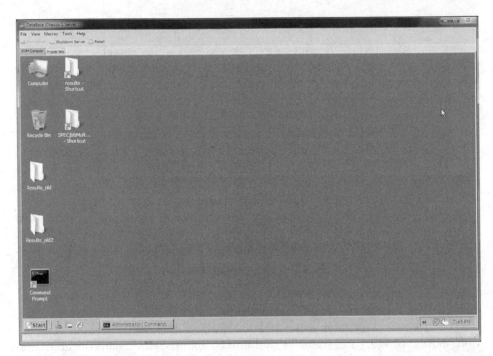

Figure 7-13 KVM session

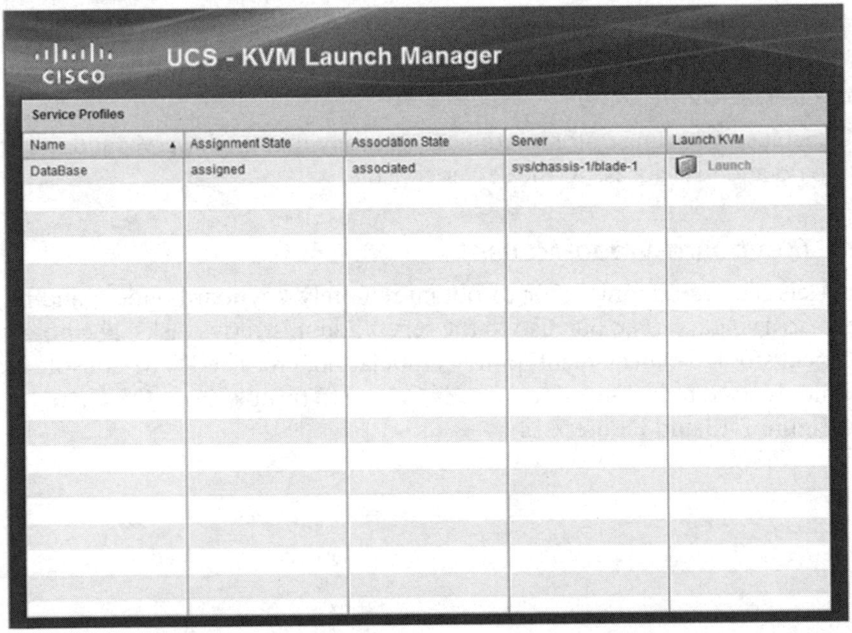

Figure 7-14 KVM launch manager

KVM also provides virtual media capabilities, which allows an administrator to mount a remote media on the server the KVM is accessing. The administrator can give the server access to image files (.iso) or physical drives like CD and DVD on the client running the KVM console session.

The KVM console can be launched from the UCS manager GUI, via the external web page KVM Launch Manager or as a standalone application. The UCS manager, independently from where the KVM session was launched, always authenticates the session and the user. The stand-alone KVM is downloadable from the UCS manager via a URL.

Standard Interfaces in a UCS

SNMP (Simple Network Management Protocol)

The UCS provides a read-only SNMP interface for external fault monitoring of UCS components via the Fabric Interconnect.

SMASH-CLP (Systems Management Architecture for Server Hardware Command-Line Protocol)

The SMASH-CLP enables administrators to use a standard command-line interface for servers, independently of vendor and model. In the UCSM implementation, this interface provides read-only access. It can be used for monitoring and debugging, inventory collection. It also provides for the information gathering of servers and chassis.

CIM-XML (Common Information Model-eXtensible Markup Language)

The CIM-XML standard interface defines a Common Information Model for servers, which allows software to exchange programmatically this well-defined information with different vendor systems. In the UCSM, this interface is implemented as read-only and can be used for monitoring, debugging, and inventory collection (server and chassis related) by frameworks that support the CIM-XML standard.

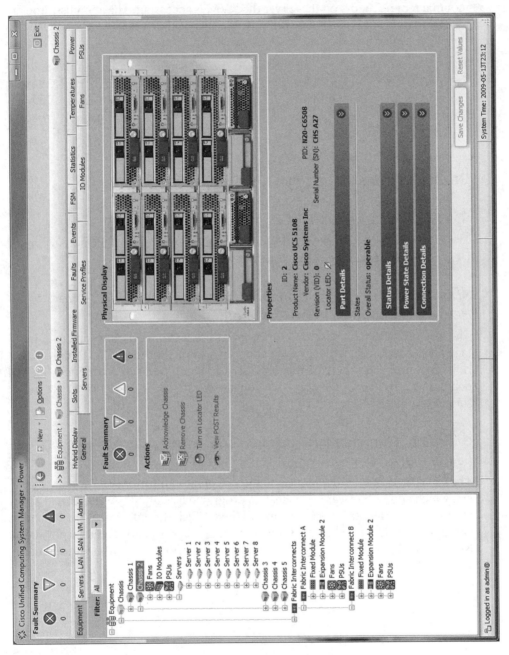

Figure 7-15   GUI

Native Interfaces in UCS

UCSM CLI (UCSM Command-Line Interface)

The command-line interface (CLI) is one of several interfaces to access, configure, and monitor the UCS. The CLI is accessible from the console port or through a Telnet or SSH session. The UCS CLI is object based and fully transactional. The CLI is fully featured, providing complete management and monitoring of all components in the UCS.

UCSM GUI (UCSM Graphical User Interface)

The UCSM GUI (see Figure 7-15) is JAVA-based and it can be started and run from any supported web browser. This interface provides a fully-featured user interface for managing and monitoring of a UCS.

XML API, eXtensible Markup Language-Application Program Interface

The XML API is the most powerful interface used to integrate or interact with a UCSM. It is generic, content-driven, and hierarchical. This is the native language for the DME and therefore there are no restrictions on what can be done through this interface, within the framework of the DME. The XML API also supports event subscription that allows a subscribing client, like monitoring software, to receive all events or actual state changes in the whole UCS, assuming that the subscriber has the right privileges. This is useful as the feed-only sends actual changes and not whole MO information; there is no need for the client to poll for current state and then differentiate what may have changed since last pull for information.

All interfaces including UCSM GUI and UCSM CLI interfaces (except cut-through interfaces) are translated into the native XML API prior to reaching the DME (see Figure 7-16). Please note that although the SNMP interface is not included in the picture, it is a native interface of the Fabric Interconnect.

Sample Integrations

Figure 7-17 is a sample of how the interfaces in the UCS can be leveraged.

All interfaces benefit from the fact that the DME is transactional, since all interfaces are translated into native XML API and the requests handled by the DME. This guarantees uniform enforcement of Role-Based Access Control.

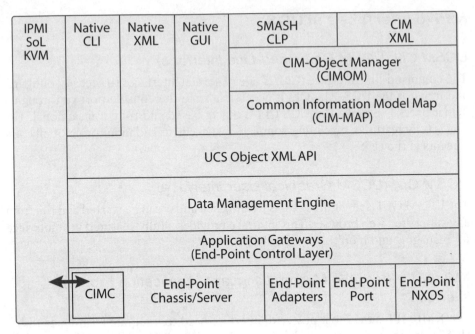

Figure 7-16   System interface stack

Syslog

Syslog is a standard protocol for forwarding log messages in a client/server fashion. The log messages include information from all the components in the UCS. The UCSM has the capability to forward log messages to up to three different syslog hosts or to a local Console, Monitor, or File (see Figure 7-18).

Operating Principles

UCSM is a policy-driven device manager. Policy-driven management is one of the key features of UCSM, allowing IT organizations the ability to define and implement their best practices as UCS policies.

Policies help to ensure that consistent, tested and compliant systems are used, reducing the risk of issues caused by repetitive manual tasks. Data centers are becoming increasingly more dynamic, and the definition, consumption, and resolution of policies is a key-enabling technology for making infrastructure devices portable and reusable. The UCSM allows subject matter experts like networking, storage, and server administrators to predefine policies within their area of expertise, which can later be selected by a server administrator when defining a compute resource.

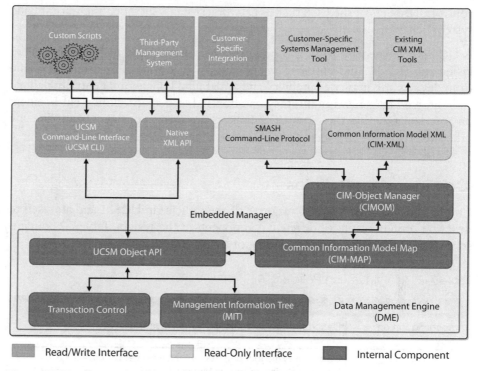

Figure 7-17   Example of integrations and interfaces

Policies control behaviors and configurations. They control how a server or other components of the UCS will act or be affected in specific circumstances. The UCSM has a large number of different policies. These policies describe and

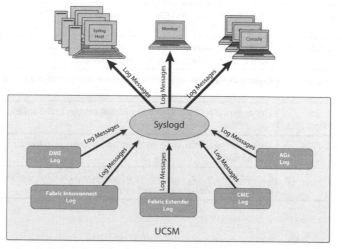

Figure 7-18   Syslog messages flow

control all aspects of the UCS such as network, storage, server configurations, and system behavior.

A UCS is managed by rules and policies. Rules are defined in form of policies inside the UCSM, and enforced in the end-point (devices). This removes state from devices and improves mobility and scalability. Policies are centrally defined and enforced at the end-point; they can be used to perform policy enforcement on any device within the same UCS. Policies are managed objects and, like any other MO, can be exported and imported to other UCSMs.

Configuration Policies

Configuration policies are the majority of the policies in UCSM and are used to describe configurations of different components of the system. Table 7-2 contains some policy examples valid at the time of this writing.

Table 7-2   Configuration Policies

Policy	Description
Autoconfiguration Policy	Describes how to configure automatically a newly discovered server.
Boot Policy	Determines the location from which a server boots, via a SAN, LAN, Local Disk, or Virtual Media.
Chassis Discovery Policy	Determines how the system reacts when a new chassis is discovered.
Dynamic Connection Policy	Determines the numbers and properties (such as queue depth, performance, etc.) of the dynamic adapters that will be utilized by Virtual Machines.
Ethernet Adapter Policy	Determines how an Ethernet adapter handles traffic (such as queue depth, failover timeout, performance, etc.).
Fibre Channel Adapter Policy	Determines how a Fibre Channel adapter handles traffic (includes flogi & plogi timeout, error handling, etc.).
Host Firmware Pack Policy	Determines a set of firmware versions that will be applied to a server via a service profile.
Local Disk Configuration Policy	Determines RAID and configuration on the optional local drives.
Management Firmware Policy	Determines a firmware version that will be applied to the CIMC on the server.
QoS Definitions Policy	Defines the outgoing quality of service (QoS) for a vNIC or vHBA (class of service, burst, and rate).

Policy	Description
Server Discovery Policy	Determines how the system reacts when a new server is discovered.
Server Inheritance Policy	Describes the inheritance from the hardware on a newly discovered server.
Server Pool Policy	Determines pool memberships of servers that match a specific "server pool policy qualifications".
Server Pool Policy Qualifications	Qualifies servers based on inventory rules, like amount of memory, Number of processors.
vHBA and vNIC Policy	Defines connectivity and QoS for a vHBA or vNIC.

Operational Policies

Operational policies determine how the system behaves under specific circumstances. Table 7-3 contains some policy examples valid at the time of this writing. Figure 7-19 contains an example of server profile policies.

Table 7-3   Operational Policies

Policy	Description
Adaptor Collection Policy	Defines intervals for collection and reporting statistics regarding adapters.
Blade Collection Policy	Defines intervals for collection and reporting statistics regarding blades.
Call Home Policies	Defines how call home profiles are used for email notification.
Chassis Collection Policy	Defines intervals for collection and reporting statistics regarding chassis.
IPMI Profile	Defines the IPMI capabilities of a server and whether the access is read-only or read-write.
Fault Collection Policy	Defines clear action and intervals for fault clearance and retention.
Port Collection Policy	Defines intervals for collection and reporting statistics regarding ports.
Scrub Policy	Determines if any state of the server should be kept during the Discovery process.
Serial over LAN Policy	Defines the serial over LAN capabilities of a server.
Threshold Policy	Sets alarm triggers for Ethernet, Fibre Channel, adapters, blades, chassis, PSUs, FEXs, FANs, etc.

Global vs. Local Policies

Some policies are global and some are local. The global policies are defined for the whole UCS; local policies are on per-organization level (organizations will be covered later in this chapter). Examples of global policies include Fault Collection Policy, Call Home Policies, and the various statistic Collector Policies.

Default vs. User-Created Policies

The UCSM has default policies that are used in the absence of user-created policies. These pre-defined policies are typically defaulting to normal system behavior.

Pools

Pools are containers for resources and ID definitions (see Figure 7-20). There are mainly two different types of pools: ID pools and blade pools. A pool contains only one type of resource. For instance, a blade pool can only contain blades and a WWPN Pool can only contain WWPNs. Pools make a system easier to manage and maintain, since they minimize the need for administrators to manage the use of resources. Multiple pools with different names can contain the same type of resources, but also the very same resources. For example, a blade can be a member of multiple pools. Once a blade is consumed and assigned by the system, the blade is no longer assignable. Pools are providers to Service Profiles and Service Profile Templates (discussed later in this chapter).

Identity Pools

Identity pools are used for server identity management and assignments. This allows the UCSM to assign automatically identities to a server and their interfaces in the UCS. This minimizes the administrative tasks needed for network, storage and server administrators. More importantly, this is one of the key components for stateless computing since the servers are stateless and any server can be assigned to any ID and workload at any time. There are four types of identity pools: MAC, WWPN, WWNN, and UUID. Figure 7-20 shows an example of system pool types.

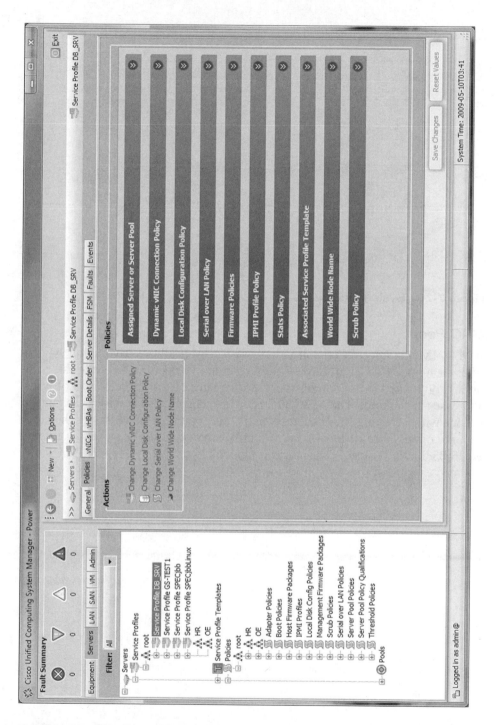

Figure 7-19   Service profile policies

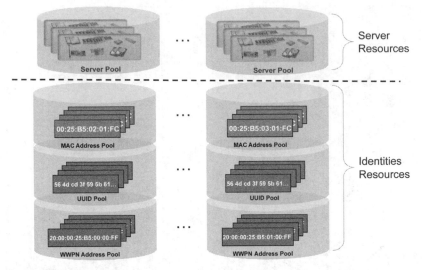

Figure 7-20   System pool types

MAC Pools

A MAC (Media Access Control) address is a hardware address that uniquely identifies each node of a LAN. A MAC pool contains blocks of MAC addresses. This pool is populated by an administrator who creates one or more blocks of MAC addresses in the pool. The MAC addresses are sequential. The block assignment is done with a starting MAC address "From" and a number of addresses the block should contain (size of block). For example, a block could be as follows: From: 00:25:B5:00:00:01 Size: 5. The block would look like Table 7-4. Figure 7-21 shows a screen capture of the MAC pool page.

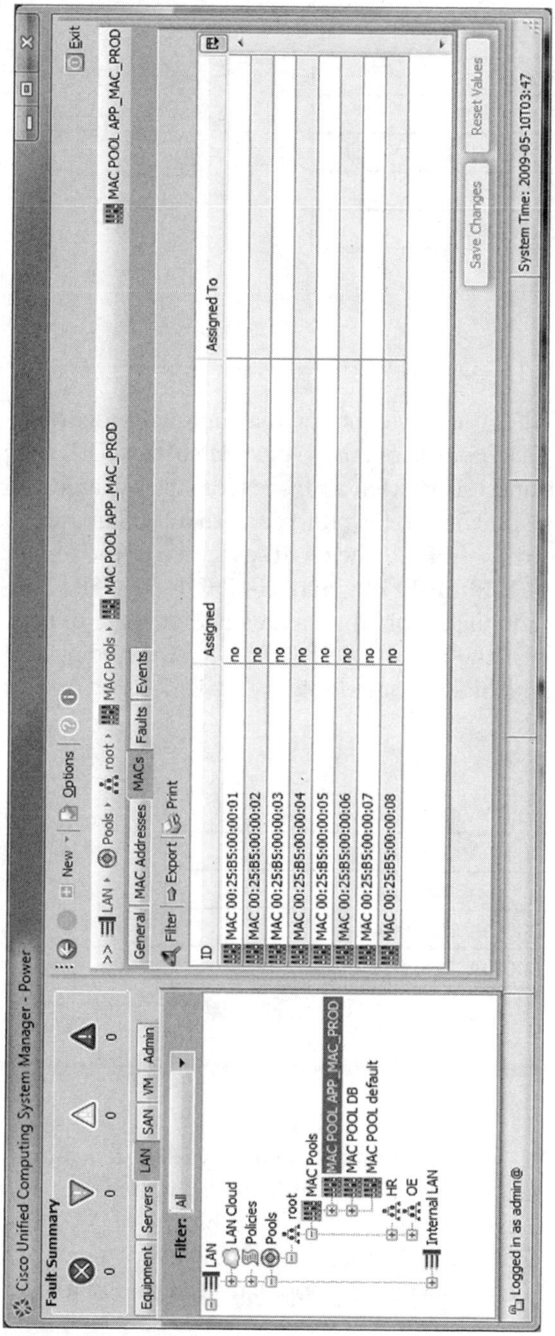

Figure 7-21 Mac pool

Table 7-4   Example of MAC Address Pool

00:25:B5:00:00:01
00:25:B5:00:00:02
00:25:B5:00:00:03
00:25:B5:00:00:04
00:25:B5:00:00:05

UUID Suffix Pool

A Universally Unique Identifier (UUID) is an identifier that uniquely identifies each compute resource (server). A UUID pool contains blocks of suffix UUIDs. In a UCSM, a suffix UUID is 8 bytes and it is written as 16 hexadecimal characters in the format "HHHH-HHHHHHHH". The pool is prefixed with a UCS unique 8 bytes in the format of "FFFFFFFF-FFFF-FFFF". The UUID assigned to the server is a "Prefix"-"Suffix", like "FFFFFFFF-FFFF-FFFF- HHHH-HHHHHHHH". The suffix UUIDs are populated by an administrator who creates one or more blocks of UUID numbers in the pool. From: "1000-0A0B0C0D01" Size: 5. Assuming the prefix is "1FFFFFFF-2FFF-3FFF", the block would look like Table 7-5.

Table 7-5   UUIDs

1FFFFFFF-2FFF-3FFF-1000-0A0B0C0D01
1FFFFFFF-2FFF-3FFF-1000-0A0B0C0D02
1FFFFFFF-2FFF-3FFF-1000-0A0B0C0D03
1FFFFFFF-2FFF-3FFF-1000-0A0B0C0D04
1FFFFFFF-2FFF-3FFF-1000-0A0B0C0D05

WWPN Pools

A World Wide Port Name (WWPN) is an address that uniquely identifies a port on a node in a SAN. A WWPN pool contains blocks of WWPN addresses, very similar to the MAC pools. A pool can contain one or more blocks of WWPN addresses; multiple pools can be created. Each block in a pool consists of a number of sequential WWPN addresses. The UCS Manager populates the pool with the addresses in a sequential order, a block is created from a starting WWPN address "From" and a number of addresses the block should contain (size of block). For example, a block could be created as follows: From: 20:00:00:25:B5:00:00:01 Size: 5. The block would look like Table 7-6.

Table 7-6   WWPNs

20:00:00:25:B5:00:00:01
20:00:00:25:B5:00:00:02
20:00:00:25:B5:00:00:03
20:00:00:25:B5:00:00:04
20:00:00:25:B5:00:00:05

A WWPN or a WWNN in the pool can also be assigned a boot target and a boot LUN, as in Table 7-7.

NOTE: All servers in this example boot from different LUNs but the configuration is the same WWPN and LUN "0". This is because storage arrays mask the real LUN IDs by using a translation layer between the back-end LUN ID and the server presented LUN ID. Therefore, the result is that all boot LUNs are physically different in the storage array but presented to the different servers as LUN ID "0".

Table 7-7   Boot Target

WWPN	Boot Target WWPN	LUN ID
20:00:00:25:B5:00:00:01	50:00:00:25:B5:60:00:A1	0
20:00:00:25:B5:00:00:02	50:00:00:25:B5:60:00:A1	0
20:00:00:25:B5:00:00:03	50:00:00:25:B5:60:00:A1	0
20:00:00:25:B5:00:00:04	50:00:00:25:B5:60:00:A1	0
20:00:00:25:B5:00:00:05	50:00:00:25:B5:60:00:A1	0

Server Pools

A server pool contains a set of available, stateless servers. This pool type allows two different ways to populate the members of the pool: manual and automatic.

Manual Population of Pools

Manual population is a very simple, but not a very efficient, way to assign pool membership for a server. The operator manually maintains and manages the server membership. In Figure 7-22, an administrator is manually evaluating the inventory of each server and then assigns the server to one or more server pools. The picture shows two different pools (Application_A and Application_B) with the same requirements of server characteristics. Therefore, the administrator manually makes them members of both pools.

Automatic Population of Pools

A pool can be automatically populated via policies (see Figure 7-23). There are two different policies that decide which pool a server should be a member of: "Server Pool Policy Qualifications" and "Server Pool Policy".

The "Server Pool Qualifications" policy describes the hardware qualification criteria for servers, like number of processors, amount of RAM, type of adapters, etc. A server that fulfills all of the defined criteria in the policy is considered a qualified server.

The "Server Pool Policy" describes which "Server Pool" the server becomes a member of, if it has qualified for a certain "Server Pool Qualification". The same server can meet multiple qualifications. Multiple "Pool Policies" can point to the same pools. Figure 7-24 shows the creation of a server pool policy qualification and Figure 7-25 shows the creation of a server pool policy.

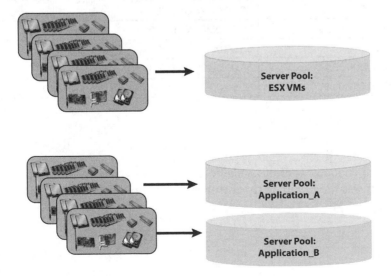

Figure 7-22   Manual pool assignment

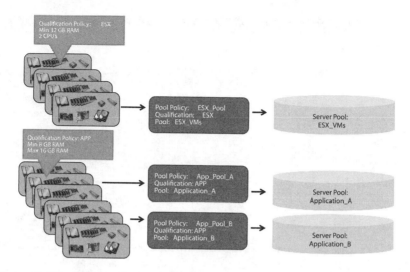

Figure 7-23 Automatic pools assignment

Figure 7-23 shows one qualification (APP) that has qualified multiple servers and two "Pool Policies" that are using the very same qualification to populate different "Server Pools".

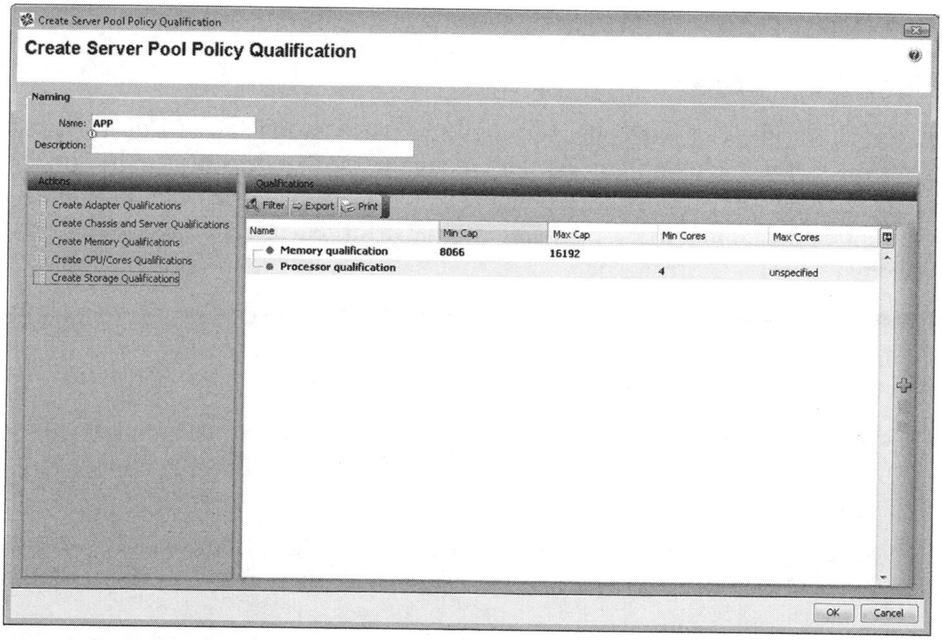

Figure 7-24 Server pool qualification

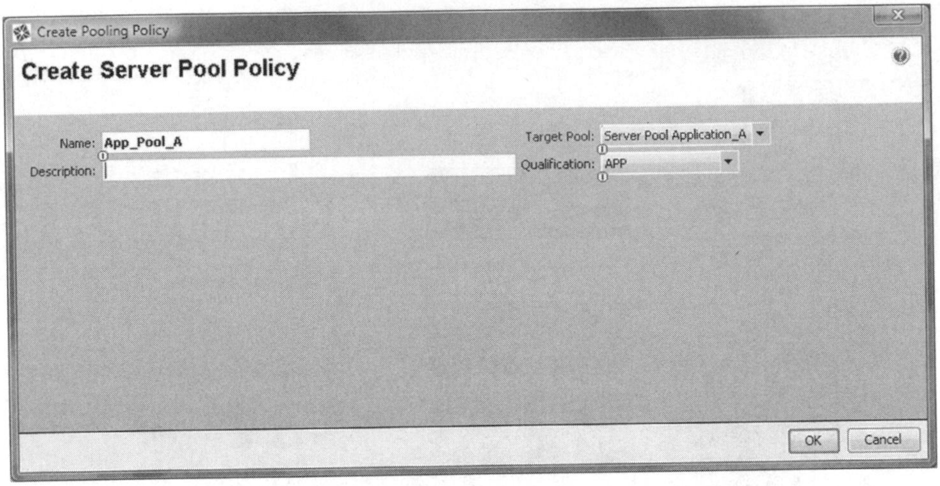

Figure 7-25   Server pool policies

Default vs. User-Created Pools

The UCSM also has default pools that are pre-defined, but not pre-populated. The default pools are used as a last resource when a regular pool has been drained out in the local organization and there are no other resources available in parent or grandparent's organizations. Organizations are discussed later in this chapter.

Service Profiles

A service profile is a self-contained logical representation (object) of a desired physical server, including connectivity, configuration, and identity. The service profile defines server hardware (configuration, firmware, identity, and boot information), fabric connectivity, policies, external management, and high-availability information (see Figure 7-26).

Every server is stateless and must be associated with a service profile to gain its identities and personality. A service profile is associated with a stateless server via manual association, or automatically via a blade pool.

A service profile ensures that the associated server hardware has the configuration, identities, and connectivity to a LAN and SAN based on the requirements from the applications the server will host.

An associated server (with a service profile) is similar to a traditional bare metal server in the way that it is ready to be used for production and to run business

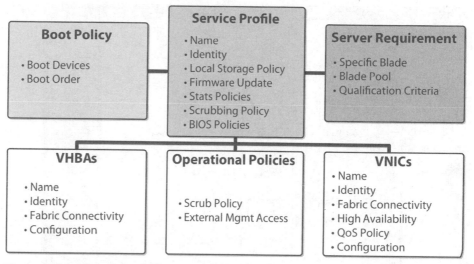

Figure 7-26   Service profile components

services or software. Once the service profile is de-associated from the server, the server is reinitialized (erased from any state) and returned to the pools (depending on current pool policies).

Servers and service profiles have a one-to-one relationship. Each server can be associated with only one service profile (see Figure 7-27). Each service profile can be associated with only one server. A service profile can be modified, cloned, or used to instantiate a template.

The UCSM uses pools, policies, and service profiles to abstract states and configuration information for all the components that define a server.

This is one of the key areas that make the UCS a stateless computing system. It allows separation of an operational state and services from the server hardware and physical connectivity.

For example, a service profile can be associated to any available server in a UCS, which automatically includes full migration of identities, firmware, and connectivity to LAN and SAN, etc. Figure 7-28 gives an example of the information that is included in a service profile.

Service Profile Templates

A service profile template is very similar to a service profile except it cannot be associated with a physical server. Templates are used for instantiation of multiple service profiles. This is useful for administrators who need to create a large

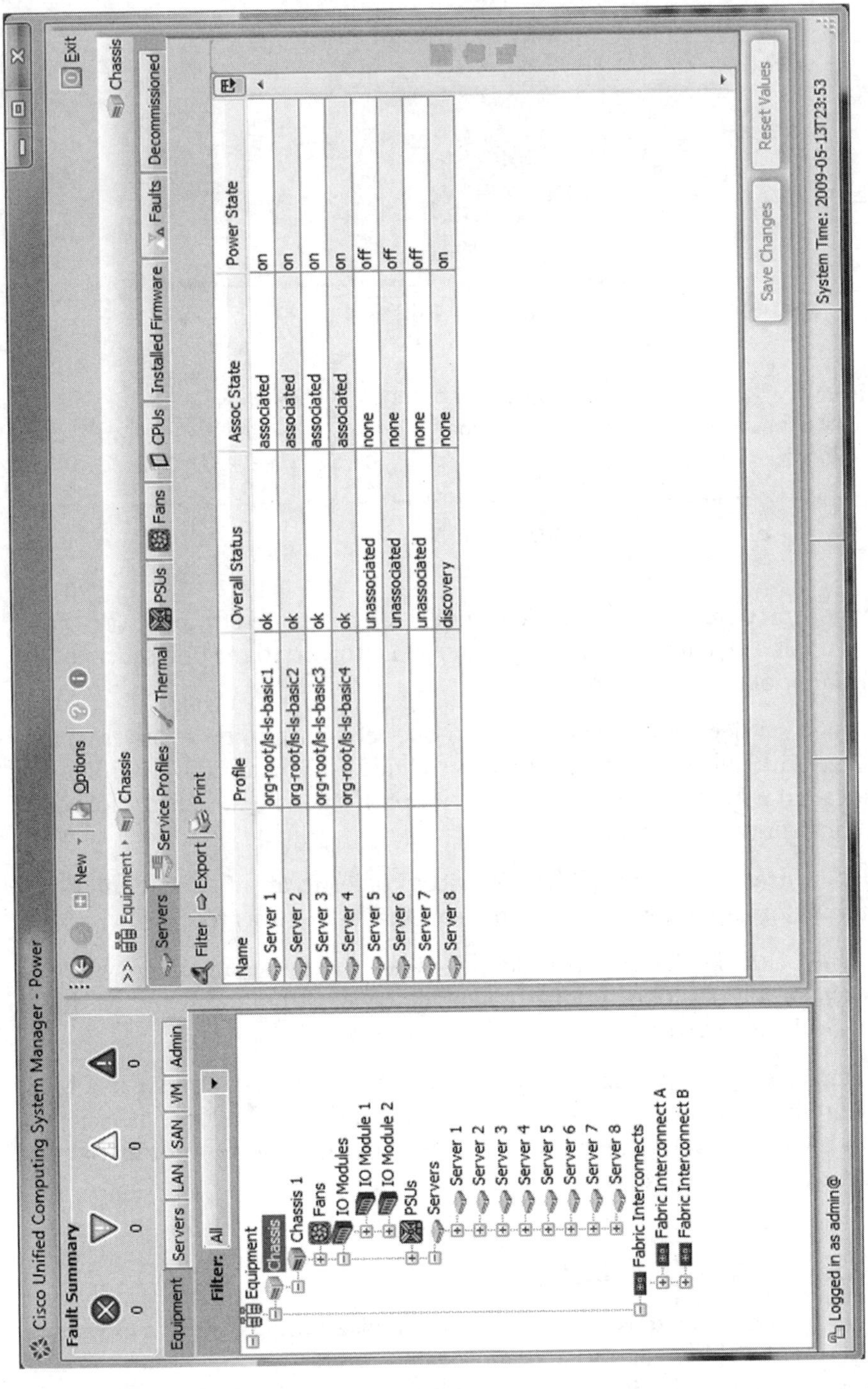

Figure 7-27   Service profile association

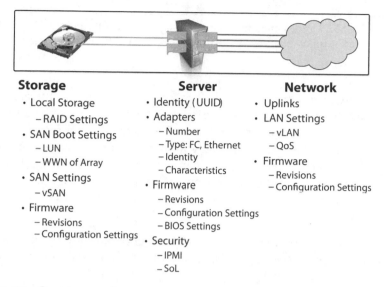

Storage
- Local Storage
  - RAID Settings
- SAN Boot Settings
  - LUN
  - WWN of Array
- SAN Settings
  - vSAN
- Firmware
  - Revisions
  - Configuration Settings

Server
- Identity (UUID)
- Adapters
  - Number
  - Type: FC, Ethernet
  - Identity
  - Characteristics
- Firmware
  - Revisions
  - Configuration Settings
  - BIOS Settings
- Security
  - IPMI
  - SoL

Network
- Uplinks
- LAN Settings
  - vLAN
  - QoS
- Firmware
  - Revisions
  - Configuration Settings

Figure 7-28   Service profile

number of service profiles. A server administrator can create a template for a certain purpose, like a database template, or an application template. This enables other administrators to instantiate new service profiles with limited expertise of requirements for a certain application or software.

There are two types of templates: "initial-template" and "updating-template". The difference is that a service profile created from an "initial-template" does not inherit any new configuration changes made to the template after the service profile has been instantiated. A service profile that has been created from an "updating-template" maintains relationship. The profile keeps inheriting any configuration changes made to the template.

Organizations

Separation of administrators and their administrative tasks can be done by the use of Organizations, Locales, and RBAC. This can be accomplished by dividing the large physical infrastructure of the system into logical entities known as organizations. As a result, administrators can achieve a logical isolation between organizations without providing a dedicated physical infrastructure for each organization. The structure of the organizations depends upon the business needs of the company. For example, organizations may represent a division within a company, such as marketing, finance, engineering, human resources, or other organizations that represent different customers, etc.

Note: The UCSM was designed for multi-tenancy environments and the XML API provides a rich set of functionalities for customers who plan to use it in multi-tenancy environments.

The "base" organization is root and all other organizations are hierarchical. All policies and other resources that reside in a root organization are system-wide and available to all organizations in the system. However, any policies and resources created in other organizations are only available to organizations in the same hierarchy. For instance, consider a system with organizations named "Finance" and "HR" that are not in the same hierarchy. "Finance" cannot use any policies from the "HR" organization, and "HR" cannot use any policies from the "Finance" organization.

Unique resources can be assigned to each tenant, or organization. These resources can include different policies, pools, quality of service definitions, etc. Administrators can also be assigned strict privileges by an organization.

Hierarchical Pool and Policy Resolution

The UCSM resolves a pool or policy name to a service profile parsing the organization tree bottom-up. Consider the organizational structure in Figure 7-29. If a user creates a service profile in Org-D and associates a boot policy called policy-1 with it, since UCSM resolves policy names by traversing the tree upwards, the policy association for the service profile will be the policy-1 policy in the root organization. However, if there was a boot policy named policy-1 in Org-D, then UCSM will use that one and not the one in the root organization. Note that, in the

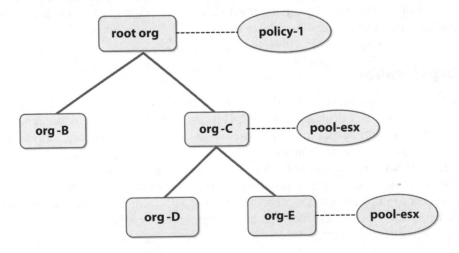

Figure 7-29   Hierarchical pool and policy resolution

absence of any user-defined boot policies, then the default boot policy associated with the organization will be used.

Another nuance in the resolution of a pool to a service profile is that UCSM will search the tree for an available resource. For example, suppose a server pool named pool-esx is associated with a service profile in the org-E. When that service profile is deployed, UCSM will search for an available blade from a blade pool called pool-esx from the org-E organization in the scope of parents and grandparents. If there is no available blade in the org-E pool, but one available in the org-C pool, then UCSM will use the blade from the org-C blade pool. Just as with policies, in the absence of a user-defined server pool, the default server pool associated with the organization will be used.

In general, resources and policies are not strictly owned by any particular organization, but instead are shared across all organizations in a sub-tree using a rule of "first-come, first-served".

Role-Based Access Control (RBAC)

Role-Based Access Control (RBAC) is a method of restricting or authorizing system access for users based on "roles" and "locales". A role can contain one or more system privileges where each privilege defines an administrative right to a certain object or type of object (components) in the system. By assigning a user a role, the user inherits the capabilities of the privileges defined in that role. Customers can create custom specific roles (see Table 7-8).

Table 7-8 Example of Roles

Role Name	Responsibilities	Privileges
server	Provision blades	Create, modify, and delete service profiles.
network	Configure internal and border LAN connectivity	Create, modify, and delete port channels, port groups, server pinning, and VLANs.
storage	Configure internal and border SAN connectivity	Create, modify, and delete port channels, port groups, server pinning, and VSANs.
AAA	Configure authentication, authorization, and accounting	Create, modify, and delete users, roles, and locales, with the exception of "admin" role.
admin	Any and all	Any and all. Only a user with "admin role", can create other users with "admin role".
read-only	None	Read-only access to all status and configuration.

Locales

A locale (not to be confused with the internationalization of character sets) in UCSM is designed to reflect the location of a user in an organization. A user is assigned all the privileges of his/her roles to all objects in the locale for the entire organizational sub-tree where the locale is associated. A locale describes where the privileges from the role can be exercised. By assigning an administrator a certain user role and a locale, administrators can exercise their privileges in the organizations and sub-organizations defined in the locale. Since users are not directly assigned privileges, management of individual user privileges is simply a matter of assigning the appropriate roles and locales. For example, Figure 7-30 shows server-related R/W privileges in each org. Based on Role and Locale, user "Bob" gets server administrative rights (R/W) in org "HR" and Read-Only (R) in "OE" and "Root" for server-related tasks, all non server-related tasks are Read-Only (R) in all organizations.

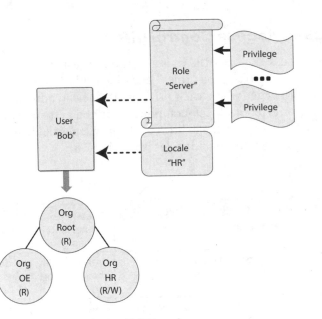

Figure 7-30   Server admin role and HR locale

Users and Authentication

The UCSM supports the creation of local users in the UCSM database as well as the integration of name services such as LDAP (AD), RADIUS, and TACACS+ for remote users. When users log into the UCSM, they are authenticated against the appropriate back-end name service and assigned privileges based on their roles.

A user assigned the "server role" performs server-related operations within the UCSM. A user assigned the network role has network privileges and manages network-related tasks. The storage role performs SAN-related operations. The scope of the AAA role is global across the UCSM. The admin role is the equivalent of the root user in a UNIX environment. The admin role has no restrictions in terms of which privileges it has on resources.

UCSM and VMware's vCenter Integration

One of many benefits with the Cisco Virtual Interface Card (VIC) (aka Palo, see "Cisco Palo®" in Chapter 4, page 124) in UCS is that it helps to off-load CPU cycles from the hypervisor, possibly removing the softswitch layer. This provides better performance and consistent network policy enforcement across the Ethernet and Fiber-Channel fabrics. This is achieved by deploying hardware-virtualized adapters in combination with the VNTag technology ("VNTag" in Chapter 3, page 86).

This section describes the support for virtualization in the management system of UCS (UCSM) and management plane integration between UCSM and VMware's vCenter (a VMware software for centralized VM and resource management).

Please note that one can deploy virtualized servers on non Cisco VIC, by using VMware's native vSwitch or Cisco's Nexus 1000 solution in a UCS environment, but that discussion is out of scope of this section, as UCSM doesn't play any active role in providing network policy control for VMs and/or providing visibility in this scenario.

Integration Architecture

The software architecture around the virtualization support can be broken in three parts:

- Virtualization support in UCSM service profile definition
- Management plane integration (UCSM and VMware vCenter)
- Runtime policy resolution for dynamic Virtual Interfaces (VIFs)

Virtualization Support

This includes discovery of VN-Link (see "FCoE (Fibre Channel over Ethernet)" in Chapter 3, page 75) hardware capable adapters, provisioning of static vNICs in service profile, and configuring VIFs (Virtual Interfaces) in Palo through the Fabric Interconnect interface. These topics and technologies have already been discussed earlier in this book. Support for integration with VMware is embedded in the service-profiles, which allows for dynamic VIFs definition and policy consumption.

Multiple dynamic vNIC connection policies can be created and each of the policies defines a number of dynamic vNICs. A service profile that consumes a dynamic vNIC connection policy, at the time of server association uses the policy to configure and pre-provision these vNIC's on the adapter in the server. For Palo, these vNICs are the pre-provisioned (stateless) uplink ports; the VM-NICs (Virtual Machine Network Interface Cards) are associated with these uplinks one-to-one dynamically as VM interfaces are created by vCenter.

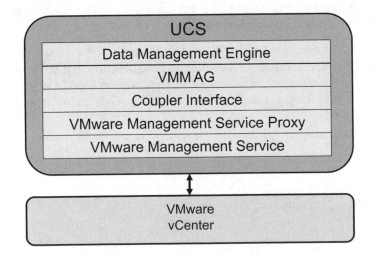

Figure 7-31   UCSM and vCenter components

Management Plane Integration

One of the benefits with the management plane integration is that it separates the role of network administrators from the server administrators in contrast to a traditional vCenter management. The network administrator can now create and define the port-profiles policies and other networking related configurations in UCSM. These port-profiles policies are visible and available to the server administrator of vCenter where he/she can choose these profiles while defining a VM or adding ESX hypervisor host in a "Data Center" (vCenter terminology for grouping and resources management of VMs). Like any policy in UCS, the profiles is identified by the names, so only the port-profile name and description are available to the server administrator. Actual network policies are opaque to the server administrator. Changes in network policy are applied to the existing set of dynamic VIFs on the Fabric Interconnect, without requiring any update in vCenter.

The integration includes a few new components (see Figure 7-31). The DME uses VMM AG (an External VM Management AG) to communicate with NX-OS components VMware Management Service Proxy (MSP) and VMware Management Service (VMS) through the Coupler Interface. VMS communicates to vCenter through VMware's SOAP APIs over HTTPS transport.

Port-Profiles

Port-profile objects within UCSM contain the properties listed in Table 7-9.

Table 7-9   Port-Profile Properties

Name	Name of the Profile
Description	Description of port profile.
Max-ports	A vCenter property, specifies maximum number of (dynamic) vNICs that can subscribe to this port-profile.
Set of networks (VLANs)	VLANs to be added as "allowed VLANs" on the corresponding VIF on the switch component.
An optional native VLAN from this set	If VM doesn't have the VLAN driver embedded in the OS, this is used as native VLAN.
QoS policy name	QoS policy to be used.
Pin group name	Pin group to be used (specifies which uplink port on the FI to be used for the given vNIC).
Port security	A flag that controls allowing forged transmission of MAC address.
Network control policy name	Network control policy to be used (various network control aspects of the adapter, such as enable / disables CDP (Cisco Discovery Protocol), behavior of the VIF when no uplink port is available in end-host-mode, etc.).

After port-profile configuration, the administrator can apply these profiles to either all the DVSes (Distributed Virtual Switches) or a subset of them. vCenter internally refers to the port-profiles by "DV Port group ID". When a profile is pushed to vCenter, UCSM obtains its corresponding port-group ID. As UCSM supports multiple DVSes, it is possible that two DVSes provide the same port-group ID for different profiles. Therefore, a combination of DVS UUID and port-group ID is treated as "profile alias", and run-time policy resolution can be done by using either port-profile names or profile aliases.

vNIC Template

A port profile is also auto created through vNIC template in UCSM. When a vNIC template with fail-over property is created, a corresponding port-profile is auto created. After that, any property changes in the vNIC template (like addition or deletion of VLANs) are reflected to that auto-generated port profile.

Runtime Policy Resolution for Dynamic VIFs

Once the port profiles are pushed to the vCenter and service profile for the ESX host is associated with a physical server, the server administrator can start managing that ESX host in the vCenter and creating Virtual Machines on the ESX host. The VMs use VMware's software vSwitch implementation by default, but in case of a UCS server with Palo adapter VMs, Service Console, and VMkernel can be "migrated" to use VN-Link in hardware. At that point, the server administrator chooses the port-profile for a given vNIC. When the VM is instantiated (or powered up) on the server, the switch software on the Fabric Interconnect receives a "VIF Create" request. This request contains port-profile name (or alias), identity of VM, hypervisor host, DVS, and DVPort. NPPM (Nuova Port Profile Manager) is a service in the DME that handles policy resolution for such VIF-Create requests (see Figure 7-32).

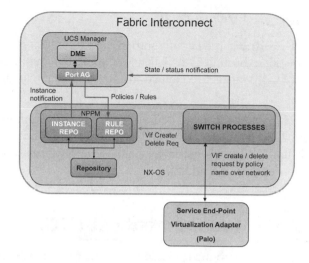

Figure 7-32   Software components of NPPM

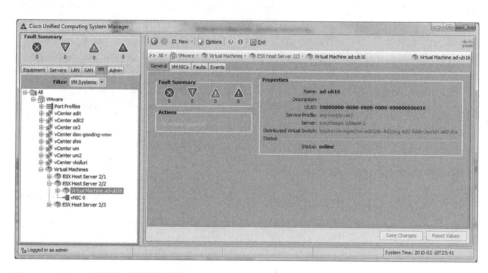

Figure 7-33   VM in UCS GUI screenshot

UCS Manager and VM in GUI

As always with UCS, the setup, configuration, and monitoring of the vCenter integration can be done through CLI, GUI, and XML API. Figure 7-33 is an example screenshot of UCS Manager expanded to show a virtual machine called "ad-ub16".

The screen also shows that the VM "ad-ub16" is currently running on an ESX host called "adit2", the ESX host is hosted by the Service Profiled called "um2" (DN=org-root/ls-um2), and it is currently running on physical server blade-2 in chassis #2 (DN=sys/chassis-2/blade-2).

Basic System Management with UCSM

The UCSM is the only component inside a UCS that contains states. All other hardware components in a UCS are stateless (except for local disk information that might contain OS and application-related states). A UCSM discovery is an ongoing process. The UCSM is always looking for new components and changes to the existing hardware configuration like insertion and removal of server, fans, power supplies, cables, etc. During the initial setup and during normal operation, an administrator can configure and change desired configurations; for example, HA vs. non-HA configuration and what ports on the Fabric Interconnect are in use for servers and infrastructure. The UCSM knows the desired configuration; for example, what ports can be connected to a chassis and what ports can be connected to the infrastructure. The UCSM leverages this information to accept or reject illegal configurations.

Hardware Management

There are two ways in which the UCSM can be updated on hardware configuration changes:

- By a discovery process typically triggered by a sensor in the system, such as a presence sensor or by a link up state change on a port
- By an AG

UCSM can ask for information from the AG, or AGs can be instructed by the UCSM to push information to UCSM when there are state changes on end-points.

Example of a Chassis Discovery Process

When a new chassis is automatically discovered, it is assigned a chassis ID. The slots, power supplies, fabric extenders, fans, etc. are all inventoried. Once the chassis is discovered and accepted, UCSM will continue to discover the presence of servers in each slot. If the presence of a server is discovered in a slot, UCSM will discover the model number, serial number, memory, number of processors, etc. The UCSM will also perform a deep discovery of the server via UCS Utility OS that also functions as a validation of components. The UCS Utility OS runs on a server prior to boot to perform diagnostics, report inventory, or configure the firmware state of the server.

Chassis Discovery

- Link on a server-facing port is discovered.
- Open basic communication to CMC (Chassis Manager Controller) in the FEX.
- Check component compatibility.
- Check that this device is supported.
- Check the serial number on the chassis, if it does exist.
  - Check if this device has been removed from management by the administrator.
  - This is a new link to existing chassis.
- If a new chassis, accept it.
- Perform discovery, such as model, firmware, fans, PSUs, slots, etc.

Discovery of Server in Chassis

- If a slot raises a state, then the slot has presence (a server is present).
- Opens communication with CIMC on the server in that slot.
- Discovers Server information, such as:
  - Vendor, model, SN, BIOS, CIMC, CPUs, memory, adapters, and local storage controller
- Boot into UCS Utility OS.
- Deep discovery via UCS Utility OS, such as:
  - Local disk info, vendor-specific adapter information
- Enforce scrubbing policies of the server.

Retirement of Hardware

Hardware can be retired by using the "Remove" function in the system. Removed components are removed from UCSM MIT (Internal Database) and, therefore, are not present in the MIM. However, UCSM does maintain a list of decommissioned serial numbers just in case an operator mistakenly reinserts a removed component. An administrator can bring decommissioned components back into control under the UCSM.

Firmware Management

Firmware management consists of keeping track of versions, dependencies, performing updates, and maintaining an inventory. It is a challenge for many data centers.

Even though a UCS has only a few types of firmware, it would still be a challenge to manage given the fact that the system supports hundreds of servers. For this reason, the UCSM has native firmware management capabilities for all the system components. For server-related firmware, these can be driven by policies and by a service profile (the firmware follows the service profile, and the blade is updated with the version specified by the firmware policy). This helps administrators perform manual or automatic firmware management of the UCS components. It also minimizes the risk of any incompatibility between the installed OS drivers and running firmware in adapters and, even in some rare cases, OS issues that are related to the BIOS version.

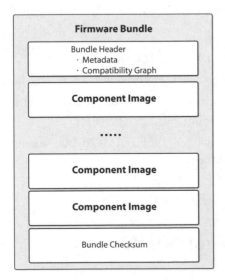

Figure 7-34   Firmware bundle

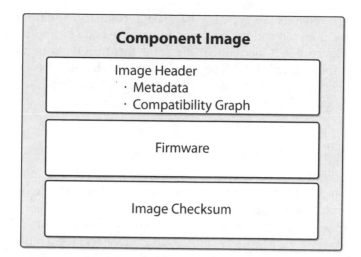

Figure 7-35 Firmware components

Firmware Download Formats

The UCS firmware images can be downloaded into two formats: as a full bundle or as a component image. A full bundle contains all the latest firmware for all supported components in a UCS (see Figure 7-34). By downloading this bundle, the administrator is guaranteed that these are the latest versions, and that they have been tested together and are supported.

A component image (see Figure 7-35) is a part of a bundle. It contains firmware for a single component type in the system, like BIOS for a server, or an adapter.

The firmware bundle and component image contain firmware, metadata, and checksum. The metadata contains information about the firmware and a compatibility graph. The compatibility graph describes the other firmware in the system that this particular firmware is compatible with. The UCS calculates a checksum for the bundle and component image. By comparing the calculated checksum against the checksum in the bundle and component image, the UCS verifies that the information in the bundle and component image is consistent and not corrupted. Corrupted bundles and component images are discarded and the administrator is notified.

New firmware versions are typically backwards compatible with at least three older versions. If an old and incompatible firmware version is detected in the system, the administrator is alerted that the component needs to be updated. The UCSM does this through a small set of golden APIs that never change between versions or during the component and firmware lifetime. Fabric Extenders are automatically upgraded to the latest version if the firmware is too old.

Firmware Life Cycle

All supported firmware for a UCS is downloadable from Cisco in the form of a bundle or component image. The operator downloads the bundle or component image from the Cisco website to a local desktop (single file). The UCSM downloads the firmware file using any of the following protocols: FTP, TFTP, SCP, or SFTP. The firmware file is stored in the Fabric Interconnect local repository. Firmware that is uploaded into the repository is automatically replicated to a standby UCSM in an HA environment.

The Fabric Interconnect unpacks the bundle or component image, verifies the checksum and reads the header. Based on the metadata in the header, the UCSM then sorts the firmware based on type and presents it to the administrator as an "installable" image.

The repository is viewed and managed using the definitions in Table 7-10.

Table 7-10 Firmware Repository Definitions

Distributable	All full bundles in the repository.
Downloaders	Where and how the UCSM downloads the firmware.
Firmware Image	A list of all components images in the repository (firmware and header).
Installables	All installable firmware in the system.

Table 7-11 and Table 7-12 are a description of firmware images in the system.

Table 7-11   UCS Firmware Images

UCS	Description/Purpose
System	This is UCSM, the embedded manager
Fabric Interconnect	Kernel
Fabric Interconnect	OS
Fabric Extenders	Chassis controller and interconnect management

Table 7-12   Server Firmware Images

Server	Description/Purpose
Management Controller	CIMC, out-of-band access to blade
BIOS	A library of basic input/output functions
Storage Controller	Local RAID controller for internal disks
Adapters	Management and protocol support
Host NIC	Third-party specific NIC firmware
Host HBA	Third-party specific HBA firmware
Host HBA OptionROM	Third-party specific OptionROM firmware

An installable image contains firmware ready to be distributed to a component. Depending on the component, the administrator typically has two ways to instruct the UCSM to install firmware to one or more components: manually or via a policy (Management Firmware Pack Policy and Host Firmware Pack Policy). Once initiated, firmware is loaded from the repository down to the component. This is fully automated and controlled by UCSM. No administrative action is needed.

Most components in the system have two firmware banks: one "Running" and one "Backup". The running bank is the current running firmware and the backup bank is the previous version of firmware. Updates to the firmware are always done to the backup firmware bank leaving the running bank untouched. The benefit with this approach is that the backup firmware bank can be updated with different firmware during production without affecting the component itself. There is a boot pointer (startup version) that identifies, to the component, which bank to load at boot time. The update procedure does not affect this boot pointer, so even

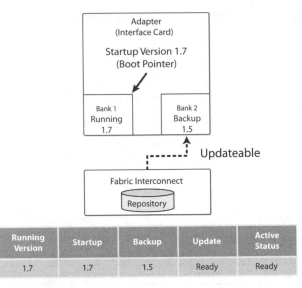

Running Version	Startup	Backup	Update	Active Status
1.7	1.7	1.5	Ready	Ready

Figure 7-36   Adapter with firmware

if the component is repowered, it will still be the same firmware as it was running previously. The boot pointer is changed via the "Activate" or "Startup" commands. When the administrator activates or starts up a certain available firmware version, the bank containing the selected firmware version will be declared startup bank.

The difference between activate and startup of the firmware is simply that activate will change the boot pointer and then reboot the component in one single command. This will force the component to boot the newly activated firmware. The startup only changes the boot pointer, but does not instruct the component to reboot, so the running version will not change.

Figure 7-36 shows an adapter with its states, including a running and backup version. The picture also shows the bank where an installable firmware would be updated.

Some components do not need two banks. For example, the firmware for the System (UCSM) and the Fabric Interconnect (OS and Kernel) do not have the concept of active and backup firmware banks. They do have the concept of a boot pointer though, and the same concept of activation and startup versions. The reason is that the firmware repository, which contains all firmware, is located in the Fabric Interconnect internal storage and therefore accessible at boot time to all of these components. They only need a boot pointer to know which firmware to boot from the repository at startup time (see Table 7-13).

Figure 7-37 shows an example of firmware activation.

Table 7-13 Firmware Status

Firmware Status	Description
Startup Version	This version will be booted at next reboot of the component. (Boot Pointer)
Running Version	This is the currently running version.
Backup Version	This is the previous running version; it is also where the installer will install the next update.

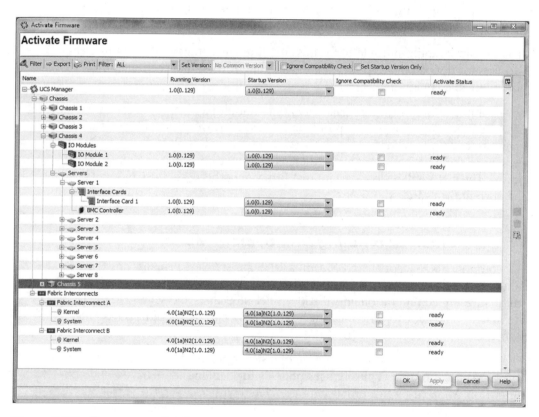

Figure 7-37 Firmware activation

Management Firmware Pack Policy

The Management Firmware Pack Policy contains management firmware images for the CIMC. A service profile that uses this policy will load the firmware to the CIMC on the server associated with that service profile.

Host Firmware Pack Policy

The Host Firmware Pack Policy contains host firmware images, like BIOS, adapters, and local storage controller. A service profile that uses this policy will load all the applicable firmware into the different components of the server associated with the service profile.

A pack can contain multiple firmwares for different components. Components that are not defined in the policy are ignored and firmware in the policy that are not applicable are ignored.

For example, a host firmware pack can contain multiple firmwares for different CNA vendors. When a service profile is associated with a particular server, the firmware pack policy (defined in the service profile) will look to see if a CNA is present in the physical server and if there is a compatible firmware defined in the policy. The CNA will be loaded with that firmware; otherwise, the CNA will keep the current firmware.

The Stateless Computing Deployment Model

All components (except the UCSM) in a UCS are stateless. This means that the components do not keep a persistent state and can be replaced at any time without losing any configuration information. Since all chassis and servers in the UCS are stateless (except for any local disk data), they can be thought of as "Just a Bunch Of Compute nodes" (JBOCs).

The service profile is a logical definition of a server personality and its connectivity. The service profile typically uses policies for defining its behavior and configuration. When a service profile gets associated with a server, the server adopts the personality and connectivity from the service profile. A service profile can be moved from one server to a different server in the same UCS (between multiple UCSes an export and import mechanism is available). To take full advantage of the flexibility of statelessness, the local disks on the servers are recommended to be used only for swap or temp space and not to store data, since it could limit the mobility of the server.

Table 7-14 Server Personality

Qualities	Number of Processors, Cores, Memory, Type of Adapters, etc.
BIOS and Firmware	The firmware running on the server and management controller.
UUID	Unique identifier of server.
MACs	MAC addresses for all defined vNICs in the service profile.
WWPNs	WWPNs for all defined vHBAs in the service profile.
WWNN	Node name for server.
Boot Settings	Where to boot from, e.g., Virtual Media, local disks, SAN, and LAN.
Local Disk Configuration	RAID level; for example, "mirror" or "best effort mirror" (if local disks are present).
vNICs	Connectivity, VLAN, HA, quality, and performance definitions.
vHBAs	Connectivity, VSAN, quality, and performance definitions.
IPMI	IPMI connectivity information.

The personality of the server includes the elements that identify that server and make it unique (see Table 7-14).

The Basic Computing Deployment Model

The UCS is very powerful due to its stateless nature. However, the UCS is also able to hide the fact that it is stateless by providing a concept of default service profiles. All configurations in the service profile are optional, except the name of the service profile itself. If a default service profile (or an empty service profile) is created and assigned to a server, the server will behave similarly to a traditional server by using pre-allocated IDs from the server itself and default values for connectivity. In this way, there is a one-to-one mapping between a physical blade and its identity. Policies can be defined so that the UCSM can automatically create default service profiles associated with newly discovered servers. That way, a UCS behaves similarly to a traditional server system.

System Setup—Initial Setup

Table 7-15 describes a few configuration questions that need to be answered before the system is ready for use.

Table 7-15   Configuration Questions

Questions	Description
Installation method	Initial installation via GUI or CLI
Setup mode	Restore from backup (Recover) or initial setup
System configuration type	Standalone or cluster configuration
System name	Unique system name, e.g., My_UCS
Admin password	Password for the initial administrator "admin"
Management port IP address and subnet mask	Static IP or DHCP

Once the initial setup is complete, the system is ready for use. From this point, all policies and configurations made by the administrator will depend on the deployment model in the data center. Basic deployment is similar to a traditional environment (via default service profiles), or of true stateless deployment (via service profiles). A hybrid implementation is also possible where certain servers are treated like a traditional server, and others are stateless.

The sections "The Default Computing Deployment Model" on page 274 and "The Stateless Computing Deployment Model", on page 275, both in Chapter 7, contain two extreme models: the very basic and the stateless model. The UCS enables the data center administrator to decide to what extent and for which system they want stateless deployment.

The Default Computing Deployment Model

In this deployment model, there is only "the administrator" of the UCS. The administrator uses the built-in admin account and can perform any operator task as needed. The administrator may set up the basic behavior of system. For example:

- Communication services (call home, interfaces, and protocols disable, enable) policies
- Faults, events, audit logs, collection retention periods, intervals, policies, etc.
- Statistical collection intervals and reporting policies

Servers are treated as traditional servers and are automatically configured for default service profiles. Each server runs its dedicated software and there is a one-to-one relationship between the service profile and the actual server. This means that the servers are using pre-defined values and IDs derived from hardware (MAC addresses, WWNNs, WWPNs, UUIDs).

If the server goes down and needs to be replaced (the software might have been protected through a cluster solution), there are probably some infrastructure components affected by the replacement of the server. A network service that depends on a MAC address needs to be reconfigured. SAN-attached storage is typically zoned based on WWPN and access layers in the storage device are typically defined based on WWPN, so this needs to be reconfigured before the production can restart on the OS instance.

The Stateless Computing Deployment Model

The administrator may change the default configuration system behavior in the following areas:

- Authorization policies (Local, LDAP (AD), RADIUS, TACACS+)
- Define an organizational structure for resource management
- Define subject matter expert administrators, for example:
  - Network administrators
  - Storage administrators
  - Server administrators
  - Operations administrators

Depending on the customer and the organization, these tasks might be performed by a subject matter expert administrator, but restricted by RBAC in his or her organization:

- Communication services (call home, interfaces, and protocols disable, enable) policies
- Faults, events, audit logs, collection retention periods, intervals, policies, etc.
- Statistical collection intervals and reporting policies

Typically, before a UCS is ready for full stateless deployments of a server and compute resource, there are policy definitions and rules that need to be configured. The configurations are mainly done upfront. They typically involve multiple different administrators. These administrators are experts in their own areas, like network, storage, server, application/software, or business service administrators.

Leveraging RBAC (users, roles, privileges, and possible organizations and locales), the administrators are responsible for setting up the wanted behavior via policies in their responsibility area.

What follows is an example of responsibilities and tasks that the administrators would set up prior to production. Once set up, the system is automatically driven by policies and rules.

Network Administration

A network administrator performs UCS internal network-related tasks by defining policies that describe the required configuration or behavior to connect servers to external networks, including:

- Configure an uplink port
- Configure port channels
- Configure PIN (PINning) groups (containing Ethernet ports)
- Create VLANs
- Configure the QoS classes (see Figure 7-38)
- Configure QoS definitions based on the QoS classes (see Figure 7-39)
- Create MAC address pools
- Create network-related threshold policies for faults, alarms, and statistics
- Create NIC adapter profiles

Storage Administration

A storage administrator performs UCS internal storage related tasks by defining policies that describe the required configuration or behavior to connect servers to an external SAN, including:

- Configure PIN (PINning) groups (containing Fibre Channel ports)
- Create VSANs
- Configure the quality of service classes (QoS Classes)
- Create storage-related thresholds, policies for faults, alarms, and statistics
- Create WWPN address pools
- Create WWNN address pools
- Create vHBA policies (see Figure 7-40)

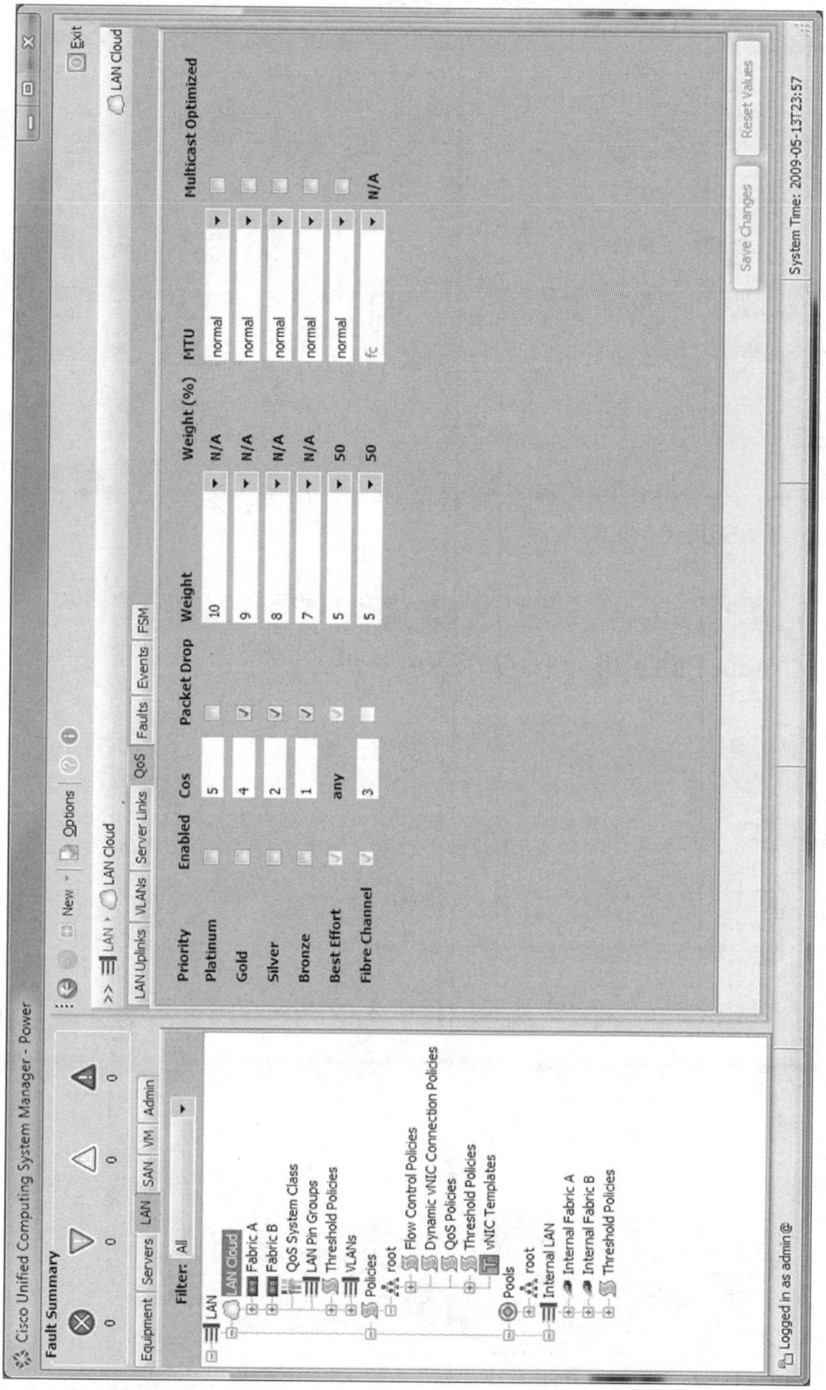

Figure 7-38 QoS configuration

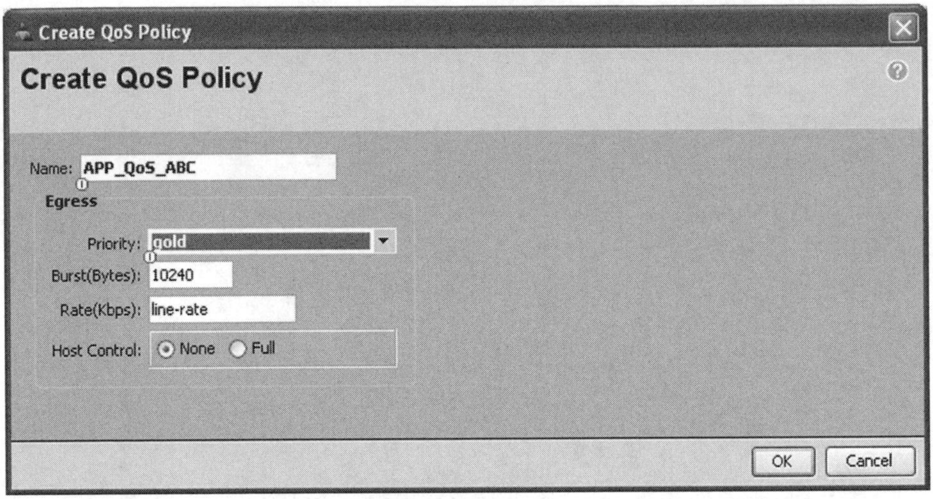

Figure 7-39   QoS policy definition

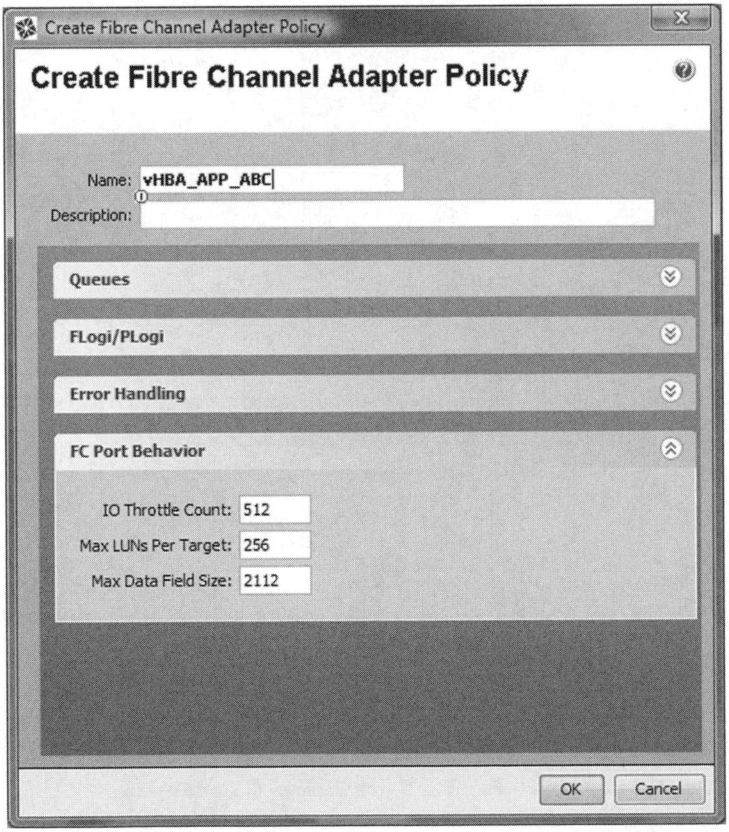

Figure 7-40   vHBA policies

Server Administration

A server administrator performs server management-related tasks by defining policies that describe the required configuration or behavior to instantiate service profiles within the system, including:

- Create server pools
- Create pool policies and pool qualification policies
- Create scrub policies
- Create IPMI policies
- Create firmware pack for host and management
- Create server-related threshold policies for faults, alarms, and statistics
- Create service profile templates

Production

The normal day-to-day production work is minimal, since most components, configurations, and system behaviors are defined prior to production. Network and Storage administrators rarely need to go in and make changes to policies.

Many policies like QoS, adapters, thresholds, and qualification policies are application-dependent. To clarify, an SLA (Service Level Agreement) related to a business service (applications like HR, Finance, Order Entry, etc.) typically dictates the required qualities (HA, performance, portability, etc.) for compute resources (servers) that host the business service. These application needs are described in the form of policies. When new applications are introduced into the UCS, it is recommended that policies describing the requirements for the particular application or business service be created. That way, the likelihood of an important business service being affected by a less-important application or software is reduced.

Day-to-Day Server Administration

Day-to-day server management-related tasks within the system include tasks like:

- Create service profiles from existing templates
- Power on/off a server
- Move a service profile between servers
- Back up the system
- Monitor the logs
- Firmware maintenance

Requirements for Stateless Service Profiles

The service profile provides a compute service for software and business services, therefore the creation of a service profile and its qualities typically originate from the requirements of the application. To illustrate this better, let's make up an application "ABC" with reasonable requirements.

It is a business-critical application that needs high availability and high performance. It also needs to be able to scale out quickly in case of unexpected production peaks. The nature of the application in this example is the one of a database that receives many SQL queries and works with large amounts of data. The application administrator understands the behavior of the application well, for example, that a particular application is storage I/O intensive and it requires a large amount of memory, but the network traffic load is average.

To summarize, the application has these requirements:

- High availability
- Memory intensive
- Storage I/O intensive
- Large amount of storage
- Average network traffic load
- Ability to scale out quickly

In this scenario, there might be up to four different administrators who define together a service profile, to accommodate all the application requirements.

High Availability

The UCS provides multiple levels of HA, from redundant Fabric Interconnects, I/O paths, power supplies, and hardware NIC failover. Table 7-17 describes different HA components, policies, etc.

Memory

The UCS supports heterogeneous memory configuration on the servers. If an application or a business service require a minimum amount of memory, this can be defined in a server pool qualification policy, as the one in Table 7-16.

Table 7-16   Example of a Server Pool Qualification Policy

Minimum RAM	Description	Policy	Admin
Server	The server admin uses the same server qualification policy "APP_HW_Req_ABC" (from the adapter requirement) to add the minimum memory requirements.	Server pool and qualification policy: "APP_HW_Req_ABC"	Server

Table 7-17 Example of HA Component Policies

Redundancy	Description	Policy	Administrator
Fabric Interconnects	The server administrator needs to confirm that the system in question is configured for Fabric Interconnect redundancy (clustered).	NA Physical requirement	Server
I/O Paths & Adapters	The server administrator needs to confirm that the system in question is configured for I/O and Adapter HA.	NA Physical requirement	Server
Power Supplies	The server administrator needs to confirm if the system has redundant power supplies.	NA Physical requirement	Server
Hardware NIC Failover	There must be at least one VLAN configured in each Fabric Interconnect; this is done through a VLAN policy. Here the network administrator creates the VLAN Policy "Prod_ABC", which defines VLANs. The hardware failover configuration is defined in a policy definition. The vNIC Template is the policy configuration; the network administrator therefore creates the vNIC Policy "APP_vNIC_ABC". Please note that the network administrator will define this policy so it get its MAC address definition from the pool "APP_MAC_PROD".	VLAN: "Prod_VLAN_ABC"* vNIC Template:"APP_vNIC_ABC"	Network

Redundancy	Description	Policy	Administrator
Storage paths, Storage, dual SAN fabrics.	This is a storage implementation requirement as well as a UCS requirement. The storage administrator needs to confirm that dual fabrics are used, as well as a fault tolerant storage array, and that proper RAID configuration is present on the LUNs. The UCS needs to provide multiple FC adapters for redundant FC paths. The server administrator creates a "server pool qualification policy". ("APP_HW_Req_ABC") to make sure the server will meets the requirements and a "Server Pool policy" ("Populate_ABC_SRV_APP") that defines which pool a qualifying server should be a member of. The storage administrator also needs to make sure there is at least one vSAN defined in each Fabric Interconnect to provide dual fabric connectivity. This is done through a vSAN policy ("Prod_VSAN_ABC").	Server Pool: "APP_SRV_ABC" Server Pool qualification policy: "APP_HW_Req_ABC" Server Pool Policy: "Populate_ABC_APP" VSAN: "Prod_VSAN_ABC"**	Server and Storage
OS and Application	The server administrator and the application administrator will need to make sure the proper drivers are installed in the OS, and that the application is configured correctly.	NA	Server and Application

continues

Server mobility via service profiles, shorten time to fix, and maintenance windows.	If the server goes down and needs to be replaced, the service profile should be able to quickly be started on a different server.	UUID Pool: "APP_UUID_PROD"****	Server
	The server administrator creates a UUID pool, to make sure the service profile can receive a portable UUID ("APP_UUID_PROD").	MAC Pool: "APP_MAC_PROD"****	Network
	The network administrator creates a MAC pool ("APP_MAC_PROD"), to make sure the service profile can receive portable MAC addresses.	WWN Pool "APP_WWN_PROD"****	Storage
	The storage administrator creates a WWN pool ("APP_WWN_PROD"), to make sure the service profile can receive portable WWN addresses.		

* Please note that multiple VLAN policies can point to the same VLAN ID.

** Please note that multiple VSAN policies can point to the same VSAN ID.

*** Please note that overlapping pools are allowed, pools can overlap other pools with same IDs, and it is possible to create a separate pool for each application if desired.

Storage I/O Intensive

This requirement, together with portability and large amount of data, builds the case for SAN attached storage (see Table 7-18).

Table 7-18   Example of Storage Policy

Component	Description	Policy	Admin
vHBA	The storage administrator creates vHBA template to describe the quality requirement for the vHBA ("APP_vHBA_ABC"). Please note that the storage admin defined this policy so it get its WWN definition from the pool "APP_WWN_PROD".	vHBA Template: "APP_vHBA_ABC"	Storage

Average Network Load

Even though the network load requirement was average, given the importance of the application, there is a need to make sure that this application has higher priority than regular applications. This may come in handy if there is an ill-behaved application or suddenly a non-important application starts to utilize the network heavily (see Table 7-19).

Table 7-19   Example of Network Policy

Component	Description	Policy	Admin
vNIC	The network administrator creates a QoS of priority class gold (second-highest priority); this ensures that any application in silver, bronze, or best-effort classes will not affect the application ("APP_QoS_ABC").	QoS Policy: "APP_QoS_ABC"	Network

Ability to Scale Out Quickly

Since all of the definitions are policies, service profiles and service templates can leverage them. A "service profile template" is a natural choice to meet this requirement of scaling out of server resources. A service profile template is similar to a service profile, with the exception that it cannot be associated with a server. It is used for instantiating new service profiles. By using a template, any administrator can easily create a compute resource that meets the requirement of the business service (see Table 7-20).

Table 7-20   Example of a Service Profile Template

Component	Description	Policy	Admin
Service Profile Template	The server administrator creates the service profile template, and defines all the policies that have been created by the various administrators for the application ABC ("APP_ABC").	Service Profile Template: "APP_ABC"	Server

No Pre-Defined Policies

Table 7-21 might be an extreme scenario with no pre-defined policies.

Table 7-21   Examples of Policies and Templates

Policy/Template	Name
MAC Pool	APP_MAC_PROD
vHBA Template	APP_vHBA_ABC
vNIC Template	APP_vNIC_ABC
QoS Policy	APP_QoS_ABC
Server Pool	APP_SRV_ABC
Server Pool Qualification Policy	APP_HW_Req_ABC
Server Pool Policy	Populate_ABC_APP
UUID Pool	APP_UUID_PROD
VLAN Policy	Prod_VSAN_ABC
VSAN Policy	Prod_VSAN_ABC
WWN Pool	APP_WWN_PROD
Service Profile Template	APP_ABC

These policies and templates have been created, by the administrators based on the application requirement. This is just to illustrate how a service profile gets defined, and some of the different policies it can include. As described earlier, the UCS allows a service profile to be created with minimum configuration and no policies.

Figure 7-41 illustrates how these definitions are related and connected to make up the service profile. This picture shows how the vHBA and vNIC templates are consuming other policies and how the server pools are automatically populated via a server pool qualification and a server pool policy.

Figure 7-42 shows how policies are related to the service profile template, and then instantiated to multiple service profiles.

Figure 7-43 shows a vNIC template. Please note that the target can be a physical server (Adapter) or a VMware virtual machine (VM).

System Logging

The UCSM logs all events, faults, and Audit information in the system. These logs can be exported to an external system. Events can also be subscribed to. This is useful for monitoring tools that integrate with the UCS.

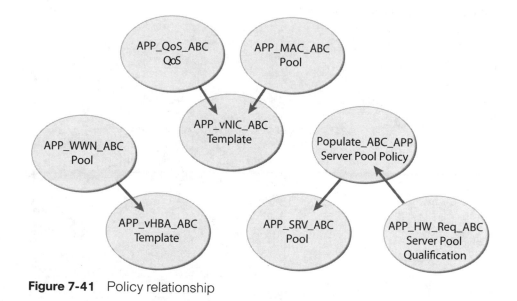

Figure 7-41   Policy relationship

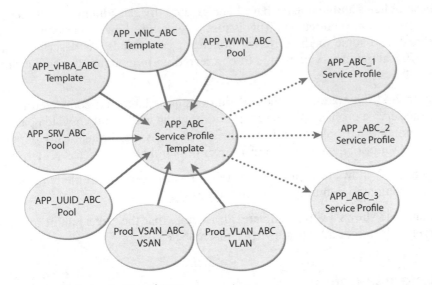

Figure 7-42 Policies in templates

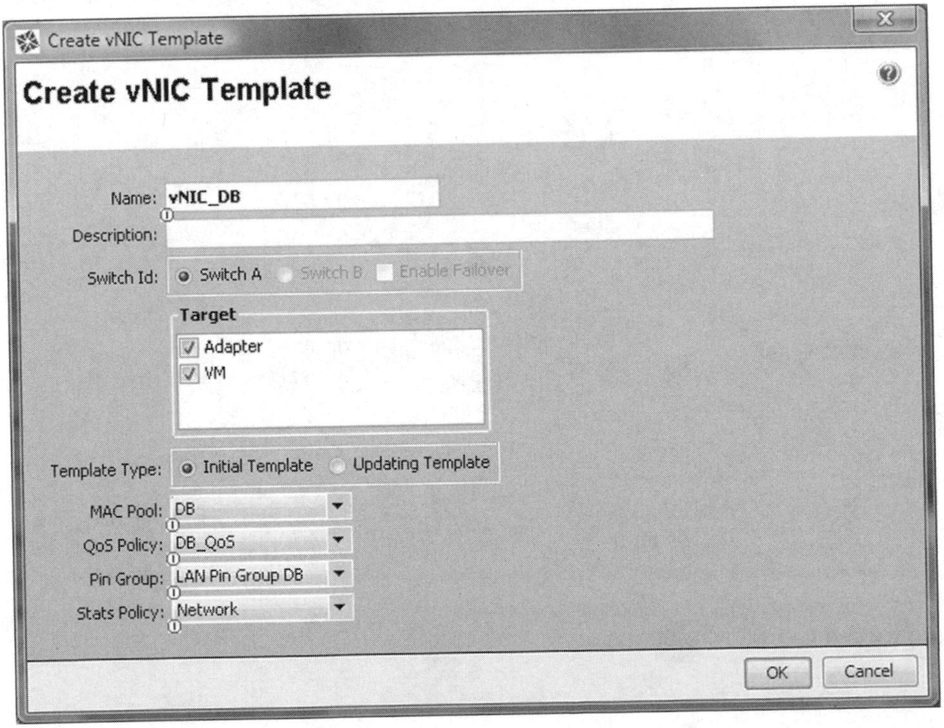

Figure 7-43 vNIC template

Faults and Events

UCS Manager exploits generic object notifications in the management of events and faults. An event is a representation of something that shortly occurred in the system. A fault represents something that failed in the system (or that got created by the triggering of an alarm threshold). Events and faults are both objects that are managed by UCS Manager and are subject to the same base set of rules as other MOs. However, events and faults have additional rules that specifically apply to them.

Events

Events are immutable as managed objects because they correspond to non-persistent conditions in the system. Once an event is created and logged, it does not change. For example, the beginning and ending states of a blade power-on request are logged as events, indicating that UCS Manager has started and completed the request (see Figure 7-44).

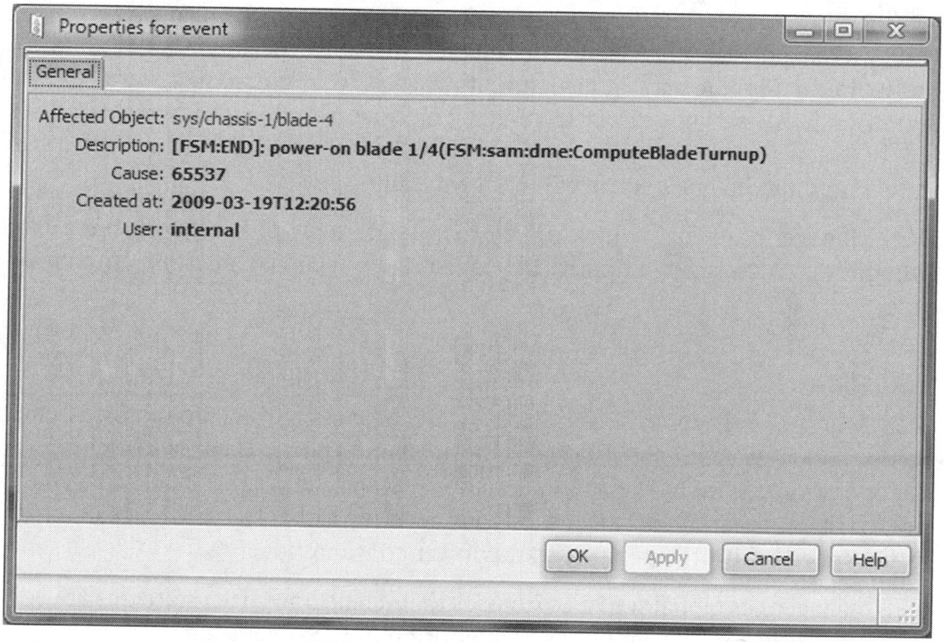

Figure 7-44   Power-on

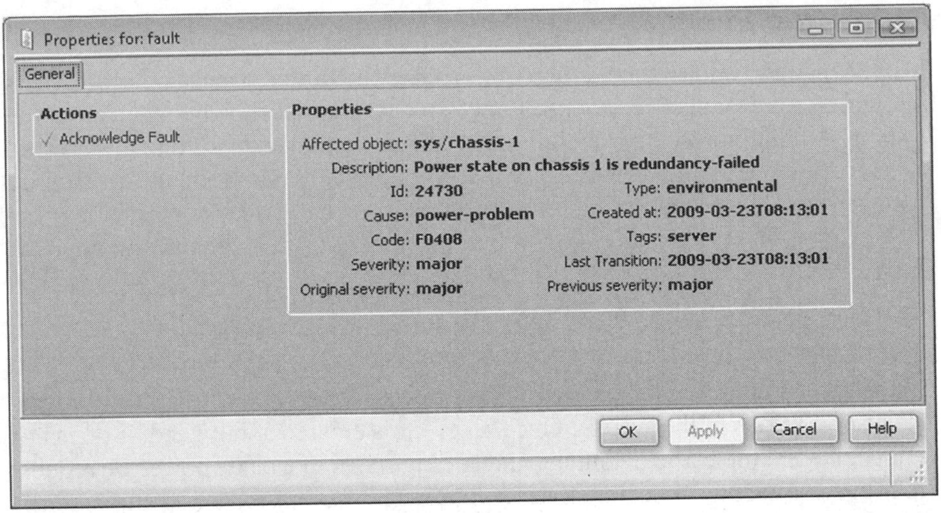

Figure 7-45 Power problem

Faults

Fault MOs, on the other hand, are mutable because the operational state of the faulted endpoint may, at any time, transition to a functioning state. A corrected fault is known as a cleared fault. For example, physically unplugging a link between a fabric extender and a switch will put the switch port into a faulted state. Plugging the link back in will clear this fault (see Figure 7-45).

UCS Manager has a global fault policy that defines how to handle cleared faults (whether to delete them automatically or to retain them for a certain amount of time).

Statistics

UCS Manager collects various device-specific statistics from the managed endpoints, including adapters, blades, chassis, hosts, and ports. These statistics reflect the operational state of the endpoints. For example, an adapter maintains counters for the number of packets it sends and receives. Other statistics include chassis fan speeds, CPU temperatures, and power consumption.

UCS manager has global statistics policies that define how often statistics are collected from each of the endpoints and reported to UCS Manager.

Thresholds

A threshold policy in UCS Manager defines values for what is considered "normal", "above normal", and "below normal" for any of the statistics that have been collected. The policy also describes the severity (e.g., warning or critical) of the deviation from the normal value. When a statistic reaches an above-normal or below-normal value (known as an escalating value), UCS Manager will create a fault MO with the corresponding severity. When the statistic value crosses a de-escalating value, UCS Manager will clear the fault.

Audit Log

The UCSM audits both direct and indirect user actions in the same way as it audits events. User actions are representative of an event that occurred "momentarily" in the system. These events can be based on a user action such as a creation, deletion, or modification of an object. As with all other objects in the system, they are exportable (see Figure 7-46).

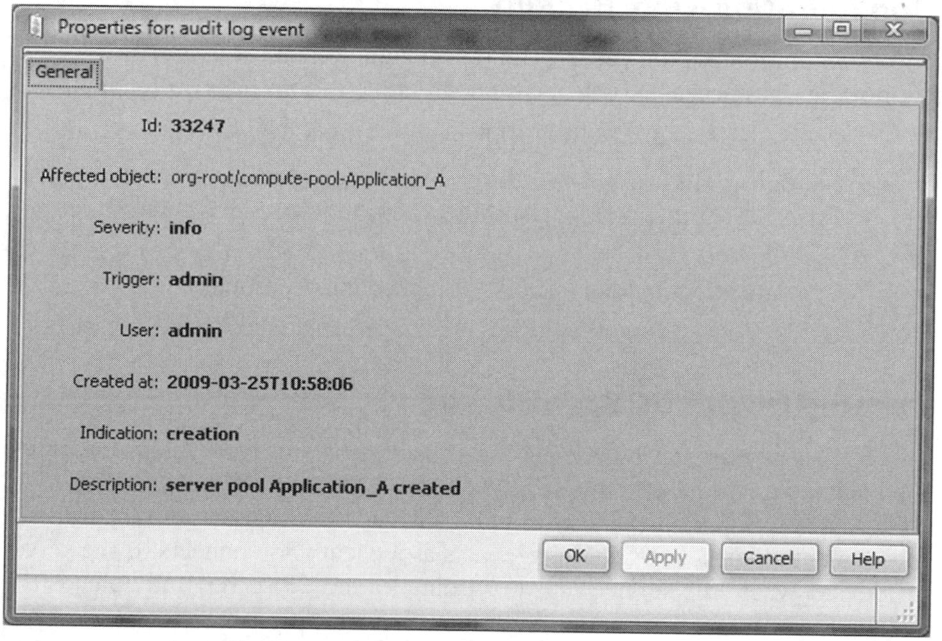

Properties for: audit log event

General

Id: **33247**

Affected object: org-root/compute-pool-Application_A

Severity: **info**

Trigger: **admin**

User: **admin**

Created at: **2009-03-25T10:58:06**

Indication: **creation**

Description: **server pool Application_A created**

OK   Apply   Cancel   Help

Figure 7-46   Audit log entry

Backup and Restore of UCS Manager

UCSM stores all the object information and their states in a local database; in a HA-configuration, the database is always replicated to the peer Fabric Interconnect, and each Fabric Interconnect contains a running database. The data stored in the database can be backed up or restored. There are currently two available options for backup:

- Full state backup
- Configuration-only backup

Full State Backup

The full state backup performs a full backup. This backup includes current operational states (Runtime states) like servers current power state, and all the configuration information (Objects like Service Profiles, Policies, Pool information, etc.). This is a complete backup of the object model.

Configuration-Only Backup

The configuration backup captures all the configuration information of the UCS, but not the runtime state. There are three different options on what to back up:

- **Configuration all**—Backs up all configuration information.
- **Configuration Logical**—Backs up up all configuration information but not AAA (Authentication, Authorization, and Accounting) related information.
- **Configuration System**—All AAA-related information.

Backing Up the UCS

The UCS Manager (see Figure 7-47) can back up to many different locations; the backups (and restores) are done via FTP, TFTP, SCP, or SFTP sessions. The UCS Manager can connect to any type of device that supports any of the protocols mentioned. The UCS Manager acts as a client and connects to the server (or device) where the service runs (for example, an FTP server) and uploads the backup file.

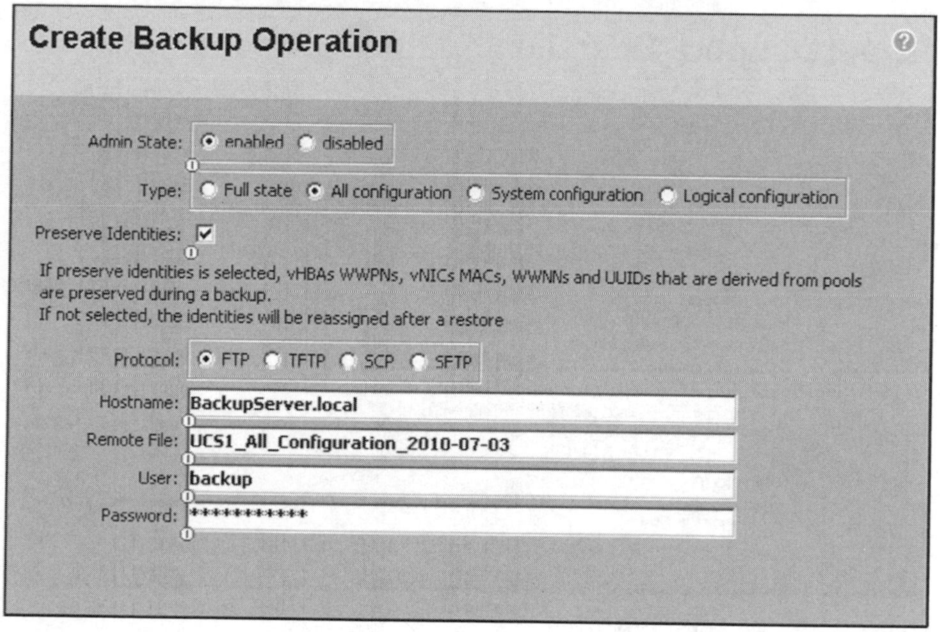

Create Backup Operation

Admin State: ⦿ enabled ○ disabled

Type: ○ Full state ⦿ All configuration ○ System configuration ○ Logical configuration

Preserve Identities: ☑

If preserve identities is selected, vHBAs WWPNs, vNICs MACs, WWNNs and UUIDs that are derived from pools are preserved during a backup.
If not selected, the identities will be reassigned after a restore

Protocol: ⦿ FTP ○ TFTP ○ SCP ○ SFTP

Hostname: BackupServer.local

Remote File: UCS1_All_Configuration_2010-07-03

User: backup

Password: ***********

Figure 7-47   Backup screenshot

Restoring a Full State Backup

The Full State Restore is a complete restore, and it is run on a non-configured UCS. One of the first options during an initial installation of a UCS is restoring from the backup.

Restoring a Configuration-Only Backup

The restore is very similar to the backup process (see Figure 7-48). The client software running inside the Fabric Interconnect downloads the specified backup file and perform the restore.

During the restore process (also known as Import Operation), there are two options available:

- **Merge**—Will merge data from backup with existing objects and create any non-existing object.
- **Replace**—Will overwrite the current configuration.

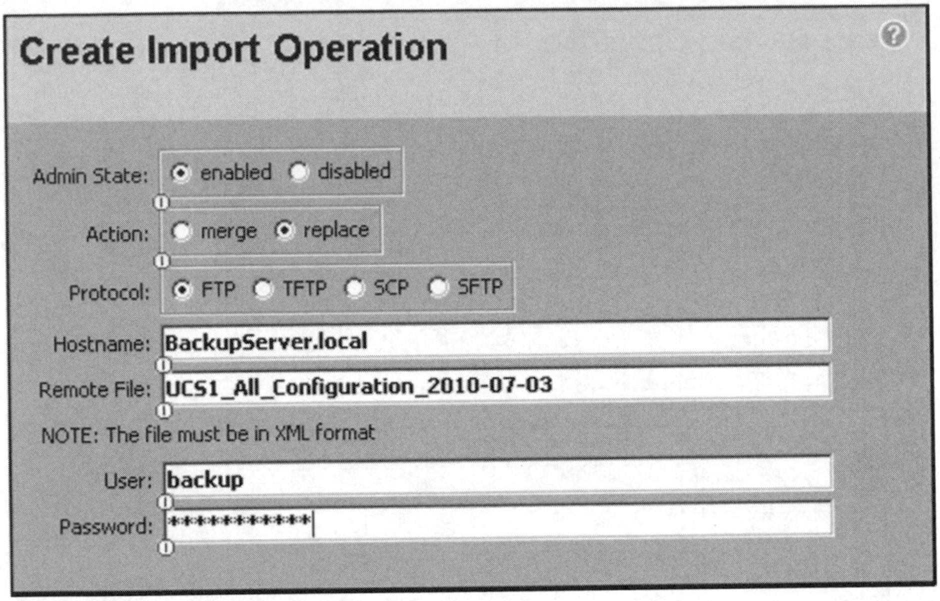

Create Import Operation   (?)

Admin State: (•) enabled ( ) disabled

Action: ( ) merge (•) replace

Protocol: (•) FTP ( ) TFTP ( ) SCP ( ) SFTP

Hostname: `BackupServer.local`

Remote File: `UCS1_All_Configuration_2010-07-03`

NOTE: The file must be in XML format

User: `backup`

Password: `***********`

Figure 7-48   Restore screenshot

Integrating with UCS

The UCS has many powerful standard interfaces for monitoring and management. The native XML (Extensible Markup Language) API is the recommended interface for integration, since it provides a full-featured interface for all features and capabilities in the UCS.

This section provides a brief overview of the XML API interface and some of the tools available to developers who are using the XML API. The XML API is fully documented and supported for customer and partners to develop and integrate third-party applications.

The XML API provides some powerful capabilities, typically not seen in other device manager software on the market.

The XML API provides complete coverage of all functionalities. It is a hierarchical, generic, and content-driven interface. The XML API terminates on a single data model that provides a single, complete object tree with all components and their functionalities in the UCS. The XML API is transactional, which means that each call is treated as a transaction, and it is rolled back in case of a failure. The transactional capability together with the hierarchical capability allows a developer to perform any number of object manipulations as a single transaction.

Let's take an extreme example. Let's say that a developer wants to create three different vLAN policies, two vSAN policies, create a service profile, power-on an existing server, all as a single transaction, and undo everything if any of the seven tasks fails.

In a traditional device manager, the developer would have to make at least seven different API calls (one for each task) from his/her code, and perform a check after each call to see if it succeeded or not. If any of the different calls failed (maybe the Service Profile already existed), the developer would need to take care of this in his own code, to delete any newly created policies, etc.

Using the XML API, this can easily be done with a single API call. The call will return success or failure for the entire call, and any rollbacks are done automatically by the UCSM.

Since the XML API is hierarchical and transactional, it allows a developer to configure and perform any operational tasks on a UCS with a single API call.

UCS Manager XML API

The UCS API interface accepts XML documents sent over HTTP or HTTPS. Client developers can use any programming language to generate XML documents containing UCS API methods.

The UCS Manager API follows an object model-based approach, which distinguishes it from a traditional function call-based API. Instead of using a unique API function for each exposed task, the UCS responds to state changes made through the API (XML documents). UCS configuration and state information is represented in a hierarchical tree structure known as the management information tree; this tree is completely exposed through the XML API.

The UCS API model is recursively driven. As an example, changes can be made to a single object, to an object subtree, or to the entire object tree. Thus, you can change a single attribute on a UCS object, or set up the entire UCS structure (including configurations for chassis, blades, adaptors, policies, and software components) using a single API call.

For additional ease of use, the UCS XML API operates in "forgiving mode." This means that any missing attributes are substituted with default values (if applicable) by the internal data management engine (DME), and incorrect attributes received by the DME are ignored. If you are configuring multiple managed objects (such as virtual NICs), and if any one of the managed objects cannot be configured, the API stops its operation, returns the configuration to its prior state, and reports an error.

The UCS XML API operates in an asynchronous fashion to improve scalability and performance. Processes that require time to complete are non-blocking so that faster API processes can proceed.

The UCS API also enables full event subscription for non-statistical data. After subscription, the DME informs of any event that occurs, and provides the attribute change and its type of state change. Updates to managed objects and properties of the UCS Manager API interface will conform to the existing object model to ensure backward compatibility. If existing properties are changed during a product upgrade, this will be handled during the database load after the upgrade. New properties will be assigned default values.

Calls are done via a HTTP post (or HTTPS). UCS uses TCP 80 for HTTP (and 443 for HTTPS) by default; however, the UCS supports configuring HTTP and HTTPS to use different port numbers. The HTTP envelope contains the XML configuration.

UCS XML API Object Naming

An object can be identified by its distinguished name (DN) or by its relative name (RN); see "Management Information Model" in Chapter 7, page 232.

Method Categories

There are mainly four method categories used to interact with the UCS. Each API is a method, and each method corresponds to an XML document. The most common methods are:

- Authentication methods
- Query methods
- Configuration methods
- Event Subscription methods

Authentication Methods

Authentication methods authenticate and maintain the session (see Table 7-22).

Table 7-22 Authentication Methods

aaaLogin	Initial method for logging into the UCS, session creation, and returns a cookie.
aaaRefresh	Refreshes the current authentication cookie.
aaaLogout	Invalidates the current authentication cookie and closes the session.

Authentication methods initiate and maintain a session with the UCS. The UCS requires that a successful authentication be performed before other API calls are allowed. XML API requests made to the UCS are cookie-authenticated. To get a valid cookie, login using the aaaLogin method, use the aaaRefresh method to maintain the session, and use the aaaLogout method to terminate the session and invalidate the cookie.

The cookie retrieved from aaaLogin method is valid for two hours. The cookie should be refreshed within the session period (10 minutes) to prevent the cookie from expiring. Each refresh operation provides a new cookie valid for the default interval.

Query Methods

Query methods obtain information on the current configuration state of a UCS object (see Table 7-23). Most query methods have the argument inHierarchical, whose value is either true or false. If true, the inHierarchical argument returns all the child objects. Many query methods also have an inRecursive argument that specifies whether the call should be recursive; that is, follow objects that point back to other objects or the parent object.

Table 7-23 Query Methods

configResolveDN	Retrieves objects by distinguished name
configResolveDNs	Retrieves objects by a set of distinguished names
configResolveClass	Retrieves objects of a given class
configResolveClasses	Retrieves objects of multiple classes
configFindDNsByClassId	Retrieves the distinguished names of a specified class
configResolveChildren	Retrieves the child objects of an object
configResolveParent	Retrieves the parent object of an object
configScope	Performs class queries on a distinguished name in the management information tree

Query Filters

The UCS XML API provides a set of filters that increase the usefulness of the query methods. These filters can be passed as part of a query and are used to identify the result set that you want. Filters are categorized as follows:

- Simple filters
- Property filters
- Composite filters
- Modifier filters

Simple Filters

There are two simple filters: the true filter and false filter. These two filters react to the simple states of true or false, respectively.

Property Filters

Property filters use the values of an object's properties as the criteria for inclusion in a result set (see Table 7-24). To create most property filters, the classId and propertyId of the target object/property are required, along with a value for comparison.

Table 7-24   Property Filters

Greater than or Equal	Restricts the result set to those objects in which the identified property is greater than or equal to the provided property value.
Greater than	Restricts the result set to those objects in which the identified property is greater than the provided property value.
Inequality	Restricts the result set to those objects in which the identified property is not equal to the provided property value.
Less than	Restricts the result set to those objects in which the identified property is less than the provided property value.
Less than or Equal	Restricts the result set to those objects in which the identified property is less than or equal to the provided property value.
Equality	Restricts the result set to those objects in which the identified property is equal to the provided property value.
Wildcard	Restricts the result set to those objects in which the identified property matches a provided property value. To create a wild-card filter, the classId and propertyId of the target object/property are required, along with a wild-card value for comparison. Supported wildcards include: "%" or "*" (meaning any sequence of characters), "?" or "-" (meaning any single character).

All bits	Restricts the result set to those objects in which the identified property has all the passed bits set. Use this only on bitmask properties.
Any bits	Restricts the result set to those objects in which the identified property has at least one of the passed bits set. Use this only on bitmask properties.

Composite Filters

Available composite filters are listed in Table 7-25.

Table 7-25   Composite Filters

AND	Restricts the result set to those objects that pass the filtering criteria of each of the composite's component filters. For example, you can use a composite filter to obtain all of the compute blades with totalMemory greater than 64 megabytes and operability of "operable." In this case, the filter is composed of one greater than filter and one equality filter.
OR	Restricts the result set to those objects that pass the filtering criteria of at least one of the composite's component filters. For example, you can use a composite filter to obtain all the service profiles that have an assignmentState of unassigned or that have an association state value of unassociated. In this case, the filter is composed of two equality filters.
XOR	Restricts the result set to those objects that pass the filtering criteria of no more than one of the composite's component filters.
Between	Restricts the result set to those objects that fall between the range of the first specified value and second specified value. For example, you could find all the faults that occurred between two dates.

Modifier Filters

Modifier filters change the results of a contained filter. Only one modifier filter is supported: the NOT filter. This filter negates the result of a contained filter. You can use this filter to obtain objects that do not match contained criteria.

Configuration Methods

The XML API interface provides several methods for making configuration changes to managed objects. You can apply changes to the whole tree or to one or more sub-trees instead of individual objects.

The configuration methods are listed in Table 7-26.

Table 7-26   Configuration Methods

configConfMo	Affects a single subtree (from distinguished name)
configConfMos	Affects multiple subtrees (from distinguished names)
configConfMoGroup	Makes the same configuration changes to multiple objects of the same class

Event Subscription Methods

Every time an object mutates (i.e., it is created, modified, or deleted) because of a user-initiated action or a system-initiated action, an event is generated. There are typically two ways for applications to get information on state changes: by polling on regular intervals or by event subscription.

Polling is easy to implement but very expensive in terms of network resources and should be used only as a last resort. Event subscription allows a client application to register for event notification from the UCS. By being subscribed, when an event occurs, the UCS informs the client application of the event and its type.

In addition, the UCS sends only the delta (actual change) and not the object's unaffected attributes. This applies to all object changes in the system.

The eventSubscribe method is used to register for events. To use event subscription, open an HTTP or HTTPS session over TCP and keep the session open; the UCS will start sending all new events as they occur. Each event has a unique event ID. These event IDs operate as counters, and are included in all method responses. Each time an event is generated, the event ID counter increases and the new event is assigned a new event ID. This enables the subscriber to keep track of the events. This also assures the subscriber that no event is missed; however, if an event is missed by the client, the client can use the eventSendEvent method to retrieve a missed event. The subscriber can also use the event sync method called logging-Sync0cns, which allows for retrieving a bulk missing events by specifying from and to event IDs.

UCS Platform Emulator

At the time this was written, the Emulator was not yet available to end customers. Currently there are a few numbers of key partners using the emulator for development.

The emulator was originally developed to enable us to start our development of UCS Manager prior to the availability of the UCS hardware. It was also used as a conceptual model of managed endpoints, and it has been around for a few years as an internal engineering tool. Its architecture is illustrated in Figure 7-49.

The emulator emulates the entire set of Device Endpoints under UCS Manager, like:

■ Fabric Interconnects

■ Board Management Controllers

■ Chassis Management Controllers

■ I/O Adapters

■ VMware Virtual Center (VM port profiles)

■ UCS Utility OS

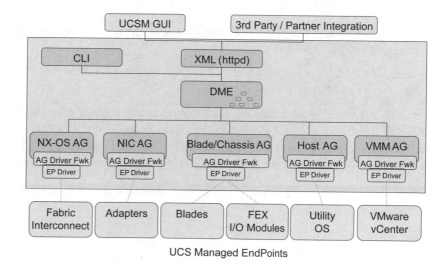

Figure 7-49 Simplified UCS Manager architecture

There are many benefits with the emulator, one of the obvious ones is that it minimizes the need to have access to real UCS hardware; however, actual test and quality assurance still need to be performed on a real system. The other benefits the emulator can bring are fault injection, emulation of large-scale deployments, and complete customizable equipment inventory that are very valuable for developers.

The emulator is built from the very same source code of the real system. The difference is that in the emulator environment the physical endpoints have been replaced by a second DME, which emulates the responses from the real endpoints (see Figure 7-50). The upper DME in the emulator is the very same DME running in a real Fabric Interconnect. The DME is not aware of the fact that it is communicating with an emulated environment, so all calls made to the emulator are identical to calls made to a UCS Manager in a real system.

In addition to XML documentation, examples, and schemas, UCS also provides some simple but very powerful tools that a developer can use to learn how to construct XML API calls.

The UCS GUI is leveraging the XML API and it has logging capabilities, so it is possible to perform a task in the UCS Manager GUI, and then look in the log to see both the XML API call and the response from the DME. On a windows system, the logs can be found at (assuming "C" is root disk):

```
C:\Documents and Settings\<user name>\Application Data\Sun\Java\
    Deployment\log\.ucsm
```

Please note that GUI has an open handle to the file, so you may have to close the GUI before you can browse the log file.

A developer can use this method to generate an example code. Please note that any security information is not logged in the GUI log (however, when using the Emulator, even security information is provided in the GUI log). Figure 7-51 contains an example of a vLAN creation in the GUI log (vLAN name is Database).

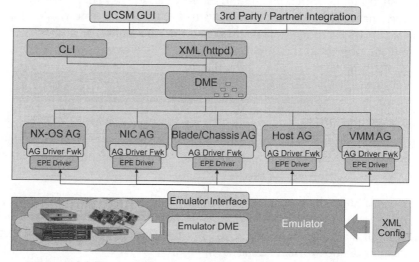

Figure 7-50   UCS Platform Emulator architecture

```
[---------- Sending Request to Server ----------
<configConfMos cookie="1265225996/ace4527d-4c97-4236-842c-c64bd7d13252" inHierarchical="true">
  <inConfigs>
    <pair key="fabric/lan/net-DataBase">
      <fabricVlan
      defaultNet="no"
      dn="fabric/lan/net-DataBase"
      id="42"
      name="DataBase"
      status="created">
      </fabricVlan>
    </pair>
  </inConfigs>
</configConfMos>
-----------------------------------------------------]

[---------- Received Response from Server ----------
HTML Headers:
    Response: HTTP/1.1 200 OK
    Date: Wed, 03 Feb 2010 19:40:39 GMT
    Server: Apache/2.2.4 (Unix) mod_ssl/2.2.4 OpenSSL/0.9.7j-fips-dev
    Content-Length: 424
    Connection: close
    Content-Type: application/soap+xml

<configConfMos cookie="1265225996/ace4527d-4c97-4236-842c-c64bd7d13252" response="yes">
  <outConfigs>
    <pair key="fabric/lan/net-DataBase">
      <fabricVlan childAction="deleteNonPresent" defaultNet="no" dn="fabric/lan/net-DataBase"
      epDn="" id="42" ifRole="network" ifType="virtual" locale="external" name="DataBase"
      peerDn=""  status="created" switchId="dual" transport="ether" type="lan"/>
    </pair>
  </outConfigs>
</configConfMos>
-----------------------------------------------------]
```

Figure 7-51   UCS Manager GUI Log vLAN

The UCS also comes with a built-in model browser. It was mainly developed for debugging purpose, but it has turned out to be a valuable tool for developers. The model browser is a read-only, web-based tool that allows an authorized user to browse the objects in the object model tree. This browser provides the same information as the GUI, but also all the internal attributes structured as the internal model tree.

The model browser allows the user to put in search criteria; the browser will display the result, but also provide the actual XML API call that was made to retrieve the information. Figure 7-52 is an example of the vLAN object "Database" in the model browser. Both the object and the actual XML API that was performed to retrieve the information are visible.

Figure 7-53 contains the same vLAN information shown in the UCS Manager GUI (under properties in the right window). Please note that the figure shows a right-click menu, highlighting the "Copy XML" option. This copy operation copies the object in an XML doc format, as shown in Figure 7-54.

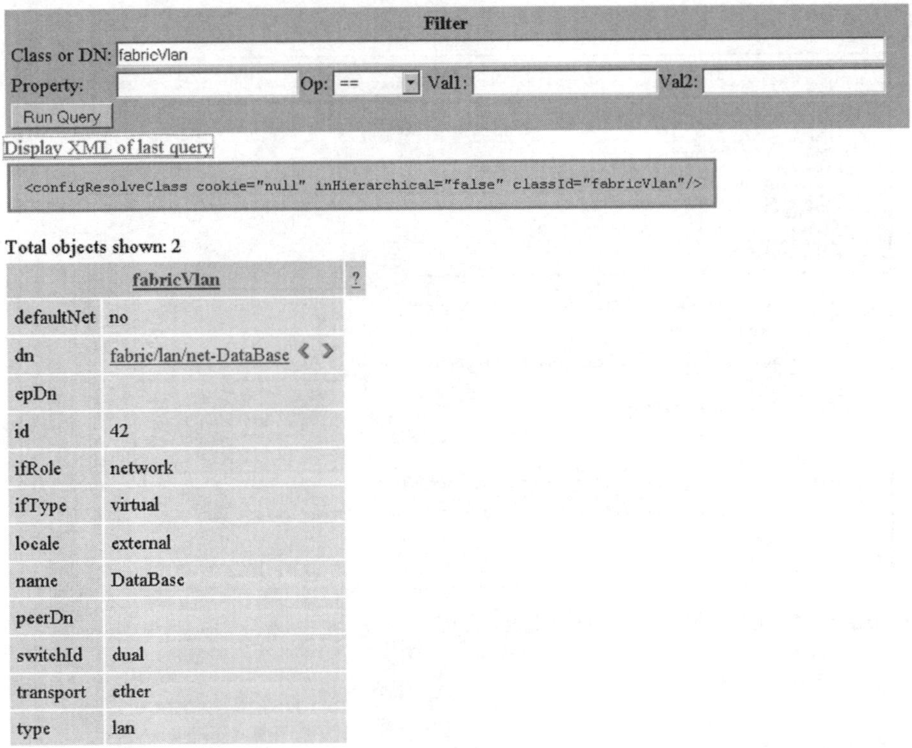

Filter

Class or DN: fabricVlan

Property: _____ Op: == ▼ Val1: _____ Val2: _____

Run Query

Display XML of last query

```
<configResolveClass cookie="null" inHierarchical="false" classId="fabricVlan"/>
```

Total objects shown: 2

fabricVlan	?
defaultNet	no
dn	fabric/lan/net-DataBase ‹ ›
epDn	
id	42
ifRole	network
ifType	virtual
locale	external
name	DataBase
peerDn	
switchId	dual
transport	ether
type	lan

Figure 7-52   UCS model browser vLAN

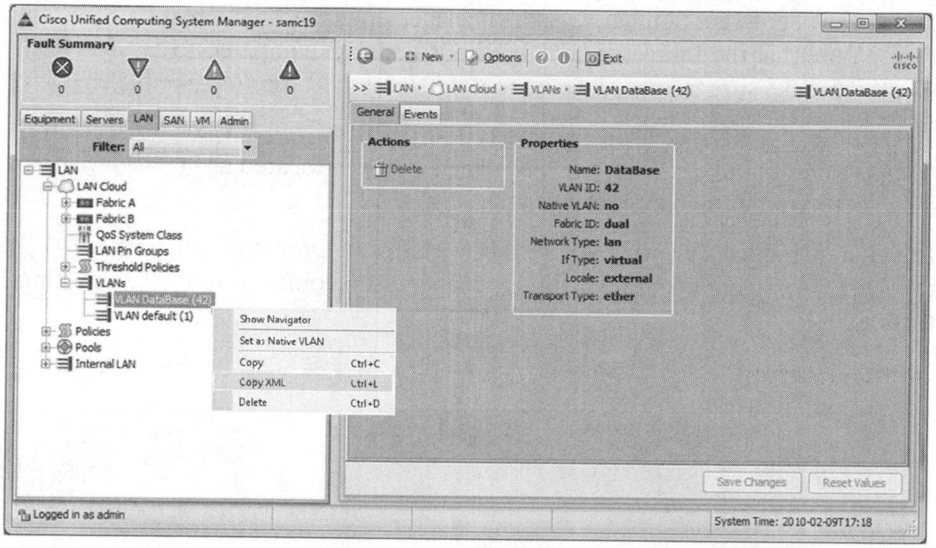

Figure 7-53 UCS Manager GUI vLAN

```
<fabricVlan
        childAction="deleteNonPresent"
        defaultNet="no"
        dn="fabric/lan/net-DataBase"
        epDn=""
        id="42"
        ifRole="network"
        ifType="virtual"
        locale="external"
        name="DataBase"
        peerDn=""
        status="created"
        switchId="dual"
        transport="ether"
        type="lan">
</fabricVlan>
```

Figure 7-54 vLAN object in native XML format

A complementary version of the Emulator (UCSPE Lite) is attached to this book in the form of a DVD. The Emulator is a lighter version that demands fewer resources on the host, has fewer tuning requirements, configuration options, and lacks the XML API tools described earlier in the book. The UCSPE Lite does provide the same capabilities of the UCS Manager and GUI. This version of the Emulator allows the user to get familiar with the management aspects of a real UCS system. Please note that the Emulator has a few shortcomings compared to a real system, so please make sure to read the release notes section of the "readme file".

To find out more about UCSPE, please visit the Cisco UCS Manager section of the Cisco Developer Network (CDN). The section is located at http://developer.cisco.com/web/unifiedcomputing.

Issues and requests relating to the UCS Platform Emulator can be posted to the UCS Manager forum at http://developer.cisco.com/web/unifiedcomputing/forums.

Chapter 8

Third-Party Management Software

Cisco is working together with many ecosystem partners to integrate and add support for Cisco UCS. The products and integrations described in this chapter are a complete description neither of our partner's products, nor of their product families. This chapter focuses only on products and components that are directly integrated with the UCS. Cisco has other important ecosystem partners, not mentioned here, that provide the same or similar capabilities; this is not considered a complete list.

Most of the integrations leverage unique UCS features, like policies and service profiles. The additional value provided by the integration differs depending on our partner's products, functionalities, and areas of expertise. These values and key product capabilities are described in each partner section.

This is an ongoing effort, and this chapter contains a snapshot taken in February 2010. Cisco is working with its partners daily to provide even greater functionality and benefits.

With a few exceptions, the partners have leveraged the UCS XML API and the UCS Platform Emulator (UCSPE) to develop their integrated solutions, and used a real UCS for testing and quality assurance. This has proven to be a very valuable and efficient way to develop integrated solutions with the UCS.

BMC®

BMC[1] BladeLogic® for Cisco UCS provides UCS customers with a complete, end-to-end management solution. With the BMC BladeLogic automation solution—natively integrated through the UCS APIs, Cisco customers can easily and efficiently manage the full scope and scale of their UCS environments. Because it provides policy-based and automated actions, and encapsulates the complexity of administering a UCS environment, Cisco customers can realize the tremendous potential for savings on both hardware and operations. This section introduces the BMC product, and explains how it integrates with UCS.

---

1   The authors are thankful to BMC® Corporation for the information and the material provided to edit this section. Pictures are courtesy of BMC®.

A Day in the Life of a System Administrator, Part 1

Chuck sipped his fourth coffee of the afternoon, sighed, and slowly looked around his office. He had just returned from a project status meeting, reviewing the rollout of their new Cisco UCS gear. This was impressive hardware, and it was going to save them a great deal of money on power and cooling, and allow them to much more efficiently and densely run their virtualized servers, with integrated compute, network, and storage.

Nevertheless, Chuck was a little worried—the company's drive toward virtualization, coupled with their enthusiastic embrace of the UCS platform, meant a dramatic increase in the number of virtual servers to be provisioned, configured, patched, audited, and monitored. These were in addition to the hundreds of physical servers he was responsible for. Moreover, although UCS was going to help them dramatically reduce the number of physical servers, it was going to enable dynamic and on-demand creation of VMs, dramatically increasing the number of virtual servers he was responsible for. Chuck picked up the phone. He needed to learn more about what Cisco could do to help.

Just-in-Time Provisioning

Just-in-time provisioning with service profiles and dynamic allocation of resources: with UCS, Cisco introduced the notion of a service profile—a software abstraction of how hardware settings (Firmware, BIOS, etc.), network resources (VLAN ID, etc.), and storage resources (WWNN, WWPN, etc.) are configured. Coupled with UCS ground-breaking design, service profiles significantly reduce administrative "touch" required—so, for example, instead of re-cabling, Chuck can simply change the VLANs or LUNs a blade is connected to, by executing a change in the management GUI.

BMC BladeLogic steps a user through a provisioning wizard, automatically creating the service profiles based on user selections. The user's choices for attributes such as NIC, HBA, and firmware are captured in the BladeLogic GUI and passed as parameters to the underlying UCS XML API calls. The combination of an advanced management system and Cisco's flexible UCS infrastructure is a clear winner for Chuck—with legacy blade hardware, he may have been given, for example, a database server that had two fixed HBAs and one fixed NIC. That would not have allowed him to build a private cloud that was elastic enough to adapt—to permit the number of virtual machines to grow or shrink in response to business users' self-service requests. With the UCS approach to stateless computing, those resources are not fixed; Chuck can use BladeLogic to re-configure adapters and resource IDs through software on the fly.

Embedded System Management

Management is uniquely integrated into all the components of the UCS, enabling the entire solution, across multiple UCS chassis, to be managed as a single entity through the UCS Manager XML API. This single API allowed easy integrate with the UCS and BladeLogic only had to integrate to this one API to manage compute, storage, and network resources, across the multiple blades and chassis that make up a UCS (which can be up to 40 chassis all connected by a pair of Fabric Interconnects). To facilitate workload mobility, BladeLogic presents Chuck with a single pane of glass across multiple UCSs—he can gather the inventory of thousands of blades at once. To achieve this, the `configResolveChildren` UCS API call is invoked so that users can browse the live views in the BladeLogic GUI (see Figure 8-1).

The code to display each blade is:

```
<configResolveChildren cookie="" inHierarchical="false" inDn="sys/chas-
sis-1" classId="computeBlade" />
```

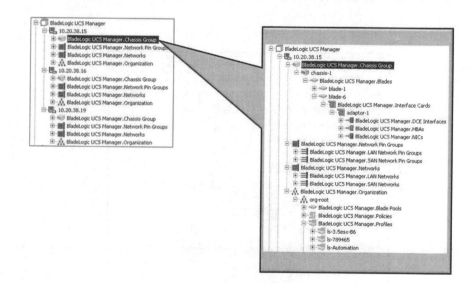

Figure 8-1   Single view across multiple UCSes

The BMC BladeLogic solution is used to rapidly provision business services on these blades—a full stack of server and application layers can be built on each blade. Since the provisioning is done to a service profile, the full stack can be rapidly moved to another blade or UCS (for example, for maintenance or failover). With other brands of hardware, BladeLogic has to tear down and rebuild the stack. However, Cisco's stateless computing enables BladeLogic to move the full stack simply by re-associating a service profile from one blade to another, as shown in Figure 8-2.

In addition, service profiles do not have to be manually built ahead of time before a hypervisor is installed by BladeLogic. BladeLogic automates hardware and software provisioning in a single operation. One job can execute the deployment (or rollback in case of error) of all of the following onto a blade:

- Hardware service profile
- Host server OS (for example, VMware ESXi or ESX)
- Virtual guest OS (for example, Red Hat)
- Application middleware (for example, WebLogic)

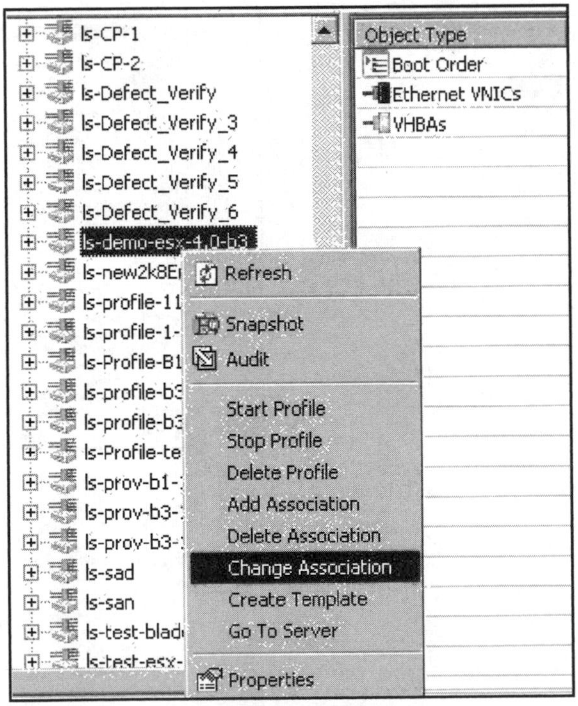

Figure 8-2   Easily move a full stack to another UCS

- Application layer (for example, a cluster of WebLogic nodes)
- Harden stack: Lock-down the layers by remediating their configuration according to SOX or PCI regulations. Patch the OS and application to thwart hackers. Apply security rules to restrict access to web forms.

To reduce costs, BladeLogic controls change by defining a policy for how each layer should be provisioned. Policy-based operations, Composite Packaging, Granular Access Control, and Closed-loop rules-based compliance are what differentiate BladeLogic for the provisioning of business services. Before these unique capabilities are explained below, Figure 8-3 contains an architecture diagram and Table 8-1 contains an overview of functionality that summarize the BladeLogic partnership with UCS.

Table 8-1   Summary of BladeLogic Functionality for UCS

Feature	Importance
Live browse of UCS infrastructure: Chassis, Blade Pool, Blade, DCB, HBA, NIC, LAN Network PIN Group, SAN Network, PIN Group, Organization, Policy, Profile, VNIC, MAC Pools, UUID Pools, WWN Pools, etc.	Real-time management improves availability of private cloud services that are built on UCS. Early warning of resource problems allows for pre-emptive reconfiguration—reduces downtime. For example, blade state values can be seen: unknown, operable, inoperable, degraded, powered off, power-problem, removed, voltage-problem, thermal-problem, etc.
Virtual awareness	With visibility into what physical or virtual machines reside on which blade, Chuck can answer what-if questions such as, "which business-services would be impacted if I took a blade off-line for maintenance?"
"UCS Template" for system-wide definition of service profiles (not tied to any particular chassis)	Enforce policies around the resources that can be assigned to service profiles. Empower junior staff to perform more complex actions—safe to delegate to them when there is a guiding policy.
SAN Provisioning—can specify a boot-from-SAN volume as a target LUN	Workload mobility—easy to move a full stack to another blade since important business data is on network storage.
"MAC Pool", "WWN Pool", and "UUID Pool"—Pool creation and management done in BladeLogic. These pools can then be used across multiple UCS Pods.	Since fixed resource IDs do not have to be specified, there is less waste and there are no conflicts.
Operator action—Start / Stop profile	Easily restart business services without having to touch cables and adaptor cards.

continues

Feature	Importance
Operator action—Change association of profile	Workload mobility—easy to move a full stack to another blade.
Operator action—Show KVM Console.	Reduce IT costs with this tool for real-time troubleshooting of the provisioning process.
"Provisioning Job"	Automated hardware provisioning and software provisioning of hypervisor layer. Scales to create many servers in parallel.
"System Packages" shipped out-of-the-box for ESX, Hyper-V, etc.	BladeLogic-tested content makes it quicker to create your hypervisor build policies.
"Virtual Guest Job"	Automated provisioning of guest containers (VMware VMs, AIX LPARs, Solaris Zones, Xen, etc.). Both Image-Based Provisioning and Script-Based Provisioning are available. Scales to create many servers in parallel.
"Virtual Guest Packages" shipped out-of-the-box for VMware, AIX LPAR, etc.	BladeLogic-tested content makes it quicker to create your virtual machine build policies.
"Deploy Job"	Automated provisioning of middleware and applications. Scales to create many web clusters in parallel.
"BladeLogic Package" wrap native packaging (rpm, msi, jar, etc.) and collect many interdependent actions in a cohesive task	Can roll-out a complex application from a single ITSM change ticket. Can roll-back deployment from a single ITSM change ticket in case of error.
"Snapshot" and "Audit" Jobs	Recording of baseline configuration. Intelligent remediation when the server configuration drifts from policy.
"Patching Job"	Protect the OS and application against vulnerabilities. Scales to remediate tens of thousands of servers in parallel.
"Patch Catalogs" shipped out-of-the-box for Red Hat Linux, Windows, etc.	BladeLogic-tested content makes it quicker to create your security policies.
"Compliance Job"	Protect the OS and application against vulnerabilities. Scales to remediate tens of thousands of servers in parallel.
"Compliance Templates" shipped out-of-the-box for SOX, PCI, etc.	BladeLogic-tested content makes it quicker to create your regulatory policies.
"Reclaim Mac," "Reclaim UUID," "Reclaim WWN"	Resource IDs are reclaimed into a pool when service profiles are decommissioned, as shown in Figure 8-4.
All jobs available from GUI, CLI, and API	Automated business service provisioning can be driven from self service private cloud portals.
ITSM integration	All jobs can optionally block waiting for approval from the change-management-board. All jobs can close the loop by updating ticket information as they complete.

Business Service Provisioning

The first layer of the stack, the UCS service profile, is automatically created by BladeLogic invoking the `configConfMos` UCS API call:

```
<configConfMos cookie=''>
      <inConfigs>
            <pair key='org-root/ls-profile-policies'>
                        <lsServer descr='' dn='org-root/ls-
profile-policies' dynamicConPolicyName='' hostFwPolicyName='host-
firmware' identPoolName='' localDiskPolicyName='local-disk'
mgmtAccessPolicyName='ipmi-pol' mgmtFwPolicyName='mgmt-fw-
pol' name='profile-policies' solPolicyName='' srcTemplName=''
statsPolicyName='stats-coll' scrubPolicyName='scrub-pol' uuid='11223344-
1111-1111-1111-112133415266'>
... etc.
```

To do so, Chuck would use a previously defined policy, guiding the service profile, called a "BladeLogic UCS Template". Using Role-Based Access Control (RBAC), he can safely enable a junior administrator to change pools and SAN adapters during the creation of the provisioning job, without fear that the junior staff member would inadvertently make a mistake. As shown in Figure 8-5, the user interface carefully controls the scope of permitted selections.

The second layer of the stack, the host OS, is equally easy to build because Chuck can use the policy templates that ship with BladeLogic. He can customize those ESXi, ESX, Hyper-V, etc. templates by leveraging the BladeLogic Property Dictionary. While building a private cloud, Chuck may use BladeLogic parallel provisioning to setup hundreds of hosts simultaneously. He will not want to hard-code server name, hard disk size, etc. in the policy and therefore, he will make heavy use of the Property Dictionary for parameterization. Values of properties can be imported from the business service context of the BMC Atrium CMDB (Configuration Management Database)—for example, `$$hard-disk-size-required-human-resources-virtual-machines$$`.

The third layer of the stack, the virtual guest OS, is built with similar tools: Property Dictionary and out-of-the-box policies for Windows, Red Hat Linux, SuSE Linux, Solaris, etc. Figure 8-6 shows an example of Image-Based Provisioning—a VMware image is cloned, but the screen can allow an operator to modify the image before cloning. Since rapid provisioning of virtual guests could lead to excessive VM proliferation, BladeLogic has a VM-sprawl job and report that regularly discovers orphaned VMs or past-expiration-date VMs.

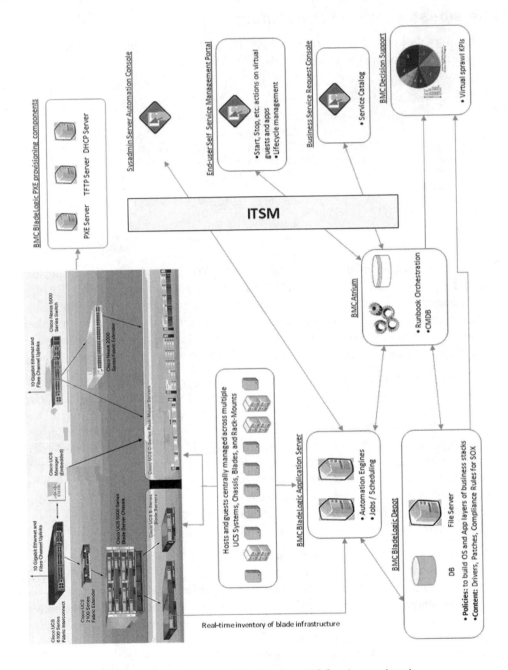

Figure 8-3 Business service provisioning in a UCS private cloud

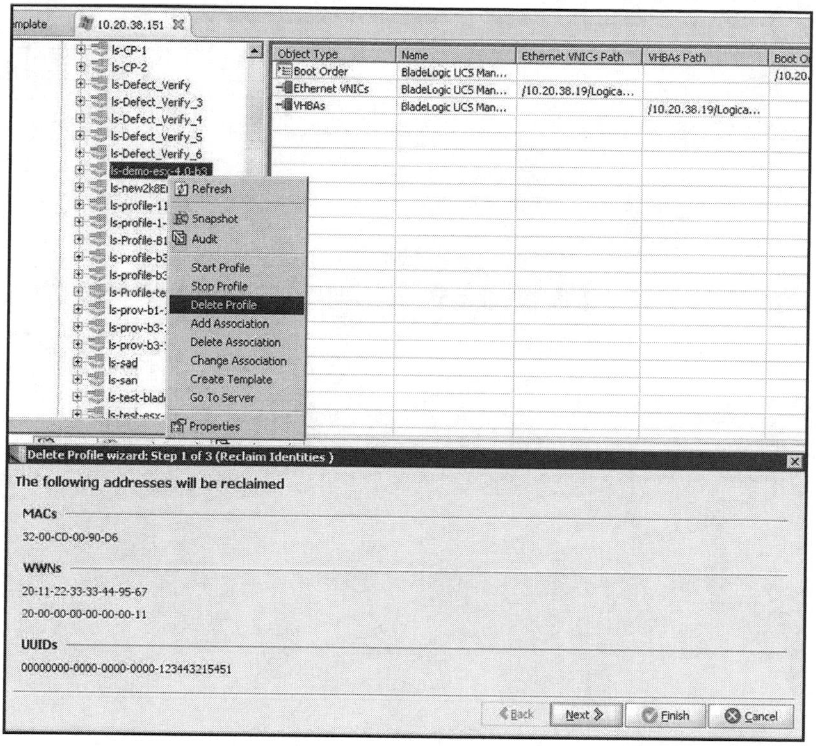

Figure 8-4   Resource IDs are reclaimed into a pool

Composite Packaging

The operations for building the application layer of the stack are also policy-based. Chuck can use a BladeLogic Package to enforce standards about how homegrown or COTS (Commercial Off-The-Shelf) applications are assembled. A BladeLogic Package wraps native packaging such as jar, rpm, and msi, and then adds value by:

- **Orchestrating complex changes into one cohesive action**—With many applications, several class files must be deployed together to satisfy dependencies. In case of an error, an IT Service Management (ITSM) change ticket can later roll back everything because it was deployed as a single change.

- **Sequencing changes in the right order**—Middleware components often have to be configured before application files will correctly install.

- **Simulate to minimize problems**—Deployment is first VALIDATED against a STAGING so that time is not wasted during the precious PRODUCTION maintenance window.

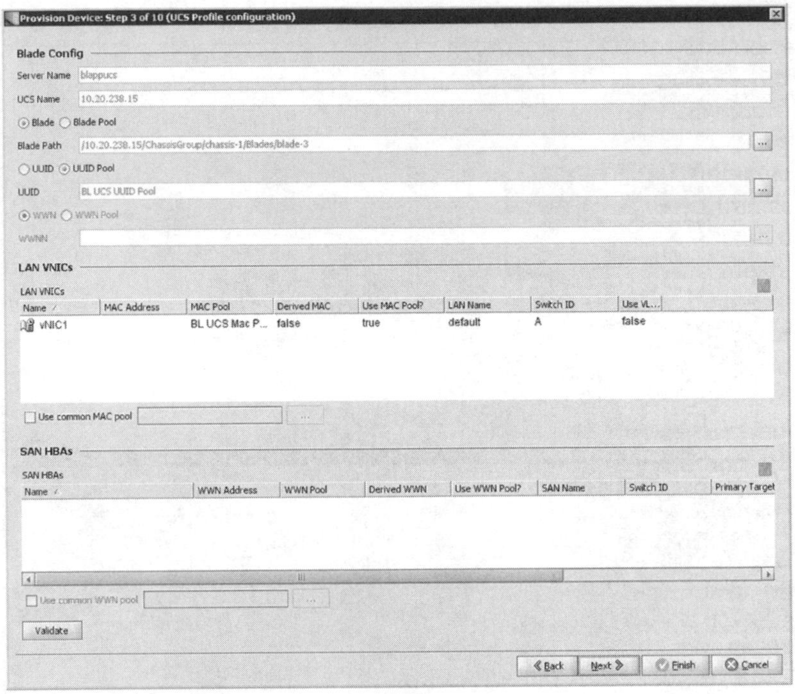

Figure 8-5 Policy-based hypervisor provisioning

Configuration Management

As soon as a business service is provisioned, it is vulnerable to uncontrolled changes that cause downtime. A common occurrence is that a user wants to expedite the addition of a product line item to a web application. In their hurry, they skip the efficient process, of filing a change ticket to add the SKU entry to the product database and have the web catalog re-generated. Instead, they manually edit web configuration files—even the simplest typo corrupts a style sheet. They leave for the day, satisfied that the web forms reflect their new product list but unaware that their customers are seeing HTML 404 errors on other parts of the website. BladeLogic protects against such out-of-band modifications with its change-tracking functionality. As a business service is provisioned, the Snapshot feature records the baseline state of configuration items, such as hypervisor resource settings, virtual machine user-group rights, and application web forms, regularly scheduled Audit Jobs detect drift from the snapshot—SNMP and SMTP notifications are triggered—and the Audit Jobs can automatically remediate to the snapshot state. The functionality is uniquely granular enough to see and make line-item changes. For example, it can detect a change in just the database connection in the configuration file of Figure 8-7, without changing the rest of the file.

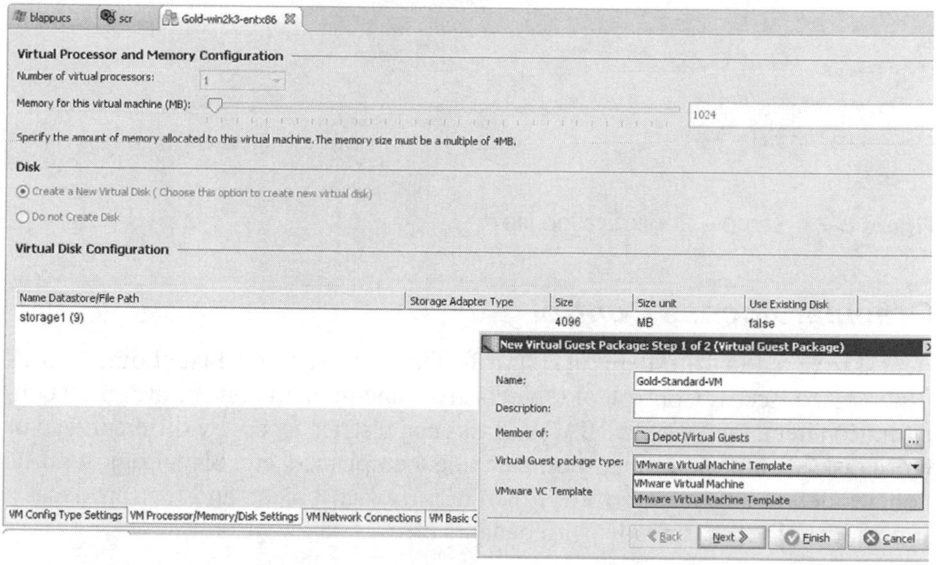

Figure 8-6   Virtual guest provisioning with BladeLogic

Entries in configuration files are not just archived into the CMDB for their historical values; the parsing of system settings into Configuration Objects also provides
live, real-time management. Since the BladeLogic Configuration Object Dictionary has a common vocabulary for configuration management across all platforms,
Red Hat password files, Windows Registry keys, and Websphere paths, are all
parsed in a similar fashion. If an unusual file does not conform to the multitude of
grammars provided out-of-the-box, the structure is easily extensible to support
in-house custom development.

```
Host=server1
IP=10.20.200.123
DB=oracle1
userid=joe
```

Figure 8-7   Sample configuration file

Granular Access Control

Access to individual line items in Figure 8-7 file can be secured. BladeLogic's RBAC (Role-Based Access Control) of Objects gives fine-grained control over each configuration item. BladeLogic RBAC of Tasks can restrict access by different read or write tasks: live-browse, snapshot, patching, compliance, etc. BladeLogic's RBAC Policies define who can perform which task to what object, and that produces a sophisticated security model with benefits of:

- **Collaboration**—Facilitate cooperation between different people working on the same servers.
- **Delegation**—Empower junior staff to perform more complex actions safely.

BladeLogic ships with several out-of-the-box policies such as "Windows Build", "Red Hat Security", "WebLogic Standard", etc., that can be customized.

Compliance

If cloned from a vendor image, a server is typically non compliant in a myriad of ways: services are enabled that do not need to be, patches are missing, and ports are open that pose a security threat. BladeLogic ships with out-of-the-box industry and government standard templates that can be used to plug these holes. BMC works with subject matter experts to encode the regulatory policies as rules—the policies meet standards such as Sarbanes-Oxley (SOX) and COBIT (Control Objectives for IT). When run through an audit job, the rules will flag all of the configuration items that do not match. An example is shown in Figure 8-8.

"Exceptions" are a unique aspect to these rules because there can often be valid reasons why a site can't conform to some rules. Exceptions document these reasons, for an auditor, when a compliance scan is run. The rules are linked with RBAC to produce multi-functional policies define WHO, WHAT, and HOW. Because they are rules-based, BladeLogic compliance policies are not tied to a specific server; they are reusable. In addition to rules, the BladeLogic certified content includes patches, and automated workflow that remediates violations and updates change-tracking tickets.

Vision for Automated and Efficient IT

With the Cisco Unified Computing System, organizations can rapidly realize the value of BMC's Business Service Management (BSM)—a comprehensive and unified platform for running IT. As shown in Figure 8-9, BMC's approach provides a complete set of management systems, covering the entire IT stack and the entire service lifecycle.

By offering rapid time-to-value products, delivered within a strategic framework, BMC helps customers meet IT's challenges at both a strategic and tactical level. For example, BMC has pre-built integration between BMC BladeLogic for Cisco UCS and the BMC Atrium CMDB. This provides IT with a business context for IT services, allowing IT to view and manage the UCS-hosted services as more than just a collection of technical resources. By applying this business context, IT can now prioritize and operate in alignment with business priorities, and be more responsive to the business.

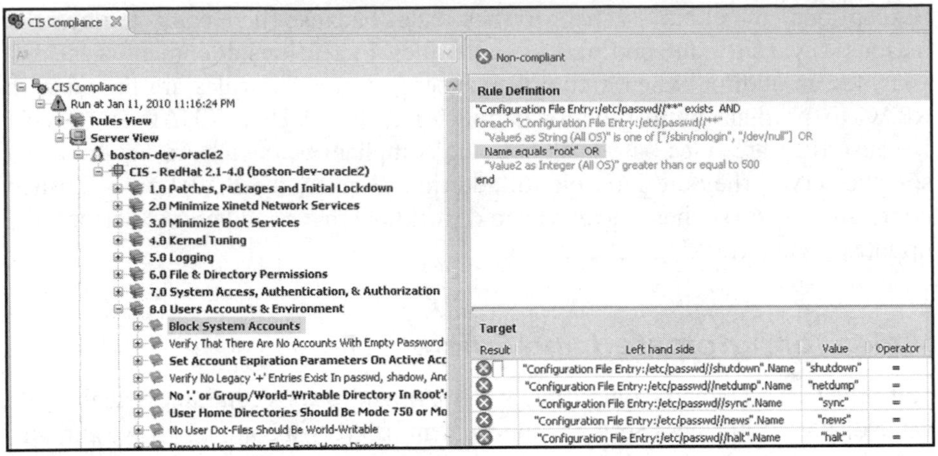

Figure 8-8   Example results where a server was non-compliant

Figure 8-9   BMC approach

As shown in Table 8-2, BMC's UCS solutions deliver value at each stage of the service lifecycle, and deliver greater value as part of an overall BMC platform.

Table 8-2 Values of BMC Solution

Phase	Benefits of BMC BladeLogic for Cisco UCS	Extended Benefits When Integrated with Other BMC Products
Plan & Govern	Define full-stack service profiles, across UCS instances. Deliver consistent services for reliable, repeatable, stable operations.	Define full-stack entries in a service catalog, for user requests. Enforce compliance with configuration policies, for reliable, repeatable, and stable operations.
Request & Support	Efficient admin UI for easily handling service requests and support. Role-based access control for robust segregation of duties.	Self-Service portal for efficient end-user service requests. Integration with IT Service Management systems, for support and tracking in compliance with ITIL.
Provision & Configure	Automated provisioning and activation of a complete service.	Provisioning integration with CMDB ensures that IT has a complete and accurate picture, for better decision-making with a business context.
Monitor & Operate	Support for automated and ad-hoc administrative tasks—without scripting—enables all admins to be as efficient as the best ones.	Proactive performance (via dynamic baselining) allows IT to predict a problem before it impacts the business. Business service context from the CMDB helps IT better assign policies and prioritize actions.
Integrate & Orchestrate	Runbook automation orchestrates activities behind-the-scenes, eliminating complexity and manual effort.	Real-time integration with CMDB and ITSM systems ensures accuracy, and enables an efficient and dynamic IT infrastructure.

As organizations embrace and deploy Cisco UCS, it's clear that they need a management system which efficiently supports its new and unique capabilities, while at the same time allows them to share common processes, tools, policies, and people with their existing infrastructure. BMC's solutions allow them to achieve this.

A Day in the Life of a System Administrator, Part 2

Chuck glanced at his watch—only twenty minutes until his monthly status meeting with the CIO, who wanted a report on how their virtualization project on the new UCS hardware was proceeding. Chuck quickly launched the Dashboard, where he could see up-to-date metrics for the systems under his management. He quickly printed out some reports showing system performance, administrative efficiency, compliance with configuration policies, and capacity trends.

The BMC management system, which was tightly integrated with the Cisco UCS platform, provided him and his staff with an efficient and reliable way of doing their jobs. By enabling end-user service requests in a self-service portal, he had significantly reduced the administrative load from his staff. And, because it was integrated with their ITSM change management system, all requests were automatically tracked and documented without manual effort. The automated provisioning, driven by the service catalog, allowed the line-of-business developers to automatically provision VMs on the UCSs, kept track of these, and enforced a decommissioning process to reclaim resources. Moreover, best of all, by tracking and centralizing all server configuration change management, their change advisory board meetings had been reduced from 6 hours a week to 30 minutes.

With his reports printed, Chuck strolled down the hallway to the CIO's office, and stole a glance at his watch. Ten minutes left. He had plenty of time to get a cup of espresso.

CA® Management Integration with Cisco UCS

CA[2] and Cisco have worked together to create integrated support for the Cisco Unified Computing System (UCS) across CA's Assurance, Virtualization Management, and Service Automation portfolio in a way that gives customers an extensive solution to handle fault, performance, and configuration management of the UCS within their infrastructure. It also addresses the increasing need for automated

---

2   The authors are thankful to CA® Corporation for the information and the material provided to edit this section. Pictures are courtesy of CA®.

policy-based provisioning of physical, virtual, and cloud resources that are key to keeping IT operation costs down as complexity in the data center increases.

The three products that directly integrate with Cisco UCS are CA Spectrum® Infrastructure Manager (Spectrum IM), CA Spectrum® Automation Manager (Spectrum AM), and CA eHealth® Performance Manager (eHealth PM). The CA Virtual Performance Management (VPM) solution provides all three products with a common management layer for multi-platform, multi-vendor virtual server technologies. The integration between these products and the UCS helps enable the provisioning of private clouds, discussed in more detail later.

In addition, CA recently certified CA Insight Database Performance Manager for proactive performance management of databases on Cisco UCS. CA Insight DPM is integrated with CA eHealth PM, CA Spectrum IM, and CA Spectrum AM and provides customers with performance visibility across database vendors.

Integration Point

CA's VPM agent is a lightweight data gatherer that is used across multiple products within CA. Its architecture allows custom modules to be written that plug into the agent itself in order to gather customized data. These modules are called Application Insight Modules (AIMs). Examples include AIMs for VMware vCenter™, Sun Solaris Zones, and Cisco UCS. The AIM gathers the information specific to it and allows that information to be queried via SNMP. Because of its generic nature, the SNMP queries can come from just about anywhere—CA Spectrum IM, CA Spectrum AM, CA eHealth PM, or even a third-party utility—so customers can leverage their investments in Cisco UCS and in other management tools. The architecture supporting UCS is shown in Figure 8-10.

CA Infrastructure Management Integration

CA Spectrum Infrastructure Manager and CA eHealth Performance Manager are the building blocks of CA's Infrastructure Management solution that provide users with the ability to achieve performance-driven root cause and impact analysis to help ensure the health and reliability of their UCS environment and the applications and services that will be delivered over a UCS-based infrastructure.

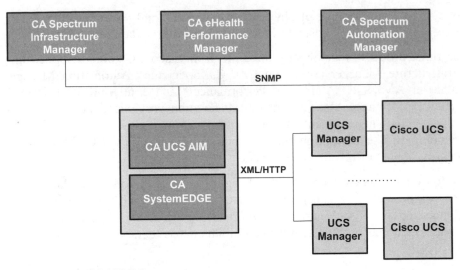

Figure 8-10   CA UCS Support

Discovery, Fault, and Service Modeling

With the integration to the UCS Manager configured and enabled, CA Spectrum IM is able to provide management for a single UCS Manager or across multiple UCS Managers. CA Spectrum IM will perform a discovery of each UCS Manager within the infrastructure and create a software model for components, including the UCS Manager, chassis, blades, and Fabric Interconnect, shown in Figure 8-11. Additionally, CA Spectrum IM also determines the connectivity between UCS components at this time.

The UCS model is placed in CA Spectrum IM's topology map as a graphical presentation of the UCS infrastructure (see Figure 8-12).

The UCS Chassis model in CA Spectrum IM's object database is designed to present to the user the overall health and the health of the blades contained within it. Each Fabric Interconnect is also topologically significant. It marks the boundary between a Fiber Channel over Ethernet (FCoE) data center network and the conventional IP network and switches between the chassis-based blades. Each blade is not topologically significant but is modeled to represent the BIOS level information available through the UCS. Alternatively, a topologically significant model of the OS or hypervisor software running on a blade can be manually associated or promoted to the chassis to take on the role of the blade.

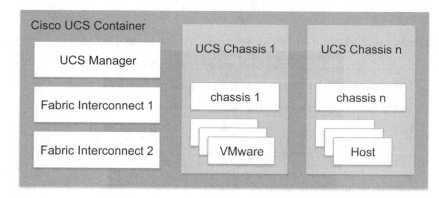

Figure 8-11 Container for the model of the UCS infrastructure

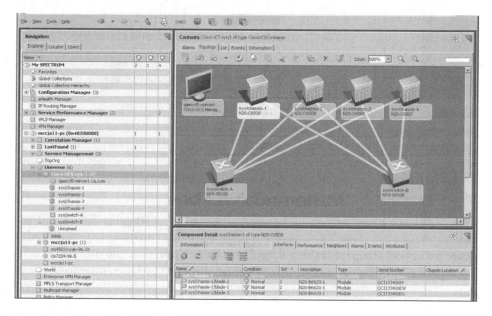

Figure 8-12 Spectrum IM topology map with UCS container

An operator can view component detail information on each UCS model.

Examples of the information views for the UCS Chassis are:

- System details, such as serial number, condition, and revision
- Environmental details, such as fans and power supplies
- Blade details, such as serial number, slot number, and condition
- Fabric extender details, such as location, serial number, and ports

Examples of the information views for the blade are:

- System details, such as serial number, operational state, and BIOS information
- Statistical information, such as CPU load, memory, and storage utilization
- Mezzanine card details, such as revision and serial number
- Memory module details, such as capacity, speed, and clock speed
- Motherboard hardware and environmental details
- Physical interface details, such as Admin and Operator status

In addition to the topology view, CA Spectrum IM's OneClick Operations Console includes a hierarchical view of the UCS environment located in the left navigation panel, as well as the ability to do Locator searches. This hierarchy shows an expandable list view of each UCS Manager, UCS Chassis, and associated components with alarm counts for each. Locator searches can be performed to find all UCS Managers, all chassis, or all Fabric Interconnects.

One of the advantages of using CA Spectrum IM for managing the UCS is the enhanced root cause analysis and alarm correlation that can quickly pinpoint root cause and eliminate unnecessary alarms that are symptoms of the root cause. CA developed CA Spectrum IM's root cause support of the UCS infrastructure to understand the UCS Chassis as a correlation domain that includes all components within each chassis. The enhanced root cause analysis identifies when UCS Fabric Interconnects and chassis issues are caused by the UCS and when they are outside of the UCS. When faults occur within the UCS correlation domain, symptomatic alarms are suppressed and a single root cause alarm is issued, eliminating extraneous "noise."

For example, if a UCS chassis power subsystem fails, affecting the blades (and services running on them), then individual alarms on all the blades will be suppressed in order to point the fault to the chassis. Suppressed alarms are preserved and listed in the alarm details tab as symptoms of the root cause.

Performance Management and Analytics

CA eHealth Performance Manager is designed to enable customers to proactively manage the performance of their infrastructure by collecting key performance indicators specific to the infrastructure technology under management. CA eHealth PM then analyzes that data, proactively identifies systemic performance issues and alerts infrastructure managers before users and services are negatively impacted. CA eHealth PM also provides insight into historical data via interactive web-based interfaces (see Figure 8-13 and Figure 8-14) in conjunction with out of the box static reports enabling the prioritization of resources based upon the health of the infrastructure components (see Figure 8-15).

CA eHealth PM supports the UCS environment as a collection of infrastructure components comprised of blade servers, Fabric Interconnect switches, fiber channel and Ethernet interfaces, and environmental components, including power, current, voltage, temperature, etc. CA eHealth PM discovers the UCS environment and collects the key performance indicators for each component, enabling proactive performance management of the UCS environment.

CA eHealth PM has the ability to detect when performance metrics "deviate from normal" and generate alerts to notify infrastructure managers that there are systemic performance issues that will impact users and services. For example, if the

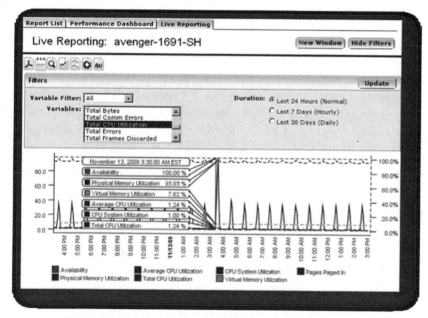

Figure 8-13   CA eHealth PM interactive reporting

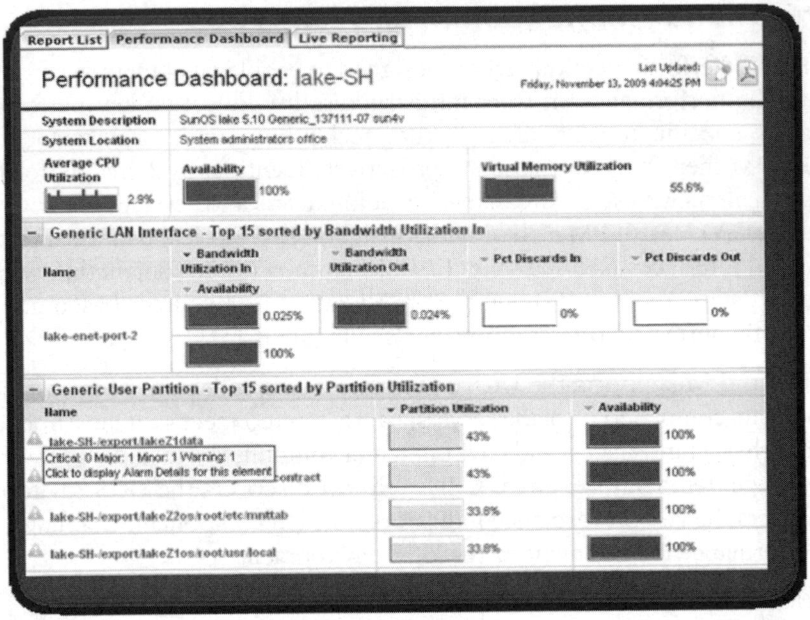

Figure 8-14   CA eHealth PM Performance Dashboard

code for an application deployed in a UCS environment is modified and introduces a memory leak, CA eHealth PM will detect the memory usage of the blade deviating from normal and will generate an alert to indicate the potential service impacting issue. The issue can be rectified before users are negatively impacted.

For implementations that include both CA Spectrum IM and CA eHealth PM, proactive performance alerts generated in CA eHealth PM can be sent to CA Spectrum IM. The operator has an integrated workflow to navigate from the CA Spectrum IM UCS model to the associated CA eHealth PM UCS performance reports, helping to increase operator productivity and providing insight into historical performance to improve MTTR.

Automation

With the integration of CA Spectrum Automation Manager and Cisco's Unified Computing System, users will be able to automate a broad range of important datacenter operations running on Cisco UCS platforms:

- Change and Configuration Detection/Remediation
- Creation of UCS Service Profile and Application Templates

- Automated Provisioning
- Policy-based Automation
- Providing a User Self-Service Capability

Change and Configuration Management

To optimize the availability and performance of applications or services, it is important to ensure that a system's configuration remains consistent over time and does not drift from its intended state. The Application Configuration Management component within CA Spectrum Automation Manager enables a user to perform continuous, automated discovery and mapping of applications and system infrastructure elements, resulting in improved accuracy of configuration management with reduced level of effort. Changes to a Cisco UCS platform and the software stack running on the platform, as compared with a user-specified

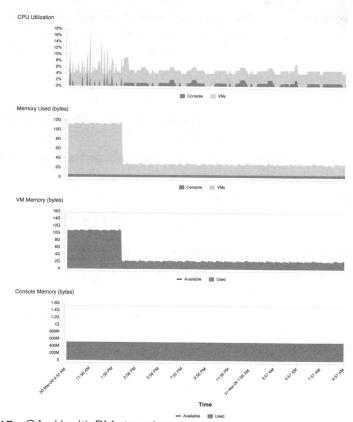

Figure 8-15   CA eHealth PM at-a-glance report

reference configuration, will be detected and then can either be reported for further action via a service desk ticket or automatically remediated based on a predetermined policy action. This reference configuration can be:

- A baseline snapshot used as a gold standard snapshot to detect servers that are out of compliance with specific corporate standards, or
- A periodic on-demand snapshot of a server's configuration settings that is compared with prior snapshots from the same server to detect changes that may impact an application's performance occurring over time.

Through process integration with service desk solutions, IT organizations can track change requests to help ensure changes are in compliance with business best practices, such as regulatory rules and procedures. An example of the level of change that can be tracked is shown in Figure 8-16.

Service Profile and Application Templates

Within CA Spectrum Automation Manager, the user will be able to create templates that associate a UCS service profile with an application stack. In this way, multiple instances of applications can be more easily created and deployed without the need for the user to replicate common configuration specifications (see Figure 8-17).

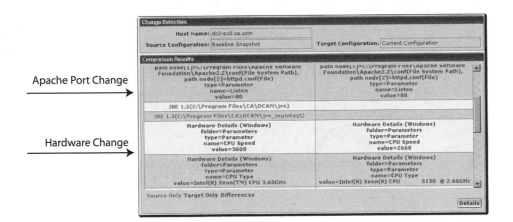

Figure 8-16   CA Spectrum Automation Manager

This streamlines and automates the process of provisioning an end-to-end service from the network layer, to the server hardware layer, to the entire software stack.

Automated Provisioning

CA Spectrum Automation Manager is designed to support the automated provisioning of software stacks (OS and application) and Cisco UCS platforms as defined by service profiles to provide services. CA Spectrum Automation Manager supports automated provisioning onto both physical and virtual server platforms.

Multiple levels of provisioning are supported to meet a range of users' needs:

- **Operator-initiated:** Manual provisioning executed by an administrator.
- **Alert-driven:** Provisioning and configuration change requests are routed through change management systems and execute upon approval.
- **Scheduled:** Resources are provisioned at a set date and time.
- **Dynamic:** Resources are provisioned in real time in response to changing business needs and performance and configuration issues.

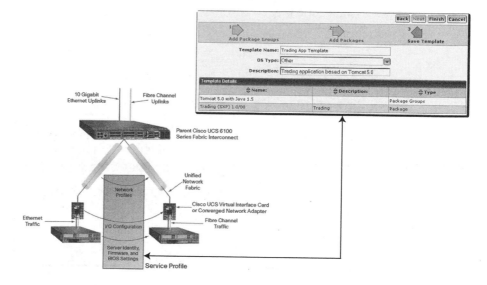

Figure 8-17   Service profile and application templates

Policy-Based Automation

Using CA Spectrum Automation Manager, users will be able to define a set of policy rules for the Cisco UCS platform on which automated system operation will take place when the rules are triggered. The rules are developed using the metrics available to CA Spectrum Automation Manager.

The rule may be simple or complex (see Figure 8-18) and are based on a user-specified combination of:

- UCS metrics or UCS events and faults
- CA Spectrum AM's rich set of metrics and events

Once a rule triggers, the user specified action takes place. This action can take many forms, as illustrated in Figure 8-19:

- Allows application services to dynamically scale up and down based on usage/performance.
- Initiates an application configuration management discovery task.
- Runs an IT Process Automation Management workflow which executes a predefined coordinated set of cross-domain IT processes (integration and data exchange, end-to-end nested processes, and coordinated on-demand process control).
- Directs a VMware action.
- Generates reports.

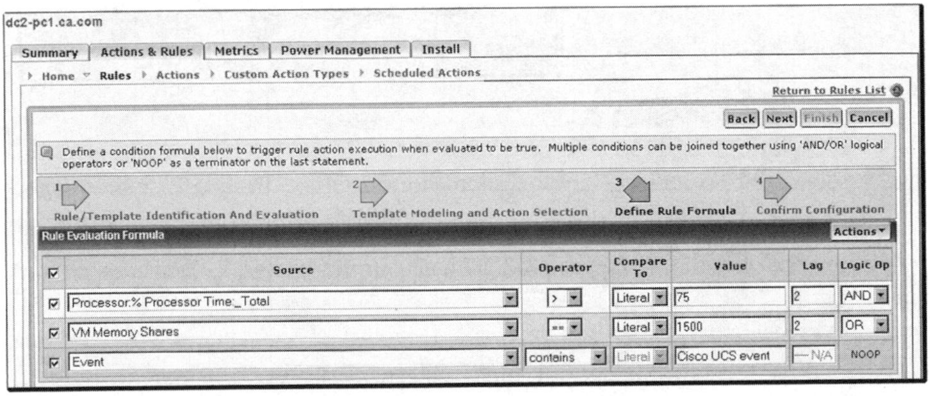

Figure 8-18 Policy rule generation

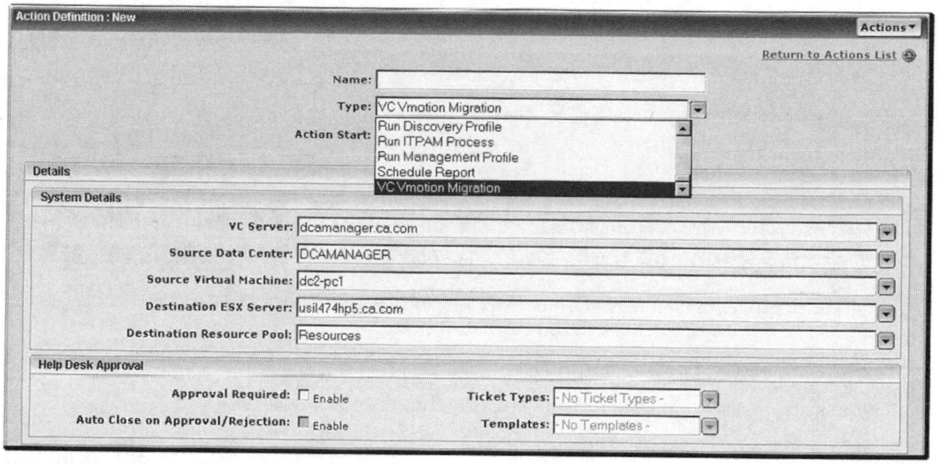

Figure 8-19 Policy actions

User Self-Service

Cisco UCS platforms can be made available as a part of an end user self-service reservation system, which allows users to quickly and securely reserve resources for application testing, development, training, production, and cloud environments without the need to directly involve IT support staff as illustrated by the following sequence:

1. Select an OS (see Figure 8-20).
2. Select the application (see Figure 8-21).
3. Specify system requirements (see Figure 8-22).
4. Specify reservation period (see Figure 8-23).

At the end of the reservation period, the resources will be returned for general use.

Private Cloud Deployments

IT organizations and their domain teams are using shared infrastructure in production today, driving the idea that cloud computing can deliver the foundation for dynamic business models, faster time to market, and the optimization of people, process and technologies. Technologies such as UCS offer IT professionals a foundational building block for delivering cloud infrastructures. The platform takes advantage of virtualization capabilities, enabling a more robust management through partner integrations, such as that with CA.

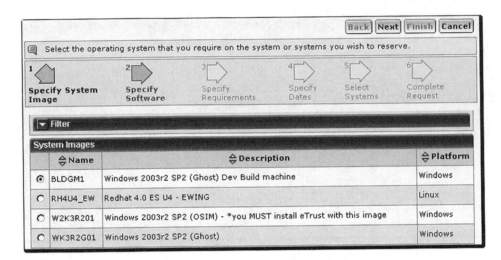

Figure 8-20   Select an OS

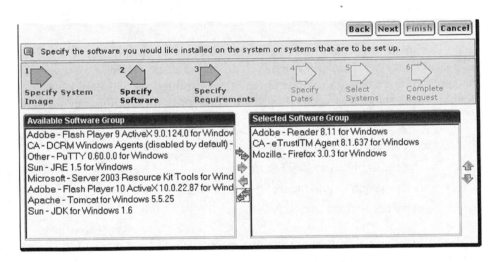

Figure 8-21   Select an application

IT executives must understand that next generation data centers will have a mixture of physical and virtual infrastructures and key technologies such as real-time performance management, root-cause analytics, self-service, models-based management, and dashboards are required to deliver highly available applications and services. UCS enables the compression and pooling of virtual storage, server and network connectivity, and resources; it recognizes that virtualization is an enabling technology. Virtualization adds several layers of control, policy, governance, performance, and security concerns that must be addressed by integrating

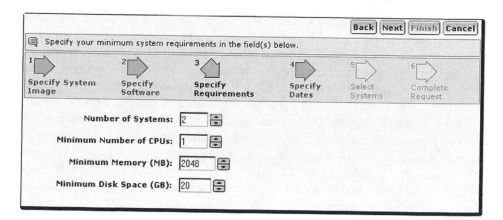

Figure 8-22 Specify system requirements

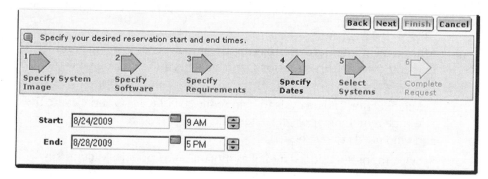

Figure 8-23 System reservation period

and automating physical and virtual processes, workflows, performance data, and other related management capabilities. The UCS platform enables users to take full advantage of virtualization, delivering policy-aware IT services that dynamically adjust and react to business demands.

The importance of management across an end-to-end service cannot be taken lightly as UCS and virtual switching is considered and deployed. Besides critical element management visibility provided by Cisco through products such as UCS Manager, CA has invested in tight integrations across the infrastructure management and automation portfolio to help reduce the business and technical risks in key areas such as integrated fault and performance management, change and configuration management, traffic management, IT process automation, self-service, and compute reservation capabilities. CA has worked with customers to identify key UCS cost containment opportunities; for example, compressing the cycles between test and development and operations through automation and self-service capabilities. Another example is integrating automated provisioning and service desk processes within UCS and integrating them with physical processes that trigger automated actions based on agreed-upon polices and process workflows. This automation helps reduce the risk of human-caused errors and speeds time to problem identification and resolution across an IT service, while maintaining deep levels of granular infrastructure visibility. The workflows intelligently react to policies (virtual and physical based) flowing through UCS. CA products aggregate polices across a virtual and physical environment, taking into account the performance parameters and SLA metrics that each application service must adhere to. As virtual machine policies are created using Open Virtualization Format (OVF) or other emerging standards, CA management technologies interact with UCS in real-time to aggregate, analyze, and, if required, trigger dynamic actions to maintain Quality of Service, availability, and performance. These customer benefits deliver cost savings, containment, and business growth.

Key considerations to enable a managed private cloud deployment using UCS and CA management include:

- Management integration across the CA management portfolio and UCS that empowers IT organizations with an application-centric view of UCS' policy-based services.

- Data collection and analysis to help reduce MTTR costs and elevate the real time requirement of understanding if there is a problem, where it is and who needs to resolve it.

- Service topology understanding as dynamic VM policies dictate key service resource parameters and the importance of topology and dependency mapping of IT service components that become critical to identifying customer impact.

- Sophisticated solutions such as root-cause analytics, models-based management, real-time dashboards, IT process automation, self-service, performance management, and self-service that help IT deliver UCS-based services that are managed and optimized to contain costs as service demands increase.

- ITIL version 2 to 3 enablement as IT moves from a process foundation to service execution capabilities based on transparency, operations, etc.

- Self-service and automated change and configuration to help drive compliance assurance, deliver application-specific actions, and empower IT to reduce costs through self-service portals for various domain expertise.

CA and Cisco are customer-driven, taking feedback into the product development cycle to enable UCS customers to manage their platform in an optimized fashion. Cisco UCS and CA management solutions complement each other to deliver on the promise of virtualization by helping to reduce risk, increase IT agility, and contain costs for the cloud-connected enterprise.

EMC® Ionix Products for Cisco UCS

EMC Ionix[3] offers two products that work with the Cisco UCS to manage and visualize multiple instances of UCS in the context of the data center:

- EMC Ionix Unified Infrastructure Manager (UIM)
- EMC Ionix Data Center Insight (DCI)

Unified Infrastructure Manager (UIM)

EMC Ionix Unified Infrastructure Manager is a single tool for managing the entire UCS ecosystem. It provides automated infrastructure deployment and provisioning as well as leverages cross-domain context that manages dependencies among software, hardware, network, and storage components. Its initial discovery, at a deep and granular level, provides a foundational basis for provisioning and configuration and change management, enabling unlimited revision history and fine-grained tracking, traceability, and reproducibility.

UIM is the element manager for the UCS and Vblock (a cloud computing system from Cisco Systems, VMware, and EMC). It models and manages all aspects of UCS and Vblock deployments offering the following:

- Configuration discovery and change auditing
- Dashboard view of UCS, Vblock, and service
- Service catalog for provisioning the UCS and Vblock
- Global management of pools

---

3 The authors are thankful to EMC® Corporation for the information and the material provided to edit this section. Pictures are courtesy of EMC®.

Configuration Discovery and Change Auditing

UIM discovers the UCS and provides combined and detailed views of devices and configurations. Configuration policies can be set and enforced to ensure system-wide compliance. It checks the UCS configurations against best practices by tying the service profile to a best practice template. UIM enforces compliancy across multiple UCS deployments by ensuring MAC addresses are not duplicated.

UIM provides views of multiple UCS devices and their configurations. This is useful for administrators who require configuration discovery for the entire data center, more than isolated views into individual UCS devices.

Figure 8-24 displays a UIM screenshot of the Devices View for the discovered UCS devices in the environment. The Properties tab makes detailed configuration data available for the selected UCS device.

Dashboard View of UCS, Vblock, and Service Offerings

The UIM dashboard provides an aggregated, read-only view of resource availability and deployed services. You create a layout of viewlets to display data.

Figure 8-25 shows a detailed view of the dashboard.

Service Catalog for Provisioning UCS and Vblock

You can select a service profile from a standard set of component profiles and apply it to a Vblock. If, for example, you have a service offering that consists of a cluster of compute blades on the UCS, external storage, and a set of VLANs, the profile captures these components and their configurations and makes it possible to create a standard catalog service profile that can be applied to similar configurations and further act as a policy.

With UIM, you can reuse the services or profiles you have configured by copying them from one Vblock to another. You can also provision the Vblock or the attached storage and SAN for an entire cluster from the service catalog.

Service Grades

Grading of services is a function that you use to constrain the quality of a service. UIM uses grades to place a service on the underlying infrastructure. Grades can be applied to physical as well as logical services such as QoS settings of an interface or the RAID level of a storage volume.

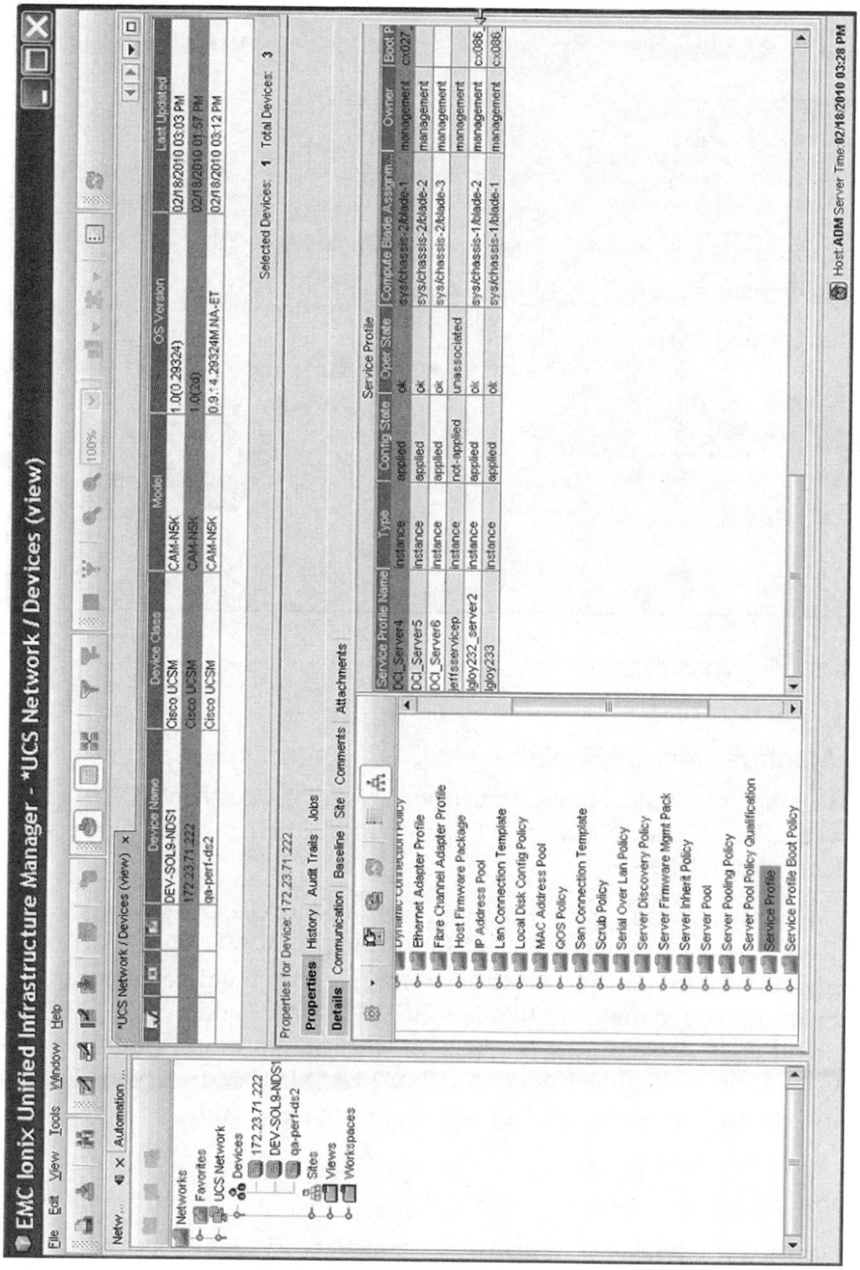

Figure 8-24 Detail view of UCS configuration

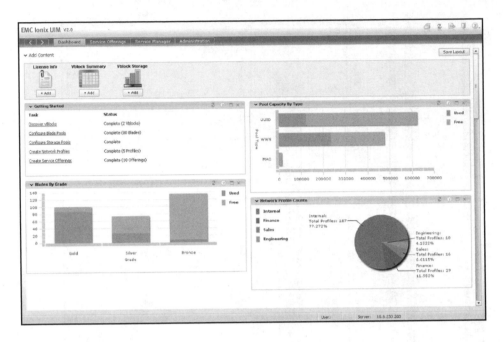

Figure 8-25   UIM dashboard

Global Management of Pools

A pool is a range of unique Fibre Channel World Wide Node Names (WWNNs), World Wide Port Names (WWPNs), Ethernet MAC addresses, or Universally Unique Identifiers (UUIDs).

With UIM, you can manage pools in multiple UCSs to avoid overlapping and unintended re-use, not simply detecting overlapping WWNN, WWPNs, MAC addresses, or UUIDs. In an enterprise environment, with multiple UCS deployments, it is possible for the same WWNN, WWPN, MAC address, or UUID to be used in different deployments. Without UIM, an administrator would have to manually track all the assigned WWNNs, WWPNs, MAC addresses, or UUIDs used across the different deployments to ensure that each value in a pool was unique.

UIM global pool management is also used to:

- Handle the complexity of managing storage for various deployment scenarios.

- Move addresses used by one UCS to another UCS in different data centers.

Data Center Insight (DCI)

DCI presents an end-to-end, near real-time view of topology in compute, storage, IP and application domains and provides full, free-form text search of configuration information across domains. Its unique offering is that it visualizes the components of UCS along with the application layer and the relationships of the application layer to the storage and network domains.

It extracts configuration information from sources using Model Supplier Adapters (MSAs) and performs identity reconciliation. MSAs can be written by customers for data sources.

It also provides for integrating this data into third-party CMDB solutions that deliver configuration management data from data sources such as the UCS, IP, storage, or application domains to the service desk.

Full Free-Form Text Search

You can search the data center environment using the following types of searches:

- **Multi-term searches**—For example, Cisco switch
- **Boolean operators**—For example, Cisco AND switch, Cisco OR switch, Cisco NOT switch
- **Field qualification**—For example, vendor: Cisco
- **Wildcard searches**—For example, EMC*
- **Fuzzy searches**—For example, NEXUS~
- **Term boosting**—For example, cisco^10 switch
- **Grouping**—For example, Cisco AND (switch OR router)
- **Field grouping**—For example, vendor: (EMC OR Cisco)

All UCS components are indexed, which returns search queries more quickly.

Figure 8-26 illustrates a sample search using the string UCS. DCI searches all data sources and returns all instances of the strings. You can click any of the search results to display the graphical map that visualizes the context for that item, as well as a detailed properties tab for the search item.

Cross-Domain Dependencies

Data Center Insight displays cross-domain dependencies in the form of graphical maps. Maps are available for a subset of the known object types in the system, including:

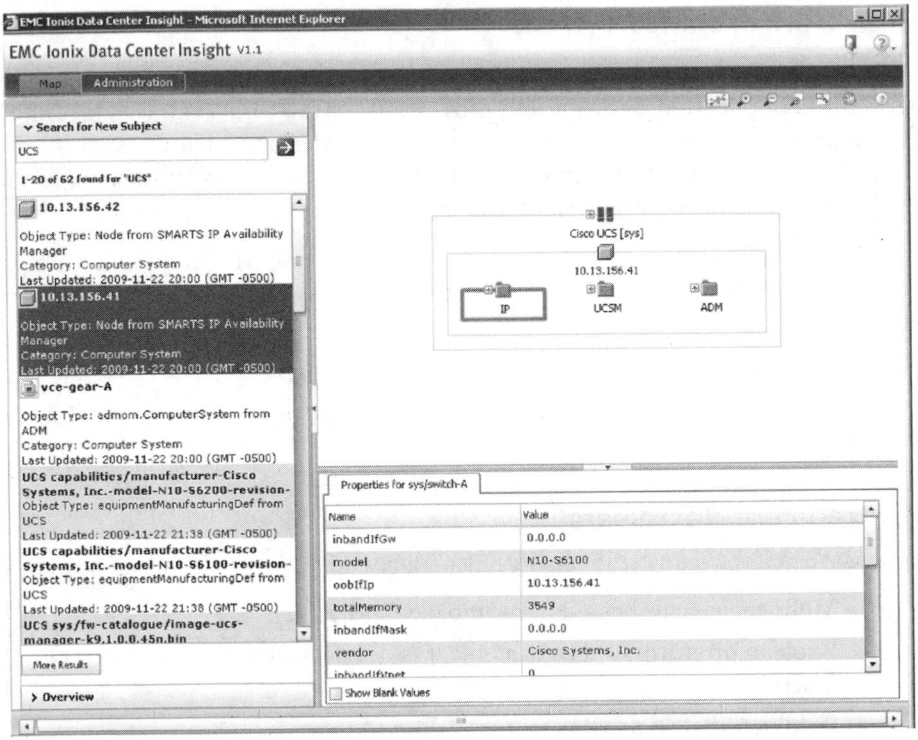

Figure 8-26 Sample DCI search

■ Cross Domain: This map displays relationships between elements in different domains. This map is the launching point for maps of the other domains.

■ UCS: This map displays the components of the UCS along with the application layer and the network connectivity for the applications and components in the UCS.

■ Application: Application maps available include services running on a server and applications running on a server.

■ Dependencies between applications.

■ Virtual machines running on an ESX host.

■ Network: Network maps available include connectivity between network devices and logical networks, physical connectivity between network devices, and VLAN membership of network devices.

■ Storage: Storage maps available include logical SAN connectivity from host to switch to array and physical SAN connectivity from host to switch to array.

One of the unique features of DCI is the ability to display the UCS topology with the application layer in the context of the data center. Figure 8-27 provides a sample map of how an application consumes computer infrastructure in the UCS and how servers consume storage volumes.

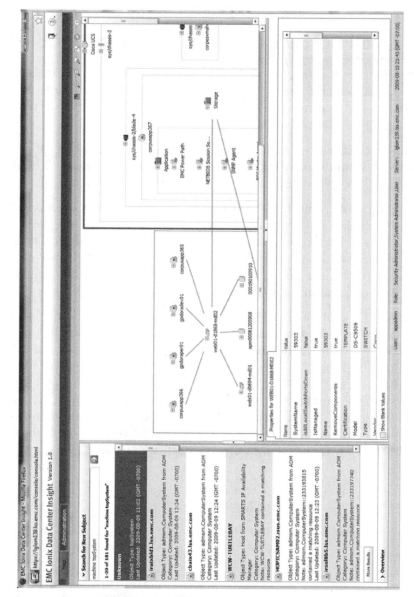

Figure 8-27   DCI graphical map of UCS

It shows a detailed view of applications such as EMC Power Path, NetBios Session, and SNMP Agent that is running on the corpusaap367 server on sys/chassis-2/blade4 in a Cisco UCS. The corpusaap367 server has storage connectivity to web-01-d1868- md02. Clicking the SNMP Agent application would display a map showing network connectivity to the host running the SNMP Manager.

IBM Tivoli Software Integration with Cisco UCS

The IBM Tivoli Software[4] portfolio provides cross-vendor service management of multiple Data Center elements, like servers, network, storage, security, software applications, and dependent services. Tivoli can be configured so it manages a UCS as an element in the Data Center.

IBM and Cisco have been working together to develop solutions for UCS in various IBM Tivoli products, specifically IBM Tivoli Monitoring (ITM) 6.2.1 IF0002 and Tivoli Netcool/OMNIbus 7.2.1.

The solution enables the Tivoli Software to monitor the UCS components like chassis and blades. Collecting and delivering fault and event information from UCS to ITM, gathering, reporting, and maintaining a longer historical dataset of statistical information, and providing event correlation on issues throughout the entire stack from hardware to application are a few areas that the integration of IBM Tivoli Service Management offers above what UCS Manager offers.

This integration enables Tivoli/Netcool OMNIbus to collect and monitor health and fault data for chassis and blades, as well as monitoring the current state watching for any raised fault conditions. The solution uses two PERL-based collector scripts to collect the UCS data. The scripts use the Cisco recommended UCS open XML API to collect the data from UCS Manager. The custom ITM agent supports multiple instances of same agent, where each instance of the agent is used to collect data from a single chassis in the UCS. The solution involves the creation of a custom ITM agent, which is the agent that will collect the events, fault data, and power and temperature usage statistics from UCS Manager.

---

4   Please note that this section only discusses the components and the actual solution that has been co-developed; there are many other functions that Tivoli Software provides, but they are not discussed here.

There are mainly three different components involved in the integration:

- A custom ITM agent
- A standard ITM OS agents
- The Tivoli Netcool/OMNIbus Exec probe

Table 8-3 describes the different data collected by the three components.

Table 8-3   Data Collected by IBM Tivoli Components

Component	UCS Data Collected
Custom ITM agent	Power, Temperature
Standard ITM OS agents	Performance and Health
Tivoli Netcool/OMNIbus Exec probe	Faults

Like most system management software's, the Tivoli Software is typically installed on one or more external management servers, like the Cisco C-Series servers.

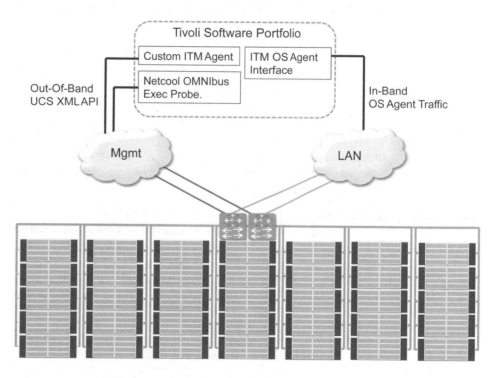

Figure 8-28   High-level integration and traffic flow

Figure 8-28 shows a high-level view of the components and data traffic flow. Please note that the OS agents are not shown in the picture as they are installed inside the OS on each blade, and communicates directly with the ITM as shown in the picture.

Microsoft System Center

Microsoft System Center Operations Manager (SCOM) enables IT administrators to monitor the health and performance of data center infrastructure including servers, devices, operating systems, and applications.

Operations Manager receives the health and performance information through management packs that are imported into Operations Manager. These management packs are written by Microsoft and other vendors to provide information, rules, and characteristics for the different services, applications, and devices being monitored.

Cisco is a partner of the System Center Alliance and works closely with Microsoft on development of management packs. Cisco has created a SCOM management pack for UCS Manager providing full health monitoring of UCS hardware and service profiles.

The SCOM software is installed on a physical or virtual server running Windows Server. Once SCOM has been configured, the management pack can be installed. During the installation, the user identifies the IP address of the UCS Manager system that they wish to monitor. The management pack enables the UCS XML object model and alerts to be presented inside of SCOM through an established connection to the UCS Manager API via a http or https. A single management pack is able to monitor all hardware objects under a Fabric Interconnect. This greatly simplifies the management within SCOM, as it only requires a single management pack to be installed and maintained.

The management is architected to poll the XML-API for the object data via a defined interval. This interval can be modified through the SCOM interface. The hierarchy of the object data is displayed with three branches of objects: hardware, operating systems, and service profiles. These objects are correlated together through comparing UUIDs. The relationship allows the health of the hardware and logical objects to be connected to show a holistic monitoring of your entire UCS.

Inside the SCOM user interface the management pack shows the state summary and visual diagram of four views: hardware, service profiles, operating systems,

---

Please note that this section only discusses the components and the actual solution that involves UCS; there are many other functions that Microsoft System Center Operations Manager provides, but they are not discussed here.

and applications. The top-level diagram shows a tree structure with all hardware and logical objects monitored by the management pack. The diagram will then draw the correlation lines between the related objects to provide a visual representation of the physical and logical system. Inside the state summary, view the management pack, and display verbose model information and alerts related to the objects. The alert details outline the source, time, location, and summary of the fault.

VMware vCenter

The VMware vCenter Server provides administrators with tools to manage all aspects of VMware vSphere operations, which can scale from tens to tens of thousands of virtual machines. It provides unified management of all hosts and VMs in the customer data center from a single console, with an aggregate-performance monitoring of clusters, hosts, and VMs.

The VMware vCenter Server gives administrator insight into the status and configuration of clusters, hosts, VMs, storage, the guest OS, and other critical components of a virtual infrastructure.

The VMware vCenter Servers lets administrators rapidly provision VMs and hosts by using standardized templates, and it ensures compliance with vSphere host configurations and host, and VM patch levels with automated remediation. The VMware vCenter Server also gives administrators control over key capabilities, such as VMware VMotion, Distributed Resource Scheduler, High Availability, and Fault Tolerance. A powerful orchestration engine allows administrators to create and easily implement best practice workflows.

The VMware vCenter Server's open plug-in architecture supports a broad range of additional capabilities from VMware and its partners. More than 200 VMware partners directly integrate with vCenter Server, allowing to extend the platform for more advanced management capability in areas such as capacity management, compliance management, business continuity, and storage monitoring. The vCenter Server APIs also allow customers to integrate physical and virtual management tools, by using their choice of enterprise management tools to connect to vCenter Server.

Chapter 7 outlined the capabilities from the perspective of the UCS Manager by presenting network policy and virtualized adapters within UCS servers to vCenter. This section illustrate specifics on how the vCenter makes use of this policy information, coupled with a control of the dynamic adapters that are present within the Cisco UCS.

The key operational advantage with this architecture is that administrators can meet service demands in both physical and virtual server infrastructures, while allowing traditional skill and toolsets with respect to the networking edge configuration, monitoring, and troubleshooting tasks. As VMware infrastructures have grown, customers have adopted new models in managing a new virtualized switching layer within the host itself. An example implementation is shown in Figure 8-29. With the Cisco VN-Link in hardware technology, inside the Cisco UCS, the virtualized switching layer can be eliminated completely, while retaining the benefits and supported technologies (VMotion, DRS, HA, etc.) within a vCenter infrastructure.

Communications

Communications between the UCSM, vCenter, and VM entities occur in a closed-loop fashion, and carry information based on the UCSM port profiles that are defined as shown in Chapter 7. These UCSM profiles include—among others—VLAN(s) membership, MAC security configuration, bandwidth, and quality of service configuration. These network configuration settings are not presented to the server administrator, only the port-profile name is, which is shown as an available port-group on vCenter. To establish communications between a given UCSM DVS instance and the vCenter server, an XML sheet is exported from UCSM and is available as a plug-in for the vCenter administrator. A view of an installed and operational plug-in is shown in Figure 8-30. This plug-in has a key value that matches the appropriate DVS instance on the UCS Manager.

Once the connection between a given UCSM DVS and the vCenter is established, the UCSM network-role administrator can select clients (DVSs) for a given port-profile, as discussed in Chapter 7. This action populates the corresponding port-groups within the vCenter for the administrators to use.

When an administrator assigns a vNIC and a port-group to a given VM, meta-data such as adapter type, MAC address, port-group, etc. are written into the .vmx file that describes the virtual machine. When the given VM is powered on or migrated onto a host, the ESX kernel interacts with UCSM via the kernel modules (to be discussed in the next section) to assign these identifiers to the dynamic adapters on a UCS server. During a live-migration event, these identifiers are moved to the gaining server, activated as part of the appropriate final steps in a VM move, and de-activated on the losing server to be utilized by other VMs.

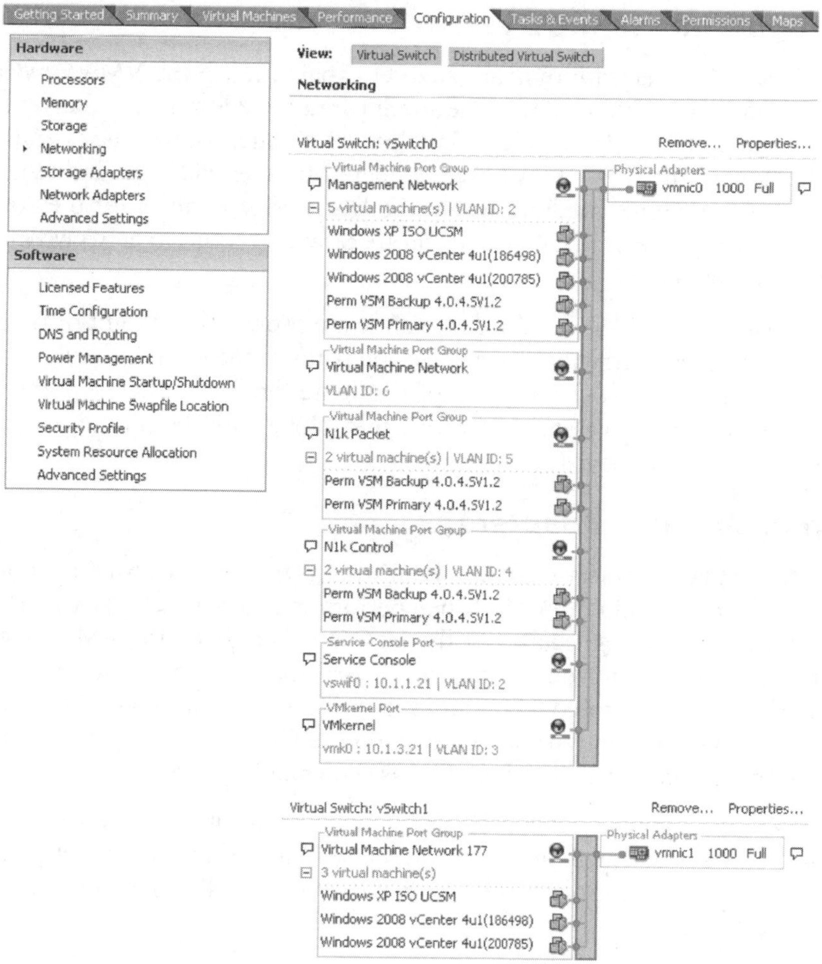

Figure 8-29 vCenter configuration

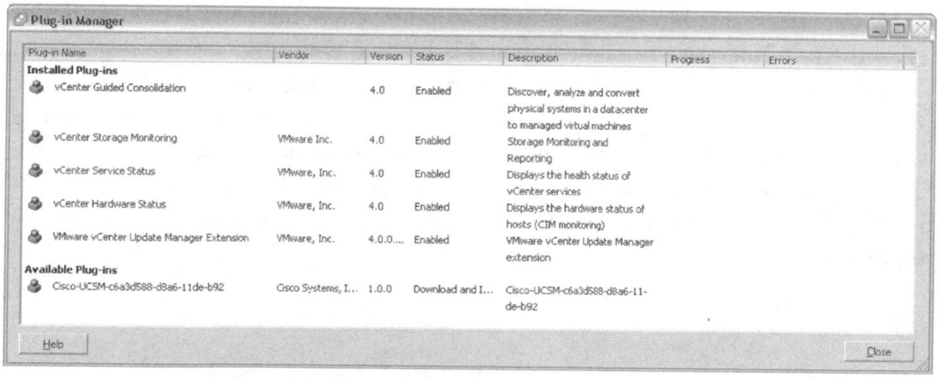

Figure 8-30 vCenter Plug-in manager

Configuration of the DVS

To add a UCS server with dynamic adapter capabilities to the VMware vCenter Distributed Virtual Switch (DVS), the administrator needs to add the server to the appropriate DVS that was configured within the vCenter. During the operation to add the host to the DVS, the VMware Update Manager will stage and remediate the appropriate kernel modules within the UCS server to allow for the communication paths between the VM and the UCS infrastructure. The view from the vCenter is shown in Figure 8-31.

Links between the UCS server and the fabric are shown on the right of the viewing pane and these carry the communication paths to the kernel modules and the UCS Manager. The entries on the left of the figure show the available port-groups that administrators can assign VM vNICs into, along with the current usage.

Virtual Machine Adapters

The VMware vCenter Server allows administrators to dynamically add, modify, or remove adapters within the VMs. When performing these functions, the administrator needs to define an adapter of the VMXNET3 type on the VM, along with the selection of a port-group to map the virtual adapter into. These vNIC definitions will be utilized to connect the machine in a direct fashion (not through a vSwitch or vDS) to the dynamic adapters on the UCS server. An administrator's view of the adapter on a virtual machine is shown in Figure 8-32.

The DVS port number is shown, and it maps to a virtual Ethernet interface on the UCS Fabric Interconnect, where networking teams can attach monitoring and management toolsets, like with traditional physical network edge port infrastructures.

Resource Checks for DRS, HA, and FT

VMware offers capabilities for Dynamic Resource Scheduling, High Availability, and Fault Tolerance to allow for load balancing and rapid service restoration, should any host within the VMware infrastructure become unavailable. A key component within these features is a resource-checking mechanism on the hosts, which includes the number of dynamic adapters available to a given UCS server. Should there be a situation where a placement decision is required in support of these technologies, no VM will be relocated or placed on a server without the required resources.

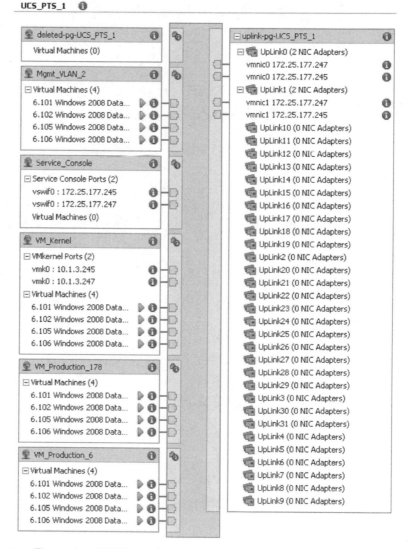

Figure 8-31 Example of UCS configuration

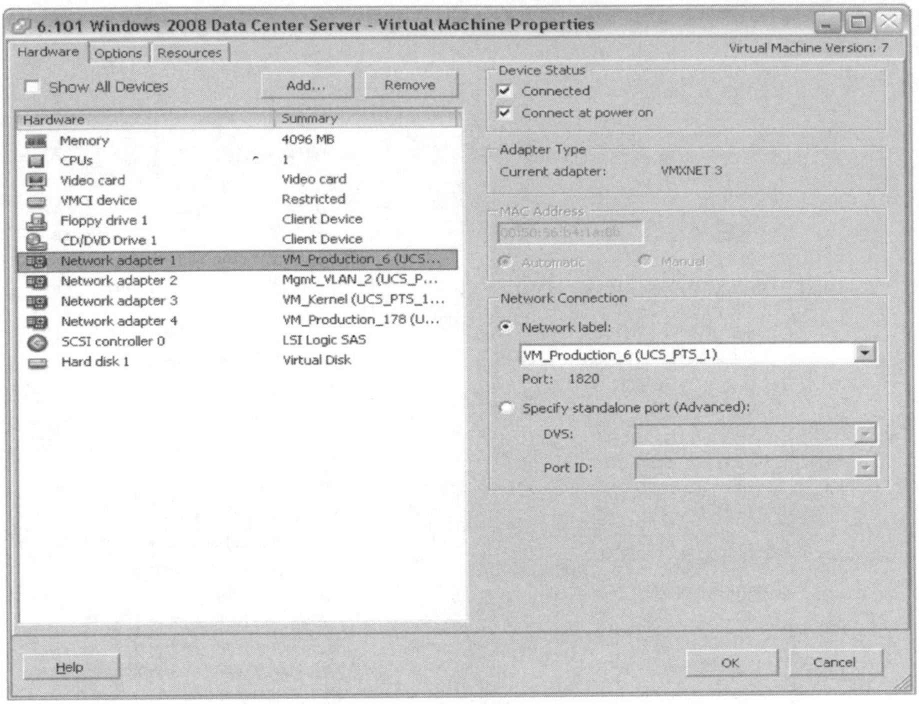

Figure 8-32 VM properties

Please note that this section only discusses the components and the actual solution that involves UCS; there are many other functions that VMware vCenter provides, but they are not discussed here..

Chapter 9

Planning a UCS Blade Server Installation

Good initial planning is the key for successful UCS deployment in data centers. Several aspects should be considered, such as who is the owner of the UCS, the network connectivity options, the power and cooling infrastructure, and the OS and application support. In this chapter, we are taking a closer look on how to plan for successful deployment of UCS blade server into customer environment.

The Owner of the UCS Domain

The UCS is a server product that combines actions of networking, storage, and server administrators under the same management domain. Therefore, a question that is usually asked is who owns the UCS domain. There is no right or wrong answer to this question, as it is mostly depending on organizational structure. In nearly all cases that we know, the owner of the UCS is the server administrator.

The flexibility that UCS allows lets UCS to be inserted into any organizational structure without breaking current models. This has been achieved by implementing role-based administration where different administrators have different roles. UCS comes with predefined roles, but users are also allowed to create their own roles, suitable for their organization. UCS also has an understanding of organizations that can be used to separate different groups from each others. These organizations allow separation of different administrator groups for security and management purposes; i.e., a network administrator in HR can only access network settings in systems that belong to HR group.

With all this flexibility, one might think that the system is complex, but that is not true as, like everything else in UCS, it is an opt-in model. One does not have to use the roles or organizations unless he wants to achieve specific purposes. Instead, this flexibility gives organizations a possibility to look at their current structure and possibly fine-tune it to better address the challenges of today's data centers.

User Authentication

After an owner and different roles have been defined, one needs to decide how he wants to authenticate the users. UCS Manager provides multiple methods for authenticating users and, in many cases, the right authentication model is easy to figure out.

Supported authentication methods in UCS include: local, LDAP, Radius, and TACACS+. In smaller environments, local authentication is sufficient, but once we start to look at authentication methods in large enterprises, local authentication might not be ideal and one might want to look for integration for their preferred authentication method. Integration to external authentication servers is generally a simple task that can be performed from UCS Manager GUI or CLI. It is also important to understand that all authentication methods give you the same functionality allowed by local authentication. In other terms, you do not lose any functionality, like roles and organizations, when using external authentication server.

Power and Cooling

A UCS has two main components that require connection to an external power source: the UCS 6100 Fabric Interconnects and the UCS 5108 Blade Server Chassis. Table 9-1 provides a view of what type of electricity is required for each component, as well as what kind of connectors are necessary.

Table 9-1   Main Components

	UCS 6100 Fabric Interconnects	UCS 5100 Blade Server Chassis
Input Voltage	100 to 240 VAC	208V to 220V
Frequency	50 to 60 Hz	50 to 60 Hz
Connector	IEC-320 C14	IEC-320-C20

UCS 5100 Blade Server Chassis uses 208-220V AC single-phase electric power and can be configured for different modes of power redundancy. In case 208-220V AC single-phase electric power is not readily available, Power Distribution Units (PDUs) can be used to convert electric power from three phases to a single phase.

The two models of Fabric Interconnects have different power consumption characteristics. Their values are listed in Table 9-2. Both models can use 100 to 240V AC power, either single or dual phase. Both Fabric Interconnects can be configured for power redundancy by having dual power supplies.

Table 9-2   Fabric Interconnect Power Consumption

	UCS 6120XP 20 Port Fabric Interconnect	UCS 6140XP 40 Port Fabric Interconnect
Normal Power Consumption	350W	480W
Maximum Power Consumption	450W	750W

Each Blade Server Chassis can hold four power supplies that are rated at 2500W each. Power supplies can be replaced from the front of the chassis, as shown in Figure 9-1.

Normal power consumption for a Blade Server Chassis depends on the blade server configuration (memory, I/O Ports, etc.) and on the load on the CPU imposed by the applications being run. Many of today's non-virtualized servers run at around 20–30% utilization. In well-utilized environments, utilization up to 70% is not unheard of.

Figure 9-1   Front of the chassis and power supply

Power consumption numbers are indicative only, since they are based upon artificial workload in lab environments on a fully loaded chassis with eight blades; they are reported in the Table 9-3. Each server blade is configured with two Intel® X5570 CPUs, six DIMMs, a single mezzanine card, and single hard disk.[1]

Table 9-3   Approximate Power Consumption

CPU Load	Combined Power Consumption for Chassis and Eight Blades
100%	2.6KW
50%	2KW
Idle	1KW

Power consumption is highly dependent on the blade configuration and workloads, and therefore these numbers represent a very limited sample. Workload that was used to create load in this test was a standards-based Java benchmark.

All power supplies in a UCS are rated at 90% power efficiency or better, and are hot swappable.

Fabric Interconnects and Blade Server Chassis are both air cooled with front to back airflow to make them suitable in a typical data center cooling environment.

They can support commonly used hot isle/cold isle cooling strategy.

The Blade Server Chassis has eight large fan modules in the back that are hot-swappable, as shown in Figure 9-2.

Power and cooling capabilities in the data center are primary considerations that determine how many UCS Blade Server Chassis can be installed per rack. This, combined with the number of blades required, provides the number of racks that are needed for the installation.

To achieve accurate cooling requirements for a UCS, it is necessary to know its power consumption. That number can then be translated into different cooling values. There is a worldwide trend among standard-setting organizations to move all power and cooling capacity measurements to a common standard, the Watt. In North America, "British Thermal Units" (BTUs) and "Tons" are still commonly used to describe cooling requirements. Table 9-4 can be helpful when translating energy consumption into BTUs and Tons.

---

1   These numbers should not be used as normal power consumption figures. Please consult the appropriate documentation.

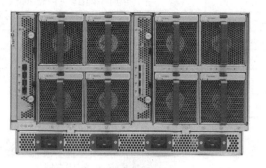

Figure 9-2   Back of the chassis and fan modules

Table 9-4   KWs, BTUs, and Tons

From KWs to	Multiply KWs by
BTUs per hour	3414
Tons	0.284

Physical Sizing and Environmental Requirements

A UCS is designed to fit into a standard 19-inch rack with square holes. Different components differ in height, depth, and weight, but their width remains the same. The following tables describe sizes for different elements.

Table 9-5   20 Ports Fabric Interconnect

Description	Specification
Height	1.72" (4.4cm) - 1 RU
Width	17.3" (43.9cm)
Depth	30" (76.2cm)
Weight with 2PS, 1 Expansion, and 2 Fan modules	35 lb (15.88 kg)

continues

Description	Specification
Temperature, operating	32°F to 104° F (0 to 40° C)
Temperature, non-operating	-40 to 158° F (-40 to 70° C)
Humidity (RH), non-condensing	5 to 95%
Altitude	0 to 10,000 ft (0 to 3,000 m)

Table 9-6   40 Ports Fabric Interconnect

Description	Specification
Height	3.47" (8.8cm) 2 RUs
Width	17.3" (43.9cm)
Depth	30" (76.2cm)
Weight with 2PS, 1 Expansion, and 2 Fan modules	50 lb (22.68 kg)
Temperature, operating	32°F to 104°F (0 to 40° C)
Temperature, non-operating	-40 to 158°F (-40 to 70° C)
Humidity (RH), non-condensing	5 to 95%
Altitude	0 to 10,000 ft (0 to 3,000 m)

Table 9-7   Compute Chassis

Description	Specification
Height	10.5" (26.7cm) - 6RUs
Width	17.5" (44.5cm)
Depth	32" (81.2cm)
Weight	250 lb (113.39 kg) fully loaded
Temperature, operating within altitude: 0 - 10k feet (0 - 3,000 m)	50 to 95° F (10 to 35° C)
Temperature, non-operating within altitude: 0 - 40k feet (0 - 12,000 m)	-40 to 149° F (-40 to 65° C)
Humidity (RH), non-condensing	5 to 93%
Altitude	0 to 10,000 ft (0 to 3,000 m)

Connectivity

Fabric Interconnects provide connectivity for management and data traffic. All I/O required by a UCS goes through the Fabric Interconnects. The two models of Fabric Interconnects provide either 20 or 40 fixed 10GE ports. Additionally, there are one or two expansion slots, respectively. These slots can be used to add more connectivity options if needed (see "UCS 6100 Series Fabric Interconnects" in Chapter 5, page 159).

Each port on the Fabric Interconnects is configured as a server or as an uplink port. Server ports are connected to the Fabric Extenders that reside in the Blade Server Chassis and uplink ports are connected to existing network infrastructure. The Fabric Interconnect is designed to plug in a 10GE backbone. If this is not available, 8 ports (6120) or 16 ports (6140) can be configured as 1 GE uplinks.

The Fabric Extenders provide connectivity from the Blade Server Chassis to the Fabric Interconnect (see Figure 9-3). Each Fabric Extender has eight internal server-facing 10GE ports and four uplink ports connecting to the Fabric Interconnects.

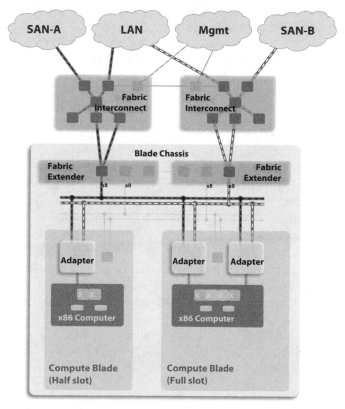

Figure 9-3 Connectivity

Different UCS blades have the capability of housing either one or two mezzanine cards. All mezzanine cards are equipped with two 10GE ports. These two ports are connected to the Fabric Extenders via the chassis mid-plane. The left port of each mezzanine goes to the left Fabric Extender and the right port of each mezzanine goes to the right Fabric Extender.

The Fabric Interconnects can work either in switch mode or in end-host mode. End-host mode is the default and recommended mode for most of the deployments. End-Host mode provides a way to connect Fabric interconnects to the network with minimal disruption. In End-Host mode, the Fabric Interconnects are not learning any MAC-addresses other than the ones from UCS blades and will not forward ARP requests to the servers. In End-Host mode, the fabric interconnects will look and operate like a giant server with multiple MAC addresses in it. There is no need to worry about Spanning tree protocol, as loops cannot be made in End-Host mode.

In some special configurations, switch mode is recommended, and one of these special circumstances happens if the configuration requires connecting the two Fabric Interconnects together, thus allowing the traffic to go from one Fabric Interconnect to another without going first to an upstream switch. In switch mode, the Fabric Interconnect behaves as a normal L2 access switch and has spanning tree enabled by default. It is important to understand that even when Fabric Interconnect can act like a normal access switch, it is not meant to be used that way. UCS 6100 Fabric Interconnects neither support third-party servers directly connected to them, nor do they give access to the NX-OS configuration to configure them like a normal switch. In switch mode, ARP requests from the network are forwarded to servers and Fabric Interconnects will learn external MAC addresses.

Another important difference in behavior is that in End-Host mode uplink tracking is on by default and if all uplinks from one Fabric Interconnect will go down, all host interfaces that are configured for failover will fail on the other Fabric Interconnect. Also by default, if there are no uplinks configured or no uplinks are up in End-Host mode, all server interfaces will also be brought down and there will be no communication between the servers. In switch mode, the uplink tracking is off and failing uplinks from Fabric Interconnect do not trigger interface failover. In addition, if there are no operational uplinks, servers can continue to talk to each others. In End-Host mode, the uplink tracking can also be turned off if necessary, and then, even without operational uplinks, servers can continue to communicate to each others.

Connectivity mode to SAN networks is done in end-host mode (aka NPV: N_Port Virtualization). In this mode, all UCS FC (Fibre Channel) ports present themselves as a host ports or N_Ports. This allows a UCS to connect to any vendor SAN without using special interoperability modes. Moreover, this mode does not consume any FC domain. Future software releases will also support FC switching on the Fabric Interconnect.

Choosing the Right Cables

Each UCS Fabric Extender can be connected to the Fabric Interconnects either with Twinax or fiber cables. There are important details that need to be considered when deciding which type of cable to use for connectivity. One of the most important factors is the number of racks the UCS Domain covers. That determines the minimum cable length required to connect all UCS Blade Server Chassis to the Fabric Interconnects.

All UCS components use standard SFP+ modules for all required network connectivity.

Twinax

Twinax is the most cost-effective solution to connect Fabric Extenders to the Fabric Interconnects, but it has limitations in length. The maximum length of Twinax cable for 10GE is 7 m. (23 ft.) and that will not be enough for all situations, particularly in a multi-rack installation.

Power consumption of Twinax connection is minimal and is currently rated at ~0.1W per cable.

Fiber

Fiber cabling is used if the distance between Fabric Interconnects and Fabric Extenders is too long for the Twinax cable. These situations could occur either when creating large UCS installations that span over multiple racks and/or if "end of the row" network design is used.

Bandwidth

The size of a UCS is dependent on bandwidth requirements. Required bandwidth dictates how many uplinks are needed from each Blade Server Chassis to each Fabric Interconnect. It is important to understand that the Fabric Extenders can be used in Active/Active fashion. There is no need to force all the traffic from blades to go to a single fabric.

Fabric Extenders and Fabric Interconnects can have one, two, or four 10GE links between them. Table 9-8 summarizes available bandwidth for a Blade Server Chassis and for each individual server slot, if they are evenly loaded.

Table 9-8   Planning for Bandwidth

Number of Uplinks from Each Fabric Extender to Each Fabric Interconnect	1	2	4
Available bandwidth for Blade Server Chassis with one Fabric Extender	10 Gbps	20 Gbps	40 Gbps
Available bandwidth for each mezzanine card with one Fabric Extender	1.25 Gbps	2.5 Gbps	5 Gbps
Available bandwidth for Blade Server Chassis with two Fabric Extenders	20 Gbps	40 Gbps	80 Gbps
Available bandwidth for each mezzanine card with two Fabric Extenders	2.5 Gbps	5 Gbps	10 Gbps

It is important to notice that the smaller number is per mezzanine card and not per blade. As new blade models come to market, they may contain more than one mezzanine card. In addition, it is equally important to understand that this value is normalized and it assumes that all mezzanine cards are simultaneously sending as much traffic as possible. All cards share unused bandwidth.

The number of links used to connect the Fabric Extenders and the Fabric Interconnects limits the size of a single UCS. Table 9-9 summarizes the maximum size of a UCS domain with different numbers of uplinks and with the different Fabric Interconnects models.

Table 9-9   Planning for Blade Server Chassis

Number of Uplinks from Each Fabric Extender to Each Fabric Interconnect	1	2	4
Maximum number of Blade Server Chassis with UCS 6120XP 20 Port Fabric Interconnect	20	10	5
Maximum number of Blade Server Chassis with UCS 6140XP 40 Port Fabric Interconnect	40	20	10

OS and Application Support

UCS is a standard X86 architecture server and therefore there are numerous applications and operating systems that can be run in UCS hardware. Many of these applications do not require hardware certification and they can be run in UCS as long as the underlying OS is supported.

Cisco does certify and test applications and Operating Systems on UCS. In general, all major Operating Systems from Microsoft and all major Linux distributions are supported. On the application side, applications like Oracle and SAP are tested and certified among other applications. Hypervisors from VMware, Microsoft, Oracle, and Xen are supported.

As the list of supported Operating Systems and Hypervisors is constantly increasing since new versions are added to the support matrix, one should check the latest certification matrix from the cisco.com website.

Supported Storage Devices and Protocols

Cisco works with all major storage vendors to provide support for UCS. Cisco's aim is to provide support for all new storage devices from major vendors at the time of their launch, as well as to support any new UCS components with all major storage vendors at the time of the launch. As the list of supported storage devices is rapidly growing, the latest list of certified solutions should be checked in the cisco.com website.

While UCS uses FCoE as its internal storage protocol, it does not mean that other protocols would not be supported. UCS works very well with all currently available mainstream storage protocols like FC, iSCSI, CIFS, and NFS.

UCS can be easily connected to any existing FC infrastructure to work as a part of existing SAN solutions. As FC connections from Fabric Interconnects work in NPV mode, they can be easily connected to any vendors SAN solutions. One should consult the certification matrix in cisco.com website for required firmwre levels for different vendors solutions. Despite not strictly necessary, it is better if the attached FC switch is capable of supporting VSANs, F_Port trunking, and F_Port channeling. Booting from FC networks is supported and can be configured in service profile. In fact, booting from SAN combined with the flexibility from service profiles gives additional benefits in terms of having flexibility to "failover" the server from one to another without having to reconfigure anything.

iSCSI, CIFS, and NFS are supported in UCS, but now none of them can be used for booting up a blade. If one would like to boot with one of these protocols, he could first boot micro OS through PXE boot process and then migrate to other protocols. When a new adapter is added to the UCS, support for iSCSI boot could be added. With IP-based protocols, UCS has some advantages over traditional blade solutions. One of them is QoS settings that can be implemented for different types of traffics. This allows users to give dedicated minimum bandwidth for certain traffic flows. For example, QoS can be used to guarantee that NFS traffic going into the blades will always have enough bandwidth available to sustain application needs. QoS settings in UCS are set per vNIC and while this might require some traffic engineering to be done, it is generally a simple task to perform. In addition, IP-based protocols can benefit from the lossless capability of the UCS fabric. This will reduce the dropped packets and retransmits, as well as the bandwidth needed for these protocols.

Planning for Redundancy

When planning for redundancy one must look at the big picture. Redundancy, in its simplest form, is avoiding single points of failures. Take, for example, power supplies: When powering normal 1RU or 2RU rack-mounted servers, it is possible to survive with one power supply, but two are needed for redundancy, in case the first happens to fail. The same rules apply to UCS as well.

Power Supply Redundancy

UCS supports multiple levels of redundancy in its power configuration. A UCS can be configured with either N+1, N+N and grid redundant configurations. A single Blade Server Chassis can survive under any load and in any configuration with just two power supplies active. Table 9-10 illustrates different levels of power redundancies in a UCS Blade Server Chassis that houses eight standard configuration blades. Standard configuration includes dual processors, dual disks, one mezzanine card, and twelve DIMMs.

Once connected, all power supplies in a UCS Blade Server Chassis become active and share the load among them. If one or more power supplies fail during operation, the load from failed power supplies is shared evenly to remaining power supplies.

Table 9-10   Power Supply Redundancy

Number of Power Supplies	Total Face Value in KW	Redundancy Achieved
1	2.5	Insufficient Power Available
2	5	None
3	7.5	N+1
4	10	N+N / Grid Redundancy

I/O Redundancy

In today's data centers, I/O redundancy is an increasingly important aspect to plan for. Connecting hosts to both Fabric Interconnects duplicates all application I/O paths and eliminates single points of failures.

UCS I/O capabilities have been designed for maximum redundancy. New technologies have been used to increase I/O availability without the introduction of added complexity. When implementing a UCS with two Fabric Interconnects, I/O redundancy is achieved by automatically creating dual fabrics. These two fabrics are separated from each other with respect to I/O, failure domain, and from a management perspective.

Ethernet Interfaces Redundancy

Today Ethernet redundancy primarily depends on Operating System drivers such as bonding and NIC teaming. For these drivers to be used, they need to be configured correctly and the switch interfaces must be configured as an EtherChannel or a similar protocol. This must be done for each node individually, which can be an error-prone and time-consuming operation, since multiple operational teams need to coordinate to make this happen.

In a UCS, if so desired, this operating model can still be used, but UCS also introduces a new and improved way of implementing Ethernet redundancy far less error-prone and labor-intensive.

When creating Ethernet interfaces in a service profile, there is an option to create them as "highly available interfaces".[2] In creating Ethernet interfaces, a primary Fabric Interconnect must be selected, which determines where that particular interface is bound. If the high-availability option is also selected, and there is a failure in the I/O path, this interface is automatically moved from one physical interface to another. This action is seamless, and it happens without the operating system being aware of it. It is fully operating system agnostic.

To ensure that this UCS feature works seamlessly, both Fabric Interconnects must have access to all required VLANs. Once this is verified, any node in the UCS can be easily configured for Ethernet redundancy by checking the high availability option. There is no need to install and configure any additional drivers in the operating systems. There is no need to change the upstream Fabric Interconnects as the configuration is programmed at the time of initial deployment. Fabric Interconnects configuration needs to be revisited only if new VLANs or uplinks are connected to the Fabric Interconnect, but in most cases, even this does not require major changes to the Fabric Interconnect configuration. This non-intrusive operation does not affect production traffic that is being processed. Once these changes to the Fabric Interconnects are done, they are available for all nodes in the UCS domain.

Working methods of this functionality are very simple. When creating Ethernet interfaces for service profiles each interface has a primary fabric interconnect that it is connected to. If the interface is configured for high availability, it has the permission to move from one Fabric Interconnect to another, in case of a failure. Once the failure condition is cleared, interfaces that were affected will automatically move back to their primary Fabric Interconnect.

This new method for creating redundant Ethernet interfaces provides multiple benefits. One obvious benefit is the simplicity of the configuration, which not only saves time but also reduces the possibility of configuration errors. Other not-so-obvious benefits range from the reduced number of interfaces required for creating highly available Ethernet connections to the agnostic operating system. This functionality can be used in any Operating System that can be run on a UCS, since it does not require a separate interface driver. This also removes the possibility of human errors in redundancy configuration and the feed for testing specific OS patch levels. If a service-profile requires high availability, then any blade that runs that profile will have high availability. This is completely dynamic. A blade that runs a non-HA service profile in the morning can run an HA profile in the afternoon.

---

2   Check the appropriate documentation as this option is supported on most but not on all adapters.

Fibre Channel Interfaces Redundancy

A UCS Domain has two distinct fibre channel fabrics when configured for redundancy. This implies a different high-availability model than a typical LAN.

Storage redundancy can be achieved by creating a vHBA (virtual HBA) per fabric. Using a storage multipathing driver then combines the vHBAs (see Figure 9-4). These drivers are available inside operating systems and from storage vendors.

Both fabrics in UCS are simultaneously active and therefore active/active configurations are possible if supported by the storage system. This gives UCS the capability to load balance storage traffic across different fabrics and to achieve higher bandwidth for storage devices.

Because these multipathing drivers differ from one another, the appropriate documentation should be referenced before implementing these drivers into a UCS.

Figure 9-4 shows the placement of a multipathing driver in the OS stack and the communications that take place between the different modules.

When configuring UCS for storage multipathing, a minimum of two vHBAs must be created in the Service Profile. Each vHBA has a virtual World Wide Name (vWWN) that can be used for fibre channel zoning and LUN (Logical Units) masking in storage arrays.

If WWN-based zoning is used, these vWWNs must be members of the appropriate zones. If port-based zoning is used, all possible uplink ports, where particular vWWNs may be pinned, must also belong to the right zones.

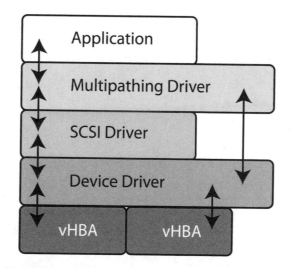

Figure 9-4 Multipathing driver

Once all zoning information is in place, hosts and storage arrays can log into the FC fabric, where it is possible to verify through management if the vWWNs are logged correctly.

The next step is to map the appropriate LUNs to vHBAs by using their vWWNs. LUN masking is performed in the storage array. Operation is very array-specific, so further information on how this is performed should be researched in the relevant storage array manuals.

Once both vHBAs have access to the necessary storage, multipathing drivers are able to configure themselves and to create the appropriate device mappings in the OS layer.

Bibliography

PCI Express

[1]   "How PCI Express Works," howstuffworks, a Discovery Company, http://computer.howstuffworks.com/pci-express.htm.

[2]   "PCI Express," from Wikipedia, the free encyclopedia, http://en.wikipedia.org/wiki/Pci_express.

[3]   "PCI-SIG Announces PCI Express 3.0 Bit Rate for products in 2010 And Beyond," OCI SIG newsroom, http://www.pcisig.com/news_room/08_08_07/.

IEEE 802.3

[4]   "IEEE 802.3: LAN/MAN CSMA/CD Access Method," IEEE Standard Association, http://standards.ieee.org/getieee802/802.3.html.

Improvements to Ethernet

[5]   "Ethernet Enhancements Supporting I/O Consolidation," Nuova Systems, http://www.nuovasystems.com/EthernetEnhancements-Final.pdf.

[6]   SFF-8431 – "Enhanced 8.5 and 10 Gigabit Small Form Factor Pluggable Module," ftp://ftp.seagate.com/sff/SFF-8431.PDF.

[7]   "Cut-Through and Store-and-Forward Ethernet Switching for Low-Latency Environments," Cisco Systems, http://www.cisco.com/en/US/prod/collateral/switches/ps9441/ps9670/white_paper_c11-465436.html.

IEEE 802.1 Activities

[8]   "802.1Qbb - Priority-Based Flow Control," IEEE Standard for Local and Metropolitan Area Networks—Virtual Bridged Local Area Networks - Amendment: Priority-Based Flow Control," http://www.ieee802.org/1/pages/802.1bb.html.

[9]   "Enabling Block Storage over Ethernet: The Case for Per Priority Pause,"
      http://www.ieee802.org/1/files/public/docs2007/new-cm-pelissier-
      enabling-block-storage-0705-v01.pdf.

[10] "Fabric Convergence from a Storage Perspective," http://www.ieee802.
      org/1/files/public/docs2007/au-ko-fabric-convergence-0507.pdf.

[11] "802.1Qau - Congestion Notification," IEEE Standard for Local and
      Metropolitan Area Networks—Virtual Bridged Local Area Networks -
      Amendment: 10: Congestion Notification, http://www.ieee802.org/1/
      pages/802.1au.html.

[12] "802.1Qaz - Enhanced Transmission Selection," IEEE Standard for Local
      and Metropolitan Area Networks—Virtual Bridged Local Area Networks -
      Amendment: Enhanced Transmission Selection, http://www.ieee802.org/1/
      pages/802.1az.html.

FCoE

[13] "FCoE (Fibre Channel over Ethernet)," http://www.fcoe.com/.

[14] "INCITS Technical Committee T11," http://www.t11.org./

[15] "Open-FCoE," http://www.open-fcoe.org/.

[16] "Fibre Channel over Ethernet in the Data Center: An Introduction,"
      FCIA: Fibre Channel Industry Association, http://www.fibrechannel.org/
      OVERVIEW/FCIA_SNW_FCoE_WP_Final.pdf.

[17] "I/O Consolidation in the Data Center," Claudio DeSanti, Silvano Gai,
      Cisco Press, 2009, ISBN: 1-58705-888-X.

TRILL

[18] "Transparent Interconnection of Lots of Links (trill)," IETF WG, http://
      www.ietf.org/html.charters/trill-charter.html.

Virtualization

[19] "VMware ESX Server 2.1: Setting the MAC Address Manually for a Vir-
      tual Machine, http://www.vmware.com/support/esx21/doc/esx21admin_
      MACaddress.html.

[20] "The Role of Memory in VMware ESX Server 3," VMware® and Kingston®
      whitepaper, http://www.vmware.com/pdf/esx3_memory.pdf.

Memory Subsystem

[21] "JESD100B.01: Terms, Definitions, and Letter Symbols for Microcomputers, Microprocessors, and Memory Integrated Circuits," JDEC standard, http://www.jedec.org/download/search/JESD100B01.pdf.

[22] "JEDEC Standard No. 21–C," JDEC Standard, http://www.jedec.org/download/search/3_07_01R5.pdf.

[23] "Future Vision of Memory Modules for DRAM," Bill Gervasi, VP DRAM Technology SimpleTech, http://www.jedex.org/images/pdf/b_gervasi_modules.pdf.

[24] "IBM® Chipkill® Memory," IBM® Corporation, http://www.ece.umd.edu/courses/enee759h.S2003/references/chipkill_white_paper.pdf.

[25] Intel® E7500 Chipset MCH Intel®x4 Single Device Data Correction (x4 SDDC) Implementation and Validation Application Note (AP-726)," Intel®, http://www.intel.com/Assets/PDF/appnote/292274.pdf.

[26] "Chipkill correct memory architecture," Dell®, http://www.ece.umd.edu/courses/enee759h.S2003/references/chipkill.pdf.

[27] "Ultimate Memory Guide: How Much Memory Do You Need?," Kingston®, http://www.kingston.com/tools/umg/umg01b.asp.

[28] Ultimate Memory Guide: Different Kinds of Memory?" Kingston®, http://www.kingston.com/tools/umg/umg05a.asp.

[29] "Server Memory," Kingston®, http://www.kingston.com/branded/server_memory.asp.

[30] "Memory technology evolution: An overview of system memory technologies," HP®, http://h20000.www2.hp.com/bc/docs/support/SupportManual/c00256987/c00256987.pdf.

[31] "FAQ on the NUMA architecture," sourceforge.net, http://lse.sourceforge.net/numa/faq/.

Intel® Processors

[32] "Next Generation Intel Core Microarchitecture (Nehalem) Processors," Rajesh Kumar: Intel Fellow, http://intelstudios.edgesuite.net/fall_idf/tchs001/msm.htm.

[33] "Intel® Core™ i7 Processor: The best desktop processors on the planet," Intel®, http://www.intel.com/products/processor/corei7/index.htm.

[34] "Intel Launches Fastest Processor on the Planet," Intel®, http://www.intel.com/pressroom/archive/releases/20081117comp_sm.htm.

Data Centers

[35] "Datacenter Power Trends," NANOG 42 Power Panel, http://www.nanog.org/mtg-0802/presentations/Snowhorn-Power.pdf.

[36] Virtualization Changes Virtually Everything," Gartner Special Report, March 28, 2008.

[37] Virtualization Evolves into Disaster Recovery Tool," eWeek, May 7, 2008.

[38] Cayton, Ken, "Choosing the Right Hardware for Server Virtualization," IDC White Paper, April 2008.

[39] IDC MultiClient Study.

Green

[40] "ENERGY STAR," U.S. Environmental Protection Agency and the U.S. Department of Energy, http://www.energystar.gov.

[41] "Climate Savers smart computing," Climate Savers® WWF, http://www.climatesaverscomputing.org/.

[42] "Average Retail Price of Electricity to Ultimate Customers by End-Use Sector, by State," Energy Information Administration, http://www.eia.doe.gov/cneaf/electricity/epm/table5_6_a.html.

Cloud Computing

[43] "Above the Clouds: A Berkeley View of Cloud Computing," Technical Report No. UCB/EECS-2009-28, Electrical Engineering and Computer Sciences, University of California at Berkeley, http://www.eecs.berkeley.edu/Pubs/TechRpts/2009/EECS-2009-28.pdf.

[44] "Above the Clouds: A Berkeley View of Cloud Computing," Blog at http://berkeleyclouds.blogspot.com/.

Glossary

10GBASE-T: A standard for 10 Gigabit Ethernet over twisted pair.

10GE: 10 Gigabit Ethernet; see also IEEE 802.3.

802.1: An IEEE standard for LAN Bridging and Management.

802.1Q: An IEEE standard for bridges, VLANs, STP, and priorities.

802.1Qau: Congestion Notification.

802.1Qaz: Enhanced Transmission Selection.

802.1Qbb: Priority-based flow control.

802.1Qbh: Port Extension.

802.3: The Ethernet standard.

ACL: Access Control List, a filtering mechanism implemented by switches and routers.

Aka: Also Known As.

AG (Application Gateway): Management process that focuses on monitoring and configuring a single elements of the system, such as the fabric extender, the server, the I/O adapter, etc.

AQM: Active Queue Management, a traffic management technique.

B2B: Buffer-to-Buffer, as in Buffer-to-Buffer credits for FC, a technique to not lose frames.

BCN: Backward Congestion Notification, a congestion management algorithm.

Blade Server Chassis: The blade server chassis provides power, cooling, connectivity (passive backplane), and mechanical support for server blades and fabric extenders, which in turn attach to fabric interconnect switch.

BMC (Baseboard Management Controller): In the UCS, this component is called CIMC (Cisco Integrated Management Controller).

Border Ports: Ports on the fabric interconnect that are connected to external LAN, SAN, and management networks.

California: See UCS and Unified Computing.

CAM: Computer Array Manager, synonymous of SAM and UCS Manager.

CIMC (Cisco Integrated Management Controller): A small processor present on servers to perform the function of baseboard management controller. It provides autonomous monitoring, event logging, and recovery control, serves as the gateway for remote system management software, hosts Keyboard-Video-Mouse, and provides remote storage media access. A CIMC consists of a processing subsystem that is independent of the computer's main CPU(s), allowing it to be reachable even when the main CPU(s) are powered off or not operational.

CMC (Chassis Management Controller): This subsystem exists on the fabric extender. It provides a management point for the chassis sensors, fans, power supplies, etc. It also establishes a connection to the Fabric Interconnect and configures fabric extender forwarding elements under its control.

CNA: Converged Network Adapter, the name of a unified host adapter that supports both LAN and SAN traffic.

CRC: Cyclic Redundancy Check is a function used to verify frame integrity.

DCB: Data Center Bridging, a set of IEEE standardization activities.

DCBX: Data Center Bridging eXchange, a configuration protocol.

DME (Data Management Engine): The core of UCS Manager, consisting of a transaction engine and an information repository (Management Information Tree).

DN (Distinguished Name): Immutable property of all MOs that provides a fully qualified (unambiguous name) for the MO.

dNS: The Fibre Channel domain Name Server.

DWRR: Deficit Weighted Round Robin, a scheduling algorithm to achieve bandwidth management.

Enode: A host or a storage array in Fibre Channel parlance.

F_Port: A Fibre Channel port that connects to Enodes.

Fabric Extender: A hardware component that connects server blades and management components of the server chassis with fabric interconnect. This subsystem also hosts the CMC.

Fabric Interconnect: The networking I/O workhorse of the UCS. The fabric interconnect is a variant of the Nexus 5000 switch and runs a version of NX-OS that is specifically designed for the UCS application. The UCS Manager runs on top of that NX-OS image.

Fabric Ports: Ports on the fabric interconnect that are connected to the Fabric Extenders.

FC: Fibre Channel.

FC-BB-5: The working group of T11 that has standardized FCoE.

FC_ID: Fibre Channel address, more properly N_Port_ID.

FCC: Fibre Channel Congestion Control, a Cisco technique.

FCF: Fibre Channel Forwarder, a component of an FCoE switch.

FCIP: Fibre Channel over IP, a standard to carry FC over an IP network.

FCoE: Fibre Channel over Ethernet.

FCS: Frame Check Sequence is a function used to verify frame integrity.

FIP: FCoE Initialization Protocol.

FLOGI: Fabric Login.

FPMA: Fabric Provide MAC Address.

FSPF: Fibre Channel Shortest Path First.

GUID (Globally Unique Identifier): A generated 16-byte number that has a very high probability of being unique within a certain context.

HBA: Host Bus Adapter, the adapter that implements the Enode functionality in the host and in the storage array.

HCA: Host Channel Adapter, the IB adapter in the host.

HOL Blocking: Head Of Line blocking is a negative effect that may cause congestion spreading.

Host Agent: Lightweight agent running on top of a customer-controlled OS (Windows, Linux, ESX), that communicates with SAM. The Host Agent is used for discovery (in particular of interfaces and I/O paths) monitoring of the general health of the server, and optionally provisioning of VLAN, VHBA, and layer-3 interfaces.

HPC: High Performance Computing.

Hypervisor: Software that allows multiple virtual machines to share the same HW platform. See also VM and VMM.

IB: Infiniband, a standard network for HPC.

IEEE: Institute of Electrical and Electronics Engineers (www.ieee.org).

IETF: Internet Engineering Task Force (www.ietf.org).

IM (Information Model): Domain-specific formal specification of the MO classes (properties, containment, inheritance, ...), rules, and service APIs used by the management framework.

IMXML (Information Model XML): XML representation of the native information model and API to access and manipulate the IM. This includes mechanisms for getting and setting MOs (RPC), as well as mechanisms to register for events.

IOC (I/O Consolidation): The ability of a network interface to provide both LAN and SAN connectivity. This effectively indicates that an interface/product/system is capable of Fibre Channel over Ethernet. Aka Unified Fabric.

IP: Internet Protocol.

IPC: Inter Process Communication.

IPMI (Intelligent Platform Management Interface): Defines interfaces and messaging for server out-of-band management. This specification covers transport and underlying protocols that consist of I2C, serial, and RCMP/

UDP/IP/Ethernet interfaces. A CIMC is an IPMI server.

ipmitool: Open source project for a utility to manage devices using IPMI 1.5 and IPMI 2.0 (see http://ipmitool. sourceforge.net).

IPv4: Internet Protocol version 4.

IPv6: Internet Protocol version 6.

iSCSI: Internet SCSI; i.e., SCSI over TCP.

ISO: The International Organization for Standardization is an international standard-setting body composed of representatives from various national standards organizations.

KVM (Keyboard-Video-Mouse): Industry term that infers access to the keyboard, video, and mouse functions of a system either directly through hardware or remotely as kvm-over-IP.

LAN: Local Area Network.

Layer 2: Layer 2 of the ISO model, also called datalink. In the Data Center, the dominant layer 2 is Ethernet.

Layer 3: Layer 3 of the ISO model, also called internetworking. The dominant Layer 3 is IP, both IPv4 and IPv6.

Layer 4: Layer 4 of the ISO model, also called transport. The dominant Layer 4 is TCP.

Layer 7: Layer 7 of the ISO model, also called application. It contains all applications that use the network.

LLDP: Link Layer Discovery Protocol, an Ethernet configuration protocol, aka IEEE 802.1AB.

LS (Logical Server): Definition of the identity, PN requirements, connectivity requirements, association policy, and storage resources used by a server. A LS is activated on a PN.

Mezzanine Card: I/O adapter installed on server blades to provide LAN and SAN connectivity.

MIT (Management Information Tree): Repository of all Managed Object instances, indexed by their Distinguished Names.

MO (Managed Object): A base class for all objects of the management framework. All MO classes are specified by the IM. All MO instances are stored in the MIT and accessed using their DN or RN.

MPI: Message Passing Interface, an IPC API.

N_Port: A Fibre Channel port that connects to switches.

N_Port_ID: Fibre Channel address, aka FC_ID.

NFS: Network File System.

NIC: Network Interface Card.

NIV (Network Interface Virtualization): Collection of HW and SW (VNTag and VIC) mechanisms that allow frames to/from vNICs to traverse the same link to a server yet have a consistent set of network policies based on source and target vNICs.

NX-OS (Nexus Operating System): Embedded Switch Software with L2, L3, and FC protocols, and a Cisco-style CLI. Based on Linux.

OOB (Out-of-Band): Typically applied to a management network deployed in data centers that is separated at some level from the production data traffic. Many customers deploy these are a completely separate physical infrastructure including switches, routers, and WAN feeds.

PCI: Peripheral Component Interconnect, a standard I/O bus.

PCIe: PCI Express, the most recent form of PCI.

PFC: Priority Flow Control, aka PPP.

PN: Processing Node.

Port Extender: A simple network device used in Top-of-Rack switches, in SR-IOV adapters, and in virtual switches. Standardized by IEEE in project 802.1Qbh.

PPP: Per Priority Pause, aka PFC.

QCN: Quantized Congestion Notification, a congestion management algorithm.

RDMA: Remote Direct Memory Access, an IPC technique.

RDS: Reliable Datagram Service, an IPC interface used by databases.

RED: Random Early Detect, an AQM technique.

RN (Relative Name): Name of an object relative to the name of its container object. Similar to the relative path of a file (where the DN would be the full pathname of that file).

RSCN: Registered State Change Notification, an event notification protocol in Fibre Channel.

SAM: Server Array Manager, synonymous of CAM and UCS Manager.

SAN: Storage Area Network.

SCSI: Small Computer System Interface.

SDP: Socket Direct Protocol, an IPC interface that mimics TCP sockets.

SFP+: Small Form-Factor Pluggable transceiver.

SMASH (Systems Management Architecture for Server Hardware): DMTF Standard to manage servers through specific set of CIM Profiles, available through either a Command-Line Protocol (CLP), or a web-based transport.

SPT: Spanning Tree Protocol, see also IEEE 802.1Q.

SR-IOV: Single Root I/O Virtualization, a PCI standard for virtual NICs.

T11: Technical Committee 11, which is the committee responsible for Fibre Channel (www.t11.org).

TCP: Transmission Control Protocol, a transport layer protocol in IP.

Twinax: A twin micro-coaxial copper cable used for 10GE.

UCS: Unified Computing System.

UCS Manager: A software providing embedded device management of an entire UCS, including the Fabric Interconnect, Fabric Extender, and server blade hardware elements; the logical servers running within the system; and all of the supporting connectivity information. Synonymous of SAM and CAM.

Unified Computing: Unified Computing unifies network virtualization, storage virtualization, and server virtualization into one, within open industry standard technologies and with the network as the platform.

Unified Fabric: See IOC.

VE_Port: An FCoE port on an FCoE switch used to interconnect another FCoE switch.

VF_Port: An FCoE port on an FCoE switch used to interconnect an Enode.

vHBA (Virtual HBA): Host-visible virtual HBA device (PCI device).

VIC (Virtual Interface Control): A SW protocol used between a NIC and a switch (in conjunction with VNTag) to provide Network Interface Virtualization.

VIF (Virtual Interface: A physical interface of a fabric interconnect supports multiple VIFs that are the policy application points.

VLAN: Virtual LAN.

VM (Virtual Machine): Hardware-level abstraction compatible with the underlying server hardware and capable of running a standard operating system (known as the guest OS) on top of a resource scheduler (known as a hypervisor).

VMM (Virtual Machine Monitor): Hypervisor that allows multiple virtual machines to share the same HW platform.

VN_Port: An FCoE port on an eNODE used to interconnect to an FCoE switch.

vNIC (Virtual NIC): Host-visible virtual Ethernet device (PCI device).

VNTag (Virtual NIC Tag): Layer-2 Ethernet header that uniquely identifies the source vNIC of packets sent by NIC and uniquely identifies the set of destination vNICs of packets sent to the NIC.

WWN (World Wide Name): A globally unique identifier assigned to Fibre Channel hosts and ports.

XAUI: Chip signaling standard for 10 Gigabit Ethernet.

Index